R C

B.M.

# A CHILD'S GARDEN OF DELIGHTS
## Pictures, Poems, and Stories for Children

# A CHILD'S GARDEN OF DELIGHTS
# Pictures, Poems, and Stories for Children

From the Collections of
The New York Public Library
Compiled by Bernard McTigue

Harry N. Abrams, Inc., Publishers, New York

For Eileen and Kerry McTigue
and
In Grateful Memory of
Elizabeth Culbert

*Frontispiece:* The Wonderful Wizard of Oz
*by L. Frank Baum, illustrated by W.W. Denslow*

*Project Director:* Darlene Geis
*Designer:* Darilyn Lowe

**Library of Congress Cataloging-in-Publication Data**
A Child's garden of delights.
"From the collections of the New York Public Library."
Summary: Eighty-five selections from the collections of the New York Public Library. Includes Mother Goose, "Wind in the Willows," Pinocchio, fairy tales, Mark Twain, Tolstoy, Blake, and other treasures.
1. Children's literature. [1. Literature—Collections
I. McTigue, Bernard. II. New York Public Library.
PZ5.C448 1987 [Fic] 86-32274
ISBN 0-8109-0791-7



Published in 1987 by Harry N. Abrams, Incorporated, New York.


Times Mirror Books

Printed and bound in Japan

# *Contents*

8 A Word to Parents
10 A Word to Children
12 Old Mother Hubbard
17 Baa Baa Black Sheep *Illustrated by E. Caldwell*
20 Mother Goose and The Old Nursery Rhymes *Illustrated by Kate Greenaway*
23 Hey Diddle Diddle *Illustrated by Randolph Caldecott*
26 The Rollo Books *By Jacob Abbott*
27 Humpty Dumpty
30 Pictorial Alphabet *By Hablôt K. Browne*
32 The History of an Apple Pie *By Z.*
36 An Alphabet from England *By Christina G. Rossetti*
40 First and Second Picture Books *By Edward Steichen and Dr. Mary Steichen Calderone*
42 About Two Squares *By El Lissitsky*
45 Mrs. Barbauld's Lessons for Children from Three to Four Years Old *By Anna Letitia Barbauld*
46 The Peacock "At Home" *By Catherine Anne Dorset*
48 The Fatal Mistake *By A. B. Frost*
52 The Butterfly's Ball and the Grasshopper's Feast *By William Roscoe*
54 A Natural History of British Quadrupeds *By W. Davison*
56 The Adventures of Bob the Squirrel
60 Animals in Costume
63 A Book of Nonsense *Written and illustrated by Edward Lear*
66 The Bosun and the Bob-Tailed Comet *Written and illustrated by Jack B. Yeats*
73 Tit, Tiny and Tittens, the Three White Kittens
74 Struwwelpeter *Written and illustrated by Heinrich Hoffman-Donner*
75 Goop Tales *Written and illustrated by Gelett Burgess*
77 Giant Otto *Written and illustrated by William Pène du Bois*
81 The Elephant's Child *Written and illustrated by Rudyard Kipling*

86 Shush, Shush, the Big Buff Banty Hen *By Carl Sandburg, illustrated by Peggy Bacon*
88 A Visit from St. Nicholas *By Clement Clark Moore, illustrated by Boyd*
91 The Ugly Little Duck *By Mark Merriwell*
96 The Farmyard Journal
98 The Big Boys' Mistake *By Anatole France, illustrated by M. Boutet de Monvel*
100 Peter and Wendy *By James M. Barrie, illustrated by F. D. Bedford*
105 Billy Bounce *By W. W. Denslow and Dudley A. Bragdon, illustrated by W. W. Denslow*
109 The Sleepamite More *By Countee Cullen, illustrated by Charles Sebree*
111 Susan and Edward; or, A Visit to Fulton Market
113 The Woodcutter's Dog *By Charles Nodier, illustrated by Claud Lovat Fraser*
116 Picture Riddler
117 The Book of Riddles
118 The Young Visiters *By Daisy Ashford*
122 Cat's Eyes *Written and illustrated by Charles Bennett*
124 Griset's Grotesques *By Tom Hood, illustrated by Ernest Griset*
126 The Wind in the Willows *By Kenneth Grahame, illustrated by Ernest H. Shepard*
128 Raggedy Andy Stories *Written and illustrated by Johnny Gruelle*
133 The Water-Babies: A Fairy Tale for a Land-Baby *By Charles Kingsley, illustrated by J. Noel Paton*
137 Pinocchio: The Adventures of a Marionette *By Carlo Collodi*
140 First Landscapes *By Maurice Denis*
142 Jack Huckaback *Written and illustrated by Wilhelm Busch*
148 The Brownies: Their Book *Written and illustrated by Palmer Cox*
151 Once in Puerto Rico *By Pura Belpré White, illustrated by Christine Price*
154 Millions of Cats *Written and illustrated by Wanda Ga'g*
157 Andy and the Lion *Written and illustrated by James Daugherty*
161 The Wonderful Wizard of Oz *By L. Frank Baum, illustrated by W. W. Denslow*
164 The Pied Piper of Hamelin *By Robert Browning, illustrated by Arthur Rackham*
167 Peacock Pie: A Book of Rhymes *By Walter de la Mare, illustrated by W. Heath Robinson*
170 In Wink-A-Way Land *By Eugene Field*
173 At the Back of the North Wind *By George MacDonald, illustrated by Jessie Wilcox Smith*
175 The Boy Who Drew Cats *By Lafcadio Hearn*
179 Fables and Fairy Tales for Little Folk *By Mary and Newman Tremearne*
182 The Piggy Girl *By Louisa May Alcott*
184 Puss in Boots *By Charles Perrault, illustrated by Gustave Doré*
189 The Rebellious Waters *By Gerald Friedlander*
190 The Golden Cockerel *By Alexander Pushkin, illustrated by Ivan Bilibin*
192 The True History of Little Golden-hood *By Andrew Lang, illustrated by Lancelot Speed*
195 Tom Thumb *By Jacob and Wilhelm Grimm, illustrated by Arthur Rackham*
199 Hop-o'my-Thumb and the Seven-League Boots *Edited and illustrated by George Cruikshank*
203 The Little Man in Gray *By Anthony Reubens Montalba, illustrated by Richard Doyle*
206 Sswanda, the Piper *By Edward Laboulaye, illustrated by Yan Dargent*
209 The Enchanted Cave of Cesh Corran *By James Stephens, illustrated by Arthur Rackham*
212 Juvenile Calendar and Zodiac of Flowers *By Mrs. T. K. Hervey, illustrated by Richard Doyle*
214 Aesop's Fables

215 Aesop in the Fifteenth Century
216 Aesop in the Seventeenth Century *Illustrated by Francis Barlow*
217 Aesop in the Nineteenth Century *By Thomas James, illustrated by John Tenniel*
218 Aesop in the Twentieth Century *By Sir Roger L'Estrange, illustrated by Alexander Calder*
219 Stories by Leo Tolstoy
221 Ivanhoe *By Sir Walter Scott, illustrated by Frank E. Schoonover*
225 The Selfish Giant *By Oscar Wilde, illustrated by Everett Shinn*
228 The Merry Adventures of Robin Hood *Written and illustrated by Howard Pyle*
231 The Golden Touch *By Nathaniel Hawthorne*
237 Adventures of Huckleberry Finn *By Mark Twain, illustrated by E. W. Kemble*
240 The Twin Heroes *Adapted by Alphonso O. Stafford, illustrated by Albert Alex Smith*
245 The Prince and the Pauper *By Mark Twain, illustrated by Harley and F. T. Merrill*
248 The King of the Golden River *By John Ruskin, illustrated by Richard Doyle*
251 The Heroes *By Charles Kingsley, illustrated by W. Russell Flint*
257 Treasure Island *By Robert Louis Stevenson, illustrated by N. C. Wyeth*
258 Songs of Innocence *By William Blake, illustrated by Geraldine Morris*
260 Tom Brown at Oxford *By Thomas Hughes*
263 Bibliography
267 Acknowledgments
269 Index

Peter and Wendy *By James M. Barrie, illustrated by F. D. Bedford*

# *A Word to Parents*

This is a book that is meant to be read. It has been compiled to serve as a family reader while highlighting a little-known aspect of the research collections of the New York Public Library. Unlike a standard treasures book, which is meant to be dipped into only on occasion or to be used as a reference work, this book is designed to provide you and your children with the opportunity to explore and delight in some of the great works written and illustrated for children over the past two hundred years—or more, since the oldest illustrated story in this collection comes from a fifteenth-century illuminated manuscript of Aesop's *Fables*.

It is most appropriate that the New York Public Library should produce such a book. For eighty years its branch library system has been providing the city's children with what has been, in many cases, their first experience of literature. It is also, in a way, appropriate that I should compile the volume, since I am a "graduate" of that system, having started at the Library's Epiphany Branch, where, at the age of four, I was introduced to the endless fascination of reading by a great children's librarian, Elizabeth Culbert, one of those to whom this book is dedicated.

While the contributions of the New York Public Library's branches to the lives of the city's children are well known, the fact that the Research Libraries have over the years been quietly assembling an important collection documenting the history of children's literature is less known. Actually, some parts of the research collections antedate the formation of the New York Public Library as we know it. James Lenox, in assembling the great collection of books pertaining to the history of the Americas that now forms the core of the Library's Rare Books and Manuscripts Division, acquired early children's books not because of their content, but because they were printed on this continent.

Similarly, other collections, such as the Spencer Collection of Illustrated Books; the Berg Collection of English and American Literature; the Arents Collections; and the Art, Prints, and Photographs Division, acquired children's books, along with manuscripts and drawings related to them, not because of what they tell us about writing and illustrating specifically for children, but because of what they tell us about the history of literature and illustration in general.

This somewhat unfocused and (uncharacteristically) random approach to collection building was briefly changed to a systematic approach in the 1930s. At that time Anne Carroll Moore, Superintendent of Work for Children and founder of the Central Children's Room, and Philip Hofer, the adviser to the Spencer Collection, made a concerted effort to add important rarities to the research collections. Through their endeavors, the Library acquired from the émigré bookseller Walter Schatzki a significant collection of eighteenth- and nineteenth-century European children's books. Part of the Pforzheimer collection of children's books printed by Harvey and Darton in England in the eighteenth and nineteenth centuries was also added in this period. In addition, major individual rarities came into the Library, a first edition of *Struwwelpeter* among them. To celebrate their juvenile acquisitions and to make this then relatively unknown area of book collecting more widely appreciated, in 1932 Moore and Hofer organized an exhibition of children's literature in two parts, one at the central building of the New York Public Library and the other at The Metropolitan Museum of Art in New York.

With Hofer's departure for the Pierpont Morgan Library in 1934, there seems to have been no one left on the staff of the Research Libraries to engage in creative collaboration with Moore. The collections continued to grow in a desultory fashion until recently, when a new generation of curators, alive to the interest in children's literature and its importance to the researcher, began collecting with renewed zest. The Schomburg Center for Research in Black Culture has recently consolidated its scattered early holdings with rare books acquired from the Branch Libraries' James Weldon Johnson Collection into a research collection representing the black experience. Indeed, a number of the items anthologized here, including the first one, *Baa Baa Black Sheep*, were acquired as late as 1985.

The eighty-five selections that form this anthology (seventy-six from the Research Libraries and nine from the rare book collection of the Central Children's Room, now located at the Donnell Library Center) owe their presence here to this pattern of collecting. I have tried to select works that emphasize the rare and unique quality of the Library's holdings, while at the same time providing enjoyable texts and appealing illustrations for young people. I have included some great old tales too delightful to pass over, but the emphasis has been on the hidden treasures rather than on those stories, pictures, and poems readily available elsewhere.

Some of the stories written in other languages appear here in new translations—the Aesop, Charles Perrault, and Anatole France versions are my own. I would particularly like to thank my colleague Mrs. Zorah Kipel, of the Research Libraries' Slavonic Division, for her translation of the El Lissitsky text, which has never before appeared in English. I have also tried to match the stories with the most apt or amusing illustrations, not always from the original edition. Full bibliographical information on both text and illustrations is given in the Bibliography at the end of the volume. My colleagues in the Branch Libraries and the Research Libraries have been heroic in their patient assistance, and I shall be forever in their debt. If this work succeeds in delighting and instructing parents and children, then it is their achievement as much as it is mine.

Bernard McTigue
August 1986

# *A Word to Children*

The stories, poems, and pictures that make up this book have been chosen to give you pleasure. It is my hope that you will find them interesting and amusing and even, occasionally, instructive. Some of the stories you may already know; some of the pictures you will almost certainly have seen. But the variety of words and pictures gathered between these covers is something you probably have not seen before.

This volume represents a very small sampling of the books owned by the New York Public Library. For more than seventy-five years its children's rooms have provided a wide assortment of events, in addition to books, for the children of New York City. At the same time, the Central Research Library and the Donnell Library's Central Children's Room have been building collections of rare children's books primarily for the use of adult scholars. This book is intended to give you young readers the pleasure of peering into those collections of rare books. It offers you the opportunity to read stories and look at pictures that you might not otherwise be able to see until you are an adult scholar yourself.

It is my hope that you will find something within these pages that you will treasure always. Perhaps it will be a story or a poem or a picture. It would be wonderful, too, if you come away from this book with the notion that the library is a treasure house and a place to which you will want to return again and again.

Bernard McTigue
August 1986

Little children in a ring,
Hear them as they gaily sing!
Red child, yellow child, black child, white—
That's what makes the ring all right.

*A Kindergarten Song* by Carrie W. Clifford
Illustration by Marcellus Hawkins

AUNT MARY'S LITTLE SERIES
OLD
MOTHER
HUBBARD
NEW
McLOUGHLIN BROS N.Y.

# *Old Mother Hubbard*

*Our way of thinking of pets as almost human is the theme of this nursery rhyme.*

OLD Mother Hubbard
Went to the cupboard,
To give her poor dog a bone;
But when she came there
The cupboard was bare,
And so the poor dog had none.

She went to the baker's
To buy him some bread,
And when she came back
Poor doggy was dead.

She went to the joiner's
To buy him a coffin,
And when she came back
The dog was a laughing.

She took a clean dish
 To get him some tripe,
And when she came back
 He was smoking his pipe.

She went to the ale-house
 To get him some beer,
And when she came back
 Doggy sat in a chair.

She went to the tavern
 For white wine and red,
And when she came back
 The dog stood on his head.

She went to the hatter's
 To buy him a hat,
And when she came back
 He was feeding the cat.

She went to the barber's
To buy him a wig,
And when she came back
He was dancing a jig.

She went to the fruiterer's
To buy him some fruit,
And when she came back
He was playing the flute.

She went to the tailor's
To buy him a coat,
And when she came back
He was riding a goat

She went to the cobbler's
To buy him some shoes,
And when she came back
He was reading the news.

She went to the sempstress
To buy him some linen,
And when she came back
The dog was a-spinning.

She went to the hosier's
To buy him some hose,
And when she came back
He was dress'd in his clothes.

The dame made a curtesy,
The dog made a bow,
The dame said, "Your servant,"
The dog said, "Bow, wow!"

# *Baa Baa Black Sheep*

*Illustrations by E. Caldwell*

*Sheep are not generally known for their generosity. In this version of the nursery rhyme we meet the very British exception to the rule.*

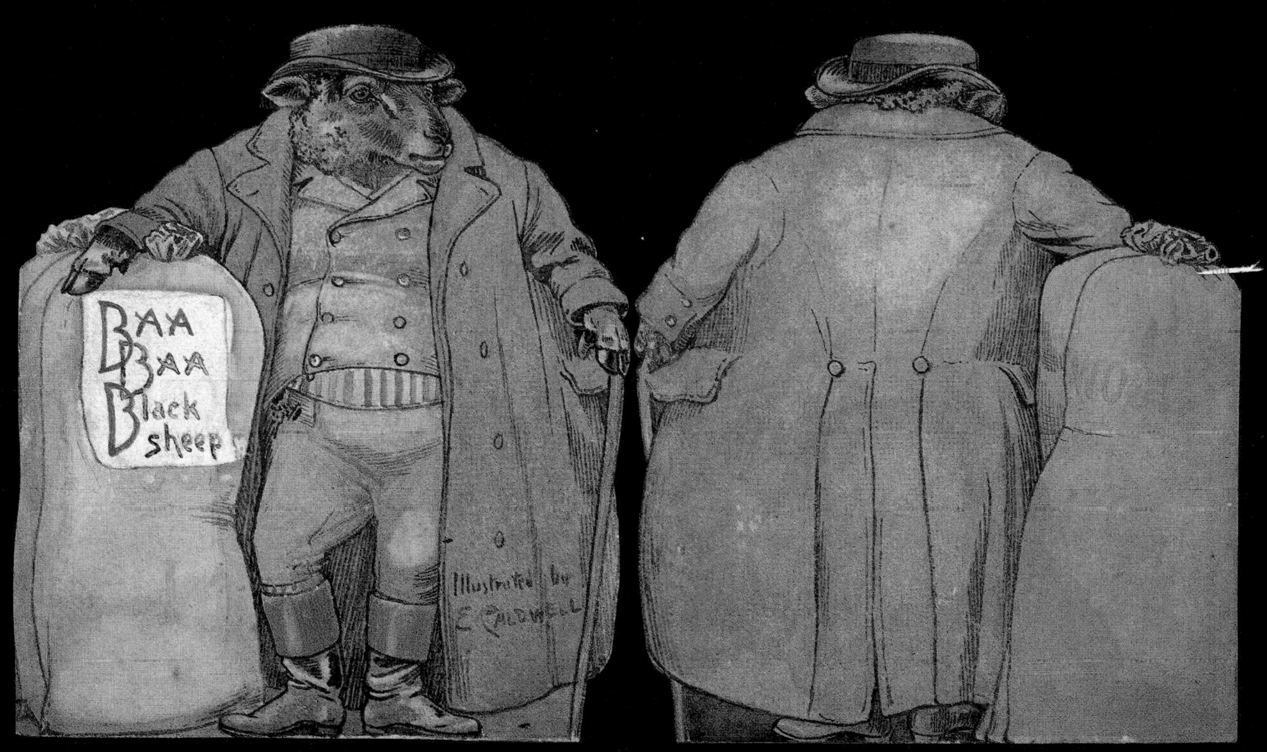

Baa, Baa! Black Sheep,
Have you any wool?
Aye, Sir; Nay, Sir;

Three bags full.
One for the master,

One for the dame,
But none for the little boy
Who cries in the lane.

# *Mother Goose and*
# *The Old Nursery Rhymes*

---

*Illustrations by Kate Greenaway*

*Perhaps these rhymes will remind you of someone you know.*

[a]

[b] There was a little man,
And he lived by himself,
And all the bread and
Cheese he got
He put upon a shelf.
But the rats and the mice
They made so much strife,
He was forced to go to
London to buy a little wife.
The streets were so crowded
And the lanes were so narrow,
He was forced to bring his little wife
Home in a barrow.

[c] Jack Sprat could eat no fat,
His wife could eat no lean;
And so between them both,
They licked the platter clean.

[a] Daffy-down-dilly
Has come up to town,
In a yellow petticoat
And a green gown.

[d] Mary, Mary, quite contrary,
How does your garden grow?
With silver bells and cockle shells
and cowslips all in a row.

[e] Polly put the kettle on
Polly put the kettle on
Polly put the kettle on
We'll all have tea.

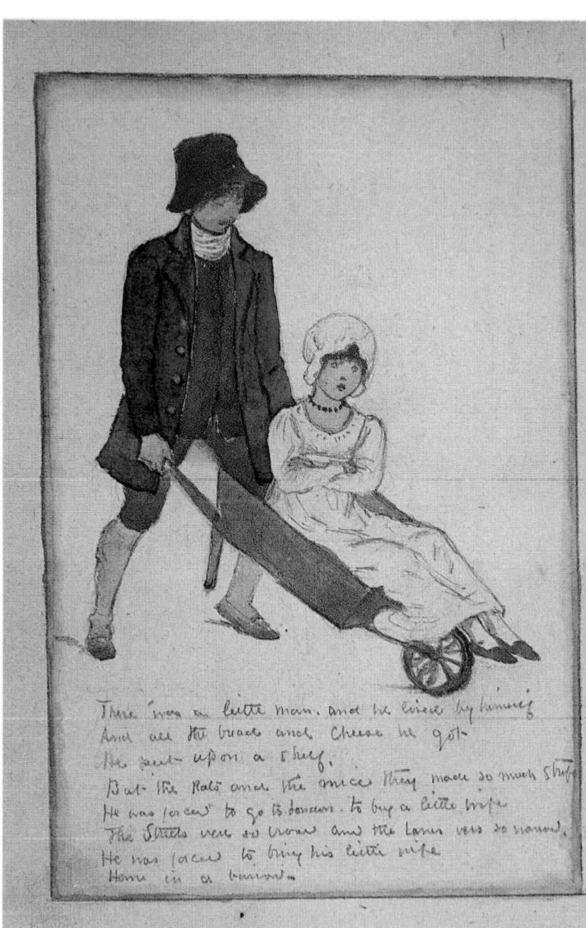
There was a little man. and he lived by himself
And all the bread and Cheese he got
But the Rats and the mice they made so much Strife
He was forced to go to London. to buy a little wife
He was forced to bring his little wife
Home in a barrow.

b

Jack. Sprat. Could eat no fat
His wife. Could eat no lean.
And so betwixt them both.
They licked the platter Clean.

Mary Mary quite Contrary
How does your Garden grow.
With Silver bells and Cockle Shells
And Cowslips all of a row.

d

Polly put the Kettle on
Polly put the Kettle on
Polly put the Kettle on
Well all have Tea.

e

f g

h

f Lucy Locket, lost her pocket,
Kitty Fisher found it;
There was not a penny in it,
But a ribbon round it.

g Ring a ring a' roses
A pocket-full of posies
Hush, hush, hush, hush,
We're all tumbled down.

h Cross Patch, lift the latch,
Sit by the fire and spin;
Take a cup, and drink it up,
Then call your neighbours in.

# *Hey Diddle Diddle*

*Illustrations by Randolph Caldecott*

*It is not entirely clear what these words mean, but they are fun to recite.*

Hey diddle, diddle,
The Cat and the Fiddle,

The Cow jumped over the Moon,
The little Dog laughed to see such fun,

And the Dish ran away with the Spoon.

# *The Rollo Books*

*By Jacob Abbott*

*Rollo learns the important difference between fact and fiction, between telling a story and "telling a story."*

## FICTITIOUS STORIES

"Father, will you tell me a story?" said Rollo, one day.

Rollo's father was sitting on the platform, leading out to the garden-yard. It was a pleasant summer evening, just before sunset.

"Shall it be a true story or a *fictitious* one?" said his father.

"What is fictitious?" asked Rollo.

"A story that is not true."

"But it would be wrong for you to tell me any thing that was not true, would it not?" said Rollo.

"Do you think it would be certainly wrong?"

"Yes sir."

"Suppose you were coming along the yard, and were riding on my cane, and should come up to me and say, 'Papa, this is my horse. See what a noble horse I have got.' Would that be wrong?"

"No sir."

"Would it be true?"

"No sir—It would not be a real horse."

"Now do you know why it would be right in this case for you to say it was a horse, when it was not?"

Rollo could not tell.

"I will tell you," said his father. "Because you would not be trying to *deceive* me. I could see your horse, as you call him, and could see that it was nothing but a cane. You would not be trying to deceive me, to make me think it was a real horse when it was not."

"No sir," said Rollo.

"If you should say any thing which is not strictly true and want to make me think it *is* true, that would be very wrong. That would be telling a lie. So it would be very wrong for me to tell you any thing which is not true, and try to make you think it is true. But it is not wrong for me to make up a little story to amuse you, if I do not try to deceive you by it."

# *Humpty Dumpty*

*This nursery rhyme, which may have started as a joke about a king's friend who fell out of favor, has been recited by generations of children amused at the crack-up of an egg.*

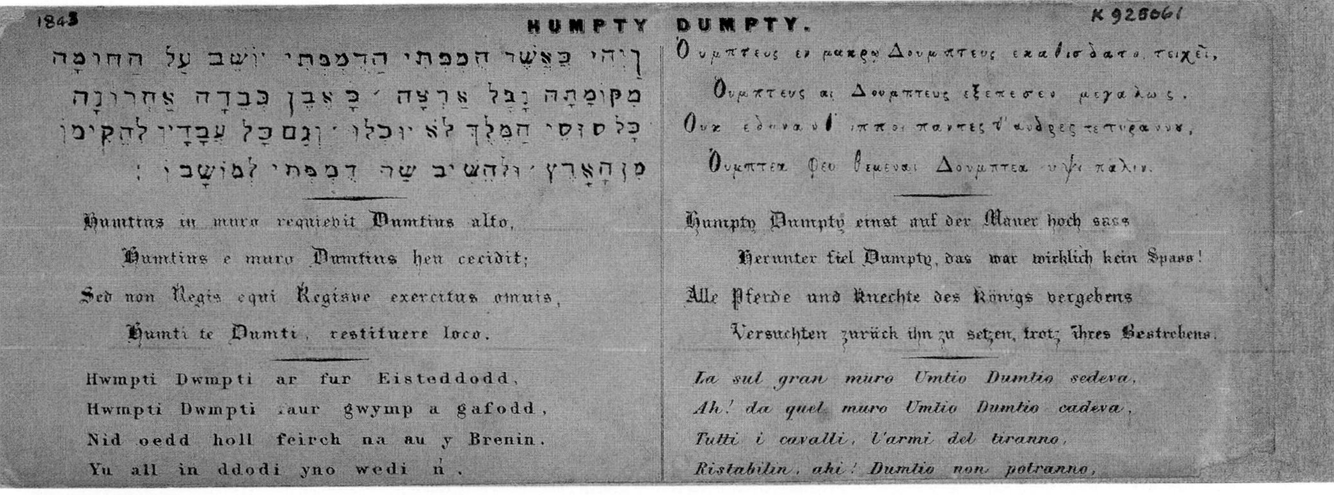

1843 HUMPTY DUMPTY. K 928061

ויהי כאשר המפתי הדמפתי יושב על החומה
מקומתה נפל ארצה כאבן כבדה אחרונה
כל סוסי המלך לא יוכלו וגם כל עבדיו להקימן
מן הארץ ולהשיב שה דמפתי למושבו :

Humtius in muro requievit Dumtius alto,
Humtius e muro Dumtius heu cecidit;
Sed non Regis equi Regisve exercitus omnis,
Humti te Dumti, restituere loco.

Hwmpti Dwmpti ar fur Eisteddodd,
Hwmpti Dwmpti ˌaur gwymp a gafodd,
Nid oedd holl feirch na au y Brenin.
Yu all in ddodi yno wedi n'.

Ὀυμπτευς εν μακρῳ Δουμπτευς εκαθισδατο τειχει,
Ὀυμπτευς αι Δουμπτευς εξεπεσεν μεγαλως.
Ουκ εδυναντ' ιπποι παντες τ' ανδρες τε τυραννου,
Ὀυμπτεα φευ θεμεναι Δουμπτεα υψι παλιν.

Humpty Dumpty einst auf der Mauer hoch sass
Herunter fiel Dumpty, das war wirklich kein Spass!
Alle Pferde und Knechte des Königs vergebens
Versuchten zurück ihn zu setzen, trotz ihres Bestrebens.

*La sul gran muro Umtio Dumtio sedeva,*
*Ah! da quel muro Umtio Dumtio cadeva,*
*Tutti i cavalli, l'armi del tiranno,*
*Ristabilin, ahi! Dumtio non potranno,*

Humpty Dumpty sat on a wall,
Humpty Dumpty had a great fall,
Not all the King's horses nor all the King's men
Could put Humpty Dumpty in his place again.

having heard of his Favorite's misfortune ordered

to the spot and superintended in person the

How the King's attempt to raise his Favorite failed.
How the weight of Humpty Dumpty w

all his horses and all his men; repaired

raising of the prostrate Humpty Dumpty.

at he dragged forward many of the Kings men, and how the rope breaking, all the rest for many miles fell backwards.

# ALPHABETS

*There have been hundreds of books printed over the years (and written out in the days before there was printing) designed to teach children their ABC's. Here are three from the Library's collection, all produced in nineteenth-century England, which suggest the variety and inventiveness of alphabet books. However much the books may change or the forms of the letters vary, the alphabet always remains essentially the same.*

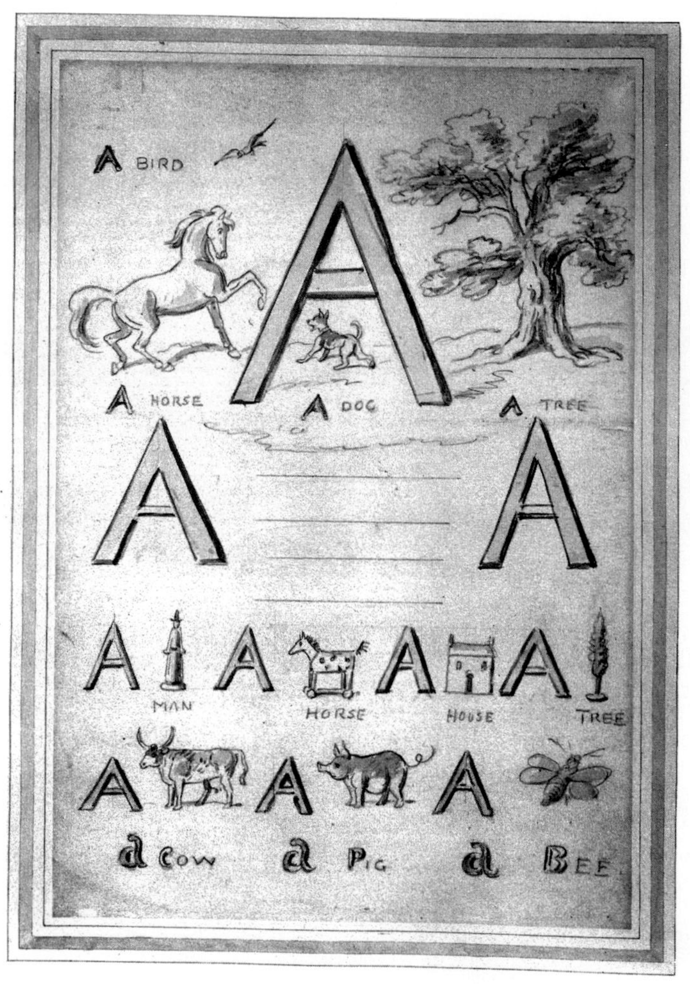

# *Pictorial Alphabet*

*By H. K. Browne*

*The artist drew these letters and pictures, perhaps to teach his own children their alphabet.*

# *The History of an Apple Pie*

*Written by Z*

*Who would have thought that so much could happen to a pie, except that it get eaten?*

THE

HISTORY

OF

AN APPLE PIE,

WRITTEN BY

Z.

LONDON:

PRINTED FOR HARRIS AND SON,

CORNER OF ST. PAUL'S CHURCH-YARD.

1823.

A B

a Apple Pie.

b Bit it.

# C D E F

c Cried for it.

d Danced for it.

e Eyed it.

f Fiddled for it.

# G H I J

g Gobbled it.

h Hid it.

i Inspected it.

j Jumped over it.

# K L M N

k Kicked it.

l Laughed at it.

m Mourned for it.

n Nodded for it.

# O P Q R

o Opened it.

p Peeped into it.

q Quaked for it.

r Rode for it.

S T U V

s Skipt for it.

t Took it.

u Upset it.

v Viewed it.

W X Y Z

w Warbled for it.

x Xerxes drew his sword for it.

y Yawned for it.

Z Zealous that all good boys and girls should be acquainted with his family, sat down and wrote the History of it.

# *An Alphabet from England*

*By Christina G. Rossetti*
*Illustrations by A. L. Stephens*

*This alphabet appeared in* St. Nicholas, *a famous American magazine for children.*

**A** is the Alphabet, A at its head;
**A** is an Antelope, agile to run.

**B** is the Baker Boy bringing the bread,
Or black Bear and brown Bear, both begging
  for bun.

**C** is a Cornflower, come with the corn;
**C** is a Cat with a comical look.

**D** is a dinner which Dahlias adorn;
**D** is a Duchess who dines with a Duke.

**E** is an elegant, eloquent Earl;
**E** is an Egg whence an Eaglet emerges.

**F** is a Falcon, with feathers to furl;
**F** is a Fountain of full foaming surges.

**G** is the Gander, the Gosling, the Goose;
**G** is a Garnet in girdle of gold.

**K** is a King, or a Kaiser still higher;
**K** is a Kitten, or quaint Kangaroo.

**L** is a Lute or a lovely-toned Lyre;
**L** is a Lily all laden with dew.

**M** is a Meadow where Meadow-sweet blows;
**M** is a Mountain made dim by a mist.

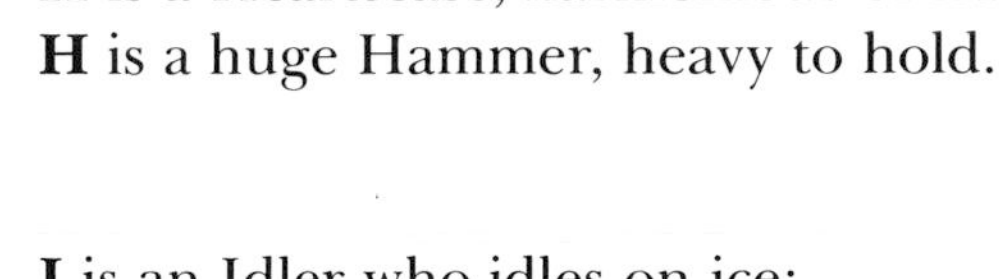

**H** is a Heartsease, harmonious of hues;
**H** is a huge Hammer, heavy to hold.

**I** is an Idler who idles on ice;
**I** am I—who will say I am not I?

**J** is a Jacinth, a jewel of price;
**J** is a Jay full of joy in July.

**N** is a nut—in a nutshell it grows;
Or a Nest full of Nightingales singing—
oh, list!

**O** is an Opal, with only one spark;
**O** is an Olive, with oil on its skin.

**P** is a Pony, a pet in a park;
**P** is the Point of a Pen or a Pin.

**Q** is a Quail, quick chirping at morn;
**Q** is a Quince quite ripe and near dropping.

**R** is a Rose, rosy red on a thorn;
**R** is a red-breasted Robin come hopping.

**S** is a Snowstorm that sweeps o'er the Sea;
**S** is the Song that the swift Swallows sing.

**T** is the Tea-table set out for tea;
**T** is a Tiger with terrible spring.

**U**, the Umbrella, went up in a shower;
Or Unit is useful with ten to unite.

**V** is a Violet veined in the flower;
**V** is a Viper of venomous bite.

**W** stands for the water-bred Whale;
Stands for the wonderful Wax-work so gay.

**X**, or X X, or X X X is ale,
Or Policeman X, exercised day after day.

**Y** is a yellow Yacht, yellow its boat;
**Y** is the Yucca, the Yam, or the Yew.

**Z** is a Zebra, zigzagged his coat,
Or Zebu, or Zoöphyte, seen at the Zoo.

# *First and Second Picture Books*

*By Edward Steichen and Dr. Mary Steichen Calderone*
*Photographs by Edward Steichen*

*The famous American photographer created these books with his daughter to show the everyday objects of a child's world. They are the first children's books illustrated with photographs.*

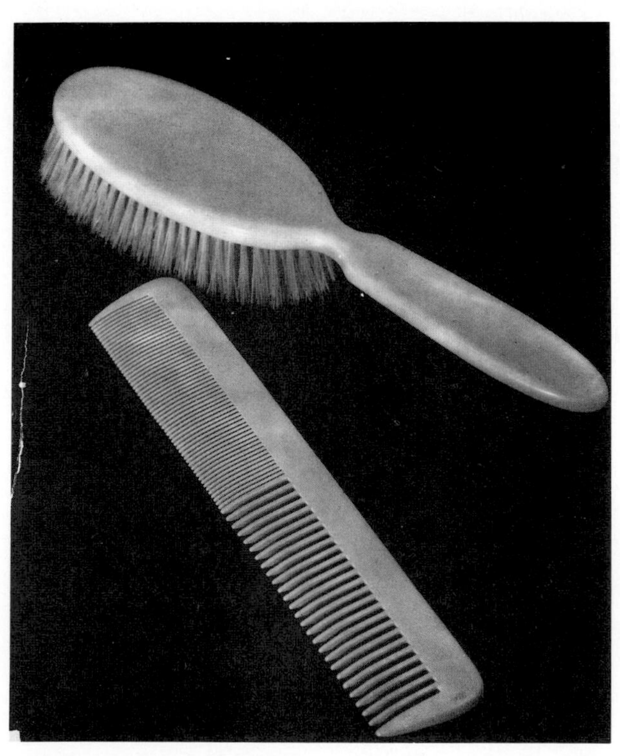

By C·B·FALLS
BEATRIX POTTER
THE TALE OF PETER RABBIT

# *About Two Squares*

*By El Lissitsky*

*In this picture book by a Russian artist and architect, the words are definitely less important than the pictures.*

- Do not read.
- Take paper, wooden pegs and blocks,
  put them together, paint with them, build things.
- Here are two squares.
- They fly together to the earth from far away.
- And they see a scary blackness.
- Bang! Everything explodes!
- And on the blackness, red sets itself up.
- And this is what it finally looks like.

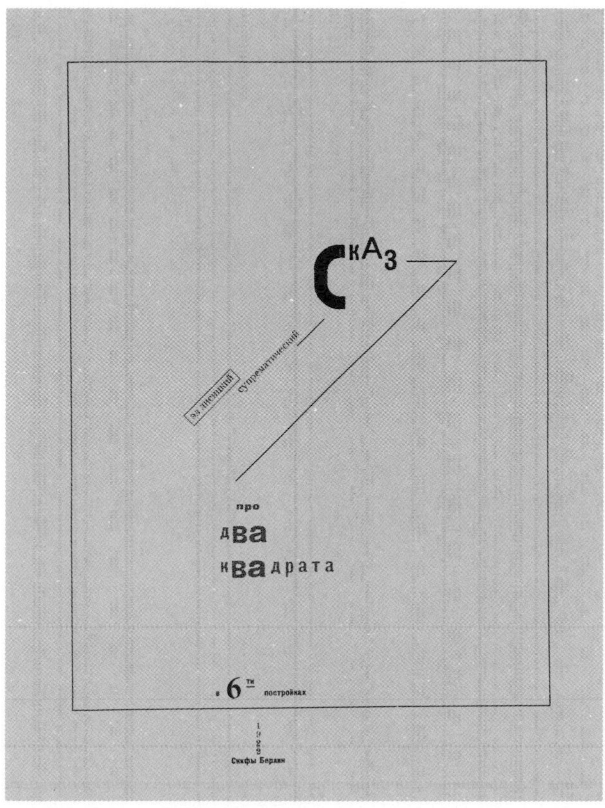
эл лисицкий
супрематический
СкАз
про
два
квадрата
в 6ти постройках
1922
Скифы Берлин

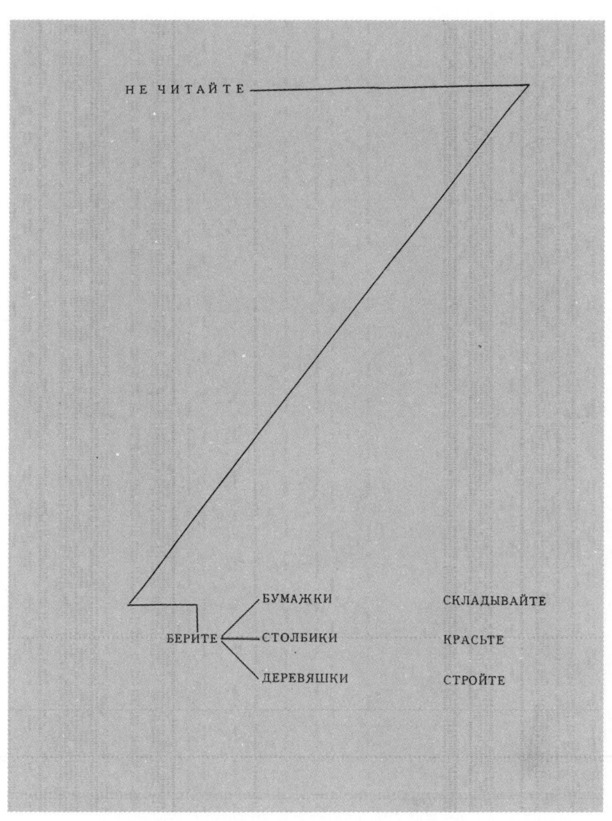
НЕ ЧИТАЙТЕ
БЕРИТЕ
БУМАЖКИ
СТОЛБИКИ
ДЕРЕВЯШКИ
СКЛАДЫВАЙТЕ
КРАСЬТЕ
СТРОЙТЕ

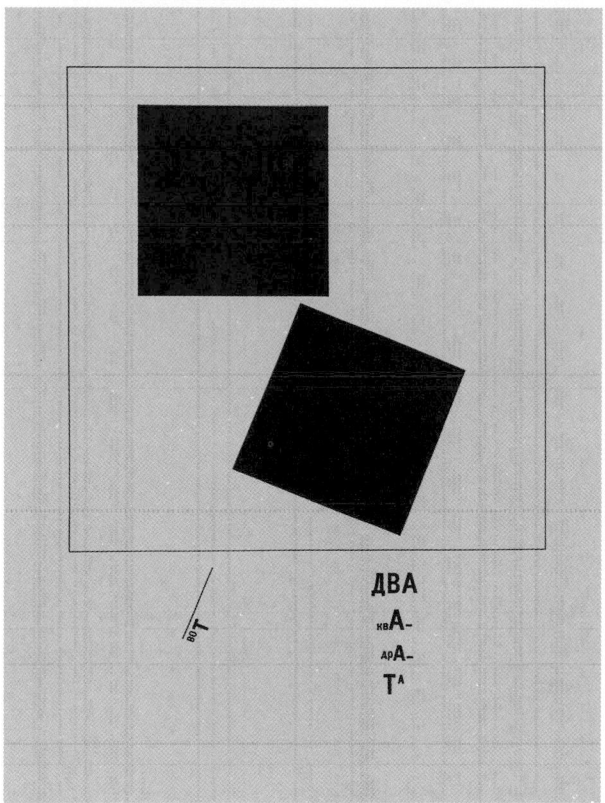
воТ
ДВА
квА-
дрА-
Тa

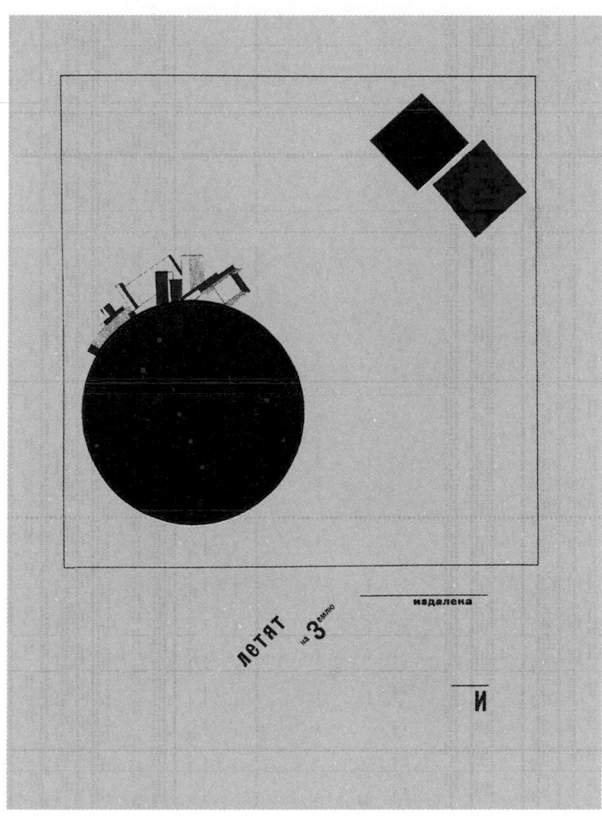
издалека
летят
на Земмлю
И

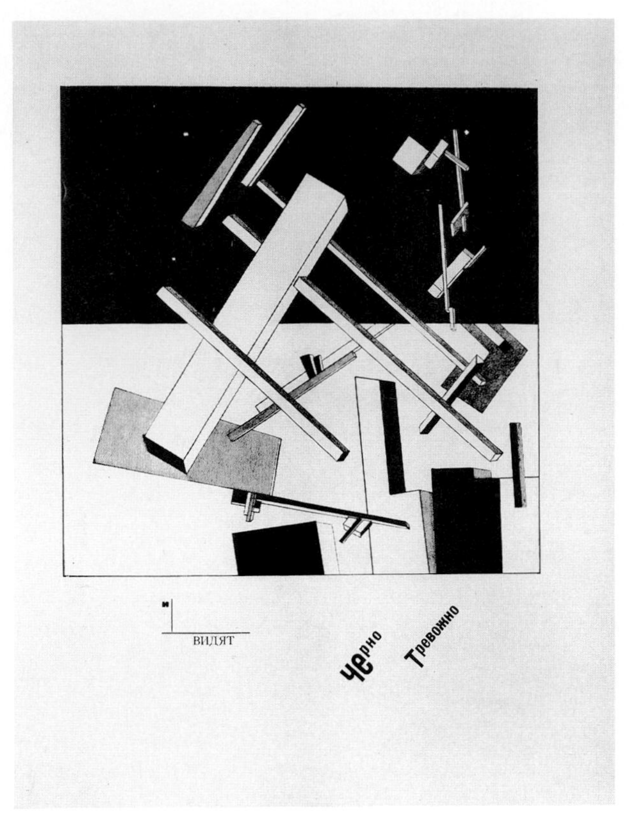
и
видят
черно
тревожно

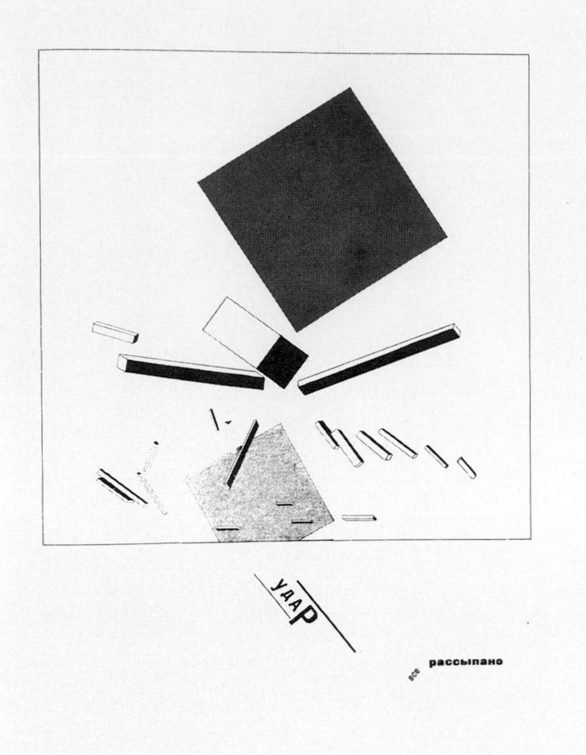
удар
все рассыпано

и По ЧЕРНОМУ
установилось
Кра
Я
сно

тут
кончено

# *Mrs. Barbauld's Lessons for Children from Three to Four Years Old*

*By Anna Letitia Barbauld*

*This is a sampling from one of the first children's books that addressed children as something other than miniature adults.*

Charles, what a clever thing it is to read! A little while ago, you know, you could only read little words; and you were forced to spell them c—a—t, cat; d—o—g, dog. Now you can read pretty stories, and I am going to write you some.

Do you know why you are better than Puss? Puss can play as well as you; and Puss can drink milk, and lie upon the carpet; and she can run as fast as you, and faster too, a great deal; and she can climb trees better; and she can catch mice, which you cannot do. But can Puss talk? No. Can Puss read? No. Then that is the reason why you are better than Puss—because you can talk and read. Can Pierrot, your dog, read? No. Will you teach him? Take the pin [pointer] and point to the words. No—he will not learn. I never saw a little dog or cat learn to read. But little boys can learn. If you do not learn, Charles, you are not good for half as much as a Puss. You had better be drowned.

What o'clock is it, Charles? It is twelve o'clock. It is noon. Come in the garden then. Now where is the sun? Turn your face towards him. Look at the sun; that is South. Always when it is twelve o'clock, and you look at the sun, your face is towards the South. Now turn to your left hand. Look forwards. That is East. In the morning, when it is going to be light, you must look just there, and presently you will see the sun get up. Always in the morning look there for the sun; for the sun rises in the East. Now turn your back to the sun. Look straight forwards. That is North. Now turn to your left hand. Look forwards. That is West. When you have had your supper, and it is going to be night, look for the sun just there. He is always there when he goes to bed; for the sun sets in the West. North, South, East, West.

# *The Peacock "At Home"*

*By Catherine Anne Dorset*

*Envy, this rhyme suggests, is not just a human vice.*

The Butterfly's Ball, and the Grasshopper's Feasts,
Excited the spleen of the birds and the beasts:
For their mirth and good cheer—of the Bee was the theme,
And the Gnat blew his horn, as he danc'd in the beam.
'Twas humm'd by the Beetle, 'twas buzz'd by the Fly,
And sung by the myriads that sport through the sky
The quadrupeds listen'd with sullen displeasure,
But the tenants of air were enraged beyond measure.
The Peacock display'd his bright plumes to the sun,
And addressing his mates, thus indignant begun:
"Shall we, like domestic inelegant fowls,
"As unpolished as Geese and as stupid as Owls,
"Sit tamely at home, hum drum with our spouses,
"While Crickets, and Butterflies open their houses?
"Shall such mean little insects pretend to the fashion?
"Cousin Turkeycock, well may you be in a passion!
"If I suffer such insolent airs to prevail,
"May Juno pluck out all the eyes in my tail;
"So a fete I will give, and my taste I'll display,
"And send out my cards for St. Valentine's Day."

The Peacock, imperial, the pride of his race,
Receiv'd all his guests with an infinite grace,
Wav'd his blue neck, and his train he display'd,
Embroider'd with gold, and with em'ralds inlaid.

# *The Fatal Mistake*

*By A. B. Frost*

*A picture story without words about a cat who swallows rat poison by mistake!*

# *The Butterfly's Ball and the Grasshopper's Feast*

*By Mr. Roscoe*
*Illustrations by William Mulready*

*This is believed to be the first story written in English simply to amuse (rather than instruct) children.*

The Trumpeter Gad-Fly has summon'd the crew,
And the Revels are now only waiting for you.

On the smooth-shaven Grass by the side of a Wood,
Beneath a broad Oak which for ages had stood,
See the Children of earth and the tenants of Air,
To an evening's amusement together repair.

And there came the Beetle, so blind and so black,
Who carried the Emmet, his friend on his back.

And there came the Gnat, and the Dragon-Fly too,
And all their relations, Green, Orange, and Blue.

And there came the Moth, with her plumage of down,
And the Hornet, with Jacket of Yellow and Brown.

Who with him the Wasp, his companion did bring,
But they promis'd that ev'ning, to lay by their sting.

Then the sly little Dormouse peep'd out of his hole,
And led to the feast, his blind cousin the Mole.

And the Snail, with her horns peeping out of her shell,
Came, fatigu'd with the distance the length of an ell.

A mushroom the table, and on it was spread,
A water-dock leaf, which their table cloth made.

The viands were various to each of their taste,
And the Bee brought the honey to sweeten the feast.

With steps most majestic the Snail did advance,
And he promis'd the gazers a minuet to dance;
But they all laugh'd so loud that he drew in his head,
And went in his own little chamber to bed.

Then, as ev'ning gave way to the shadows of night,
Their watchman, the Glow-worm, came out with his light.

So home let us hasten, while yet we can see;
For no watchman is waiting for you or for me.

# *A Natural History of British Quadrupeds*

*By W. Davison*
*Illustrations by Thomas Bewick*

*This instructional book can still teach children a thing or two about wild animals. It is one volume from* A Cabinet of Natural History *published in 1809 "containing pretty pictures of Birds, Animals, Fishes, Reptiles, Serpents, and Insects."*

## THE PHEASANT

The pheasant is said to have been first brought into Europe from the banks of the Phasis, in Asia Minor, and to have been at first artificially propagated in this country. However, notwithstanding the coldness of our climate, and the tenderness of its constitution, it has multiplied in a wild state; and, as if disdaining the protection of man, has left him, to take shelter in the thickest woods and the remotest forests. In fact, this spirit of independence seems to attend the pheasant even in captivity. In the woods the female lays from eighteen to twenty eggs in a season; but in a domestic state she seldom produces above ten. This bird seems better adapted to range at large in the woods than to be brought up in a state of captivity.

## THE BADGER

The badger is a solitary, stupid animal, that seeks refuge remote from man, and digs itself a deep winding hole, with great assiduity; its legs being very strong, and its claws stiff and horny. It seldom ventures far from its habitation, as it runs but slowly, and can find safety only in the strength of its retreat. When surprised by dogs at some distance from its hole, it falls upon its back, combats with desperate resolution, and seldom dies unrevenged on its enemies. The badger sleeps the greatest part of the time, and is particularly fat during the winter season. Its flesh is eaten by the poor of some countries, but is very rank and ill-tasted. When taken young the badger is easily tamed, and after a short time, will play with the dogs, and follow its master about the house.

## THE FOX

The fox has ever been famous for his cunning and arts, and he partly merits his reputation. He generally keeps his kennel at the edge of a wood, and yet within a short distance from some cottage; from thence he listens to the cackling of the fowls, scents them at a distance, makes an attack with the first opportunity, and seldom returns without his booty. If he be able to get into the yard, he begins by leveling all the poultry, and carrying off a part of the spoil, hides it at some convenient distance, and again returns to the charge. The she fox produces but once a year, and seldom has more than four or five cubs at a litter. To these she is peculiarly attentive, and if she suspects that the place of their retreat has been discovered, and that her young have been disturbed during her absence, she removes them, one after another, in her mouth to a place of security.

## THE BLACK GROUSE

This bird is usually about one foot ten inches in length, and weighs about four pounds. The general colour of the plumage is a deep black, glossed with violet and green. These birds are found chiefly in high and wooded situations. They feed principally on the leaves and buds of the birch tree, berries, and other fruits, the produce of wild and mountainous places. The black grouse is found in the mountainous parts of the north of England and Scotland, in Norway, Sweden, Russia, and Poland. In Norway they pass the winter beneath the snow in a state of torpor.

The female makes an artless nest upon the ground, laying six or seven eggs, rather less than those of the common hen.

# *The Adventures of Bob the Squirrel*

*Here is one youngster who learns, the hard way, the dangers of straying too far from one's parents.*

Come listen to my little book,
  And all of you shall know,
The story of a Squirrel,
  That a travelling would go,
Of all the sad disasters,
  And the dangers that he past,
And how he travelled far and wide,
  And came home safe at last.

Beside the margin of a lake,
  There stood a large Oak Tree,
Where Gaffer Scug, and Goody Scug,
  Lived happy as could be,
Except that Bob, their only son,
  Would never stay at home,
But like many naughty boys,
  Resolved abroad to roam.

So of a piece of willow bark,
 A boat he soon did make,
And having stor'd it well with nuts,
 He launch'd it on the lake,
Tho' his Father, and his Mother,
 Both begg'd that he would stay,
He spread his tail to catch the gale,
 And boldly sail'd away.

For two long days, and two long nights,
 He gaily on did float,
But on the third a storm arose,
 And sunk his little boat,
All drench'd and cold and weary,
 He struggled with the tide,
Till almost gone with swimming on
 He reach'd the farther side.

---

Now night was fast approaching,
 The storm was past away,
And toward a neighbouring forest,
 Poor Bobby bent his way,
When meeting Mrs. Bun, by chance,
 A Rabbit kind and good,
She made him stay, until next day,
 And treated him with food.

And being now recovered he,
 To Bunny bade adieu,
Resolved to climb a lofty hill,
 Which he far off could view,
But e'er he reach'd the mountain foot,
 The Sun had long been set,
And he was glad with Mr. Hare,
 A lodging for to get.

Next morning up the mountain side,
His way he gaily bent,
But weary did he find himself,
E'er half the day was spent,
And as night came the rain did fall,
And shelter found he none,
But drenched with wet and shivering cold,
He past the night alone.

Again as soon as it was light,
He urged his toilsome way,
For still the storm that raged all night
Continued thro' the day,
And nearly did he fall into,
The clutches of a Fox,
From which he was, to save himself,
Obliged to climb the rocks.

---

At length all faint and hungry,
With weakness nigh to drop,
With draggled tail and miry feet,
He reach'd the mountain top,
Which spread around with barren rocks,
All desert seem'd to be,
Nor could he meet with aught to eat,
Or water could he see.

And now with tears and sighs he cried,
Oh were I but at home,
I ne'er would leave my native tree,
Or e'er abroad would roam,
But whilst he mourn'd his hapless fate,
A Raven past that way,
And being hungry seiz'd on Bob,
And bore him far away.

But as the wicked Raven,
  With Bobby flew away,
An Eagle saw them and resolved,
  To make them both his prey,
With which he seized the Raven,
  And struck him such a blow.
That made him let go Bob, who fell,
  Into a tree below.

But who can tell how happy,
  And rejoiced poor Bobby felt,
On finding he was in the tree,
  Where both his parents dwelt,
And now he has determined,
  No more abroad to roam,
But in the future to be good,
  And always stay at home.

# *Animals in Costume*

*By dressing animals in clothes and putting them in human situations, the author of these verses hoped to avoid the smugness of righteous advice.*

## CLEANLINESS

Little Kitty nice,
Who catches all the mice,
Washes beard and ear,
In water pure and clear,
Her clothes from stains are free,
Child try like her to be.

## THEFT

"Out knave into thy hole with thee,
Nor steal my valued property!"
"Neighbour, which of the two is worst?
I only steal what you stole first."

## IMITATION

To shave himself
Ape thinks he's able,
And draws a chair
Up to the table;
He takes the razor
From the case,
And in a moment
Cuts his face.

## GOSSIP

Clatter, clatter,
Chatter, chatter,
Tattle, rattle,
Tittle, tattle,
Scandalizing friends and foes,
'Tis all the same with prating Crows,
I'd like to pull them by the nose.

## DISORDER

"Brother do not be
So disorderly,
Clothes and books are found
Lying on the ground.
How can you see them lie?
Pick them up, Oh fye!"

## FIDELITY

Upon his master's grave all day,
Consumed with sorrow, sits poor Tray;
In vain to tempt him off we try,
Oh could he there with master lie!

## HAUGHTINESS

"Have pity on my poverty,
A bit of bread pray give to me!"
The lord and lady dressed so gay,
Move haughtily along their way,
A neighbour poor who heard the prayer,
Comes his last mite with her to share.

## SELF-SATISFACTION

The donkey plays on his guitar,
The neighbours half distracted are.

## GENEROSITY

"The waters rise upon the land,
Can no one lend a helping hand?
Can no one from a watery grave,
My precious darling Kitty save?"
The watch-dog heard as near he stood,
And nobly leaped into the flood,
And saved the child of her who oft
In former times his life had sought.

## HEEDLESSNESS

The little lamb has stumbled,
  And her tears are sadly flowing,
She never would have tumbled
  Had she looked where she was going.

# *A Book of Nonsense*

*By Derry down Derry*
*Written and illustrated by Edward Lear*

*Edward Lear wrote these nonsense rhymes, called limericks, to entertain the grandchildren of his patron, the Earl of Derby.*

*There was an old Derry down Derry,*
*Who loved to see little folks merry:*
*So he made them a Book,*
*And with laughter they shook,*
*At the fun of that Derry down Derry!*

THERE WAS A YOUNG LADY OF HULL, WHO WAS CHASED BY A VIRULENT BULL;
BUT SHE SEIZED ON A SPADE, AND CALLED OUT—"WHO'S AFRAID?"—
WHICH DISTRACTED THAT VIRULENT BULL.

THERE WAS AN OLD MAN OF THE ISLES, WHOSE FACE WAS PERVADED WITH SMILES;
HE SUNG HIGH DUM DIDDLE, AND PLAYED ON THE FIDDLE,
THAT AMIABLE MAN OF THE ISLES.

THERE WAS AN OLD MAN OF THE DEE, WHO WAS SADLY ANNOYED BY A FLEA;
WHEN HE SAID, "I WILL SCRATCH IT,"— THEY GAVE HIM A HATCHET;
WHICH GRIEVED THAT OLD MAN OF THE DEE;

THERE WAS A YOUNG LADY OF NORWAY, WHO CASUALLY SAT IN A DOORWAY;
WHEN THE DOOR SQUEEZED HER FLAT, SHE EXCLAIMED "WHAT OF THAT?"—
THIS COURAGEOUS YOUNG LADY OF NORWAY.

# *The Bosun and the Bob-Tailed Comet*

*Written and illustrated by Jack B. Yeats*

*In this story a sailor's shore leave includes his first space flight. You might like to know that a "plum duff" is a pudding and a "tuck shop" is what the English call a candy store.*

**When the Bosun was paid off by his ship, the Bold Plum Duff, he found himself with thirty pounds, so**

he bought a nice stout pony

and everything went very well until they met

a little Comet.

But the Bosun secured that little Comet,

**and continued his journey on its back.**

**Of course people**

**were rather astonished.**

**Then the tail of that silly little Comet used to catch in the tops of the trees,**

until the Bosun made it shorter by tying it in a knot.

After that they went along finely till

they came to the Edge.

Then the Bosun really was frightened;

**when suddenly he saw his own old ship, the Bold Plum Duff, lying becalmed upon the ocean.**

**So they hailed each other,**

**and the Bosun very kindly towed the Bold Plum Duff to**

**port; where he was received with great honour,**

**and they presented him with the freedom of the Tuck Shop. And he and his little Comet lived happily ever afterwards.**

# *Tit, Tiny and Tittens, the Three White Kittens*

*In this poem the kittens learn that to act happy is to become happy.*

TITTENS growled over a ducking he'd had;
Tit he complained that the weather was bad:
Up started Tiny with, "Never be sad;
  Let's have a see-saw together,
  Together how merry we'll be!

"You in your corner, all shivering and wet,
The longer you stay there the more you will fret:
Jumping will warm you and make you forget;
  Let's have a see-saw together,
  Together how merry we'll be!

"Tit, though the shower may heavily fall,
We can be happy in spite of it all."
Tittens and Tit they sprang up at the call,
  Gaily they gambolled together,
  As merry as merry could be.

# *Struwwelpeter*

*Written and illustrated by Heinrich Hoffmann-Donner*

*This famous German children's book teaches neatness through the horrible example of slovenly Peter.*

## SHOCK-HEADED PETER

Just look at him!
There he stands,
With his nasty
hair and hands.

VI. Der Struwwelpeter

Sieh einmal, hier steht er,
Pfui! der Struwwelpeter!
An den Händen beiden
Ließ er sich nicht schneiden
Seine Nägel fast ein Jahr;
Kämmen ließ er nicht sein Haar.
Pfui! ruft da ein Jeder:
Garst'ger Struwwelpeter!

(15)

See! his nails
are never cut;
They are grim'd
as black as soot;

And the sloven, I declare,
Never once has comb'd his hair;
Any thing to me is sweeter
Than to see Shock-headed Peter.

# *Goop Tales*

*Written and illustrated by Gelett Burgess*

*You may have never met Goops before, but you will surely recognize them.*

## ASKALOTTE

Children, Behold Miss ASKALOTTE,
A most Attractive little Tot;
She was not Rude, nor yet Unkind,
I Never Knew her Not to Mind;
Yet she was always Asking Questions,
And Making most Ill-Timed Suggestions.

(This Goop is called ASKALOTTE because
she asks such a lot of needless questions)

## GOBLICK

When GOBLICK was but Four Years Old
His Parents seldom had to Scold—
They seldom Called him "GOBLICK don't!"
He did not Scowl, and say, "I won't!"
Yet Now 'tis Sad to see him Dine—
His Table Manners are not Fine!

(This Goop is called GOBLICK because
he gobbles his food and licks his fingers)

# INKFINGA

INKFINGA, a Cherubic Child,
Was never Rough, or Rude, or Wild.
Forbidden Sweets he would not Touch,
Though he might Want them Very Much!
But Oh, Imagination Fails
When I Describe his Finger Nails!

(This Goop is called INKFINGA because his fingers are as black as ink)

# DESTROYA

You'd never Think, to See DESTROYA,
That Anything could much Annoy her;
She'd Lend her Toys, she'd Help her Brother,
She'd Run on Errands for her Mother;
But Books and Papers, Every Day,
She'd Tear, in quite an Awful Way!

(This Goop is called DESTROYA because she destroys so many things)

# *Giant Otto*

*Written and illustrated by William Pène du Bois*

*This is the story of a very large dog who, even when friendly, is dangerous to be around.*

In a strange-looking house in a little French town lived a man and a dog.

There was nothing very funny about the man.... His name was Duke.

But the dog was enormous.... His name was Otto and he was an otter hound.

Otto was SO BIG that when he wagged his tail, it made so much wind that trees bent to the ground.

And children would "crack the whip" on his tremendous tail.

One day Duke decided that Otto was too big for such a little French town, so he decided to join the Foreign Legion in the big Sahara desert in Africa.

But Otto was also too big for the boat which sailed to Africa, so he traveled on a barge which was pulled by a tugboat.

Just as soon as they arrived in Africa, Otto stretched his legs and began to run all over the desert.

"It's wonderful," said Otto, "and the sun is hot."

"Too true," said Duke, and he reported at once at the Legion post.

The French Legion was having trouble with the Arabs because they were expecting an attack from them and they did not have half as many men as the Arabs. So Duke said: "Otto and I will conquer the Arabs alone." The legionnaires thought that was very funny because they did not know what a good dog Otto was.

So Otto and Duke set out to conquer eight hundred and fifty-two Arabs and eight camels. At first they worried and wondered how they would do such an enormous feat.

"If the Sphinx were here," suggested Otto, "I could hide behind it and pounce on the Arabs when they came."

"But it isn't," said Duke.

"And here are the Arabs," said Otto, and they both started some very fast charging.

And as they charged, Otto thought of a wonderful way to capture all the Arabs and all the camels, so he charged ahead alone faster, faster, and faster straight towards the Arabs.

Just before meeting them, he turned to the right and ran still faster around, around, and around the Arabs, wagging his tail and making lots of wind.

Otto ran still faster, and STILL FASTER, and then he stopped. The wind he had made was extraordinary. It whirled around and AROUND with such speed and strength that it swept the Arabs off their feet and they all spun around in the air.

Duke and Otto watched them whirl around and around and felt very proud.

"That was wonderful, Otto," said Duke.

Otto smiled and said: "It was really quite easy."

After a while the Arabs stopped spinning and all fell in a big pile covered with sand. And one by one they crawled out, feeling very dizzy and very scared, and they ran away into the desert.

"We must go home," said Duke.

"I think we must," said Otto, so they walked back to the Legion post.

When they arrived they were met by the company of soldiers, who carried Duke on their shoulders and cheered Otto loudly. Duke was then given a medal for bravery.

But the next day there was a special celebration all for Otto. There were soldiers, bugles, and flags; and he was given a medal for extraordinary courage in the face of extreme danger.

Otto was so happy that he wagged his tail, making a great wind. And as the people cheered louder, he wagged it harder and harder until all of a sudden he saw Duke running towards him and cheering *very* loudly. At this he was so happy that he wagged his tail with such speed that the wind blew the soldiers off the ground way up in the air.

It was a beautiful sight: soldiers, flags, and bugles flying through the air and everybody cheering Duke and his dog Otto, who, for extraordinary courage in the face of extreme danger, had just received a superb medal.

# *The Elephant's Child*

*Written and illustrated by Rudyard Kipling*

*This is one of the* Just So Stories, *which Kipling wrote in 1902 to entertain his little daughter. Generations of children since then have read them with pleasure.*

In the High and Far-Off Times the Elephant, O Best Beloved, had no trunk. He had only a blackish, bulgy nose, as big as a boot, that he could wriggle about from side to side; but he couldn't pick up things with it. But there was one Elephant—a new Elephant—an Elephant's Child—who was full of 'satiable curtiosity, and that means he asked ever so many questions. *And* he lived in Africa, and he filled all Africa with his 'satiable curtiosities. He asked his tall aunt, the Ostrich, why her tail-feathers grew just so, and his tall aunt the Ostrich spanked him with her hard, hard claw. He asked his tall uncle, the Giraffe, what made his skin spotty, and his tall uncle, the Giraffe, spanked him with his hard, hard hoof. And still he was full of 'satiable curtiosity! He asked his broad aunt, the Hippopotamus, why her eyes were red, and his broad aunt, the Hippopotamus, spanked him with her broad, broad hoof; and he asked his hairy uncle, the Baboon, why melons tasted just so, and his hairy uncle, the Baboon, spanked him with his hairy, hairy paw. And still he was full of 'satiable curtiosity! He asked questions about everything that he saw, or heard, or felt, or smelt, or touched, and all his uncles and his aunts spanked him. And still he was full of 'satiable curtiosity!

One fine morning . . . this 'satiable Elephant's Child asked a new fine question that he had never asked before. He asked, "What does the Crocodile have for dinner?" Then everybody said, "Hush!" in a loud and dretful tone, and they spanked him immediately and directly, without stopping, for a long time.

By and by, when that was finished, he came upon Kolokolo Bird . . . and he said, "My father has spanked me, and my mother has spanked me; all my aunts and uncles have spanked me for my 'satiable curtiosity; and *still* I want to know what the Crocodile has for dinner!"

Then Kolokolo Bird said, with a mournful cry, "Go to the banks of the great gray-green, greasy Limpopo River, all set about with fever-trees, and find out."

That very next morning . . . this 'satiable Elephant's Child took a hundred pounds of bananas (the little short red kind), and a hundred pounds of sugar-cane (the long purple kind), and seventeen melons (the greeny-crackly kind) and said to all his dear families, "Good-bye. I am going to the great gray-green, greasy Limpopo River, all set about with fever-trees, to find out what the Crocodile has for dinner." And they all spanked him once more for luck, though he asked them most politely to stop.

Then he went away, a little warm, but not at all astonished, eating melons, and throwing the rind about, because he could not pick it up.

He went . . . east by north, eating melons all the time, till at last he came to the banks of the great gray-green, greasy Limpopo River, all set about with fever-trees, precisely as Kolokolo Bird had said.

Now you must know and understand, O Best Beloved, that till that very week, and day, and hour, and minute, this 'satiable Elephant's

Child had never seen a Crocodile, and did not know what one was like....

The first thing that he found was a Bi-Coloured-Python-Rock-Snake curled round a rock.

" 'Scuse me," said the Elephant's Child most politely, "but have you seen such a thing as a Crocodile in these promiscuous parts?"

"*Have* I seen a Crocodile?" said the Bi-Coloured-Python-Rock-Snake, in a voice of dretful scorn. "What will you ask me next?"

" 'Scuse me," said the Elephant's Child, "but could you kindly tell me what he has for dinner?"

Then the Bi-Coloured-Python-Rock-Snake uncoiled himself very quickly from the rock, and spanked the Elephant's Child with his scalesome, flailsome tail.

"That is odd," said the Elephant's Child, "because my father and my mother, and my uncle and my aunt... have all spanked me for my 'satiable curtiosity—and I suppose this is the same thing."

So he said good-bye very politely to the Bi-Coloured-Python-Rock-Snake... and went on ... till he trod on what he thought was a log of wood at the very edge of the great gray-green, greasy Limpopo River, all set about with fever-trees.

But it was really the Crocodile, O Best Beloved, and the Crocodile winked one eye—like this!

" 'Scuse me," said the Elephant's Child most politely, "but do you happen to have seen a Crocodile in these promiscuous parts?"

Then the Crocodile winked the other eye, and lifted half his tail out of the mud; and the Elephant's Child stepped back most politely, because he did not wish to be spanked again.

"Come hither, Little One," said the Crocodile. "Why do you ask such things?"

" 'Scuse me," said the Elephant's Child most politely, "but my father has spanked me, my mother has spanked me, not to mention my tall aunt, the Ostrich, and my tall uncle, the Giraffe, who can kick ever so hard, as well as my broad aunt, the Hippopotamus, and my hairy uncle, the Baboon, *and* including the Bi-Coloured-Python-Rock-Snake, with the scalesome, flailsome tail, just up the bank, who spanks harder than any of them; and *so*, if it's quite all the same to you, I don't want to be spanked any more."

"Come hither, Little One," said the Crocodile, "for I am the Crocodile," and he wept crocodile-tears to show it was quite true.

Then the Elephant's Child grew all breathless, and panted, and kneeled down on the bank and said, "You are the very person I have been looking for all these long days. Will you please tell me what you have for dinner?"

"Come hither, Little One," said the Crocodile, "and I'll whisper."

Then the Elephant's Child put his head down close to the Crocodile's musky, tusky mouth, and the Crocodile caught him by his little nose, which up to that very week, day, hour, and minute, had been no bigger than a boot, though much more useful.

"I think," said the Crocodile—and he said it between his teeth, like this—"I think to-day I will begin with Elephant's Child!"

At this, O Best Beloved, the Elephant's Child was much annoyed, and he said, speaking through his nose, like this, "Led go! You are hurtig be!"

Then the Bi-Coloured-Python-Rock-Snake scuffled down from the bank and said, "My young friend, if you do not now, immediately and instantly, pull as hard as ever you can, it is my opinion that your acquaintance in the large-pattern leather ulster" (and by this he meant the Crocodile) "will jerk you into yonder limpid stream before you can say Jack Robinson."

This is the way Bi-Coloured-Python-Rock-Snakes always talk.

Then the Elephant's Child sat back on his little haunches, and pulled, and pulled, and pulled, and his nose began to stretch. And the Crocodile floundered into the water, making it all creamy with great sweeps of his tail, and *he* pulled, and pulled, and pulled.

And the Elephant's Child's nose kept on

stretching; and the Elephant's Child spread all his little four legs and pulled, and pulled, and pulled, and his nose kept on stretching; and the Crocodile threshed his tail like an oar, and *he* pulled, and pulled, and pulled, and at each pull the Elephant's Child's nose grew longer and longer—and it hurt him hijjus!

Then the Elephant's Child felt his legs slipping, and he said through his nose, which was now nearly five feet long, "This is too butch for be!"

Then the Bi-Coloured-Python-Rock-Snake came down from the bank, and knotted himself in a double-clove-hitch round the Elephant's Child's hind legs, and said, "Rash and inexperienced traveller, we will now seriously devote ourselves to a little high tension, because if we do not, it is my impression that yonder self-propelling man-of-war with the armour-plated upper deck" (and by this, O Best Beloved, he meant the Crocodile), "will permanently vitiate your future career."

That is the way all Bi-Coloured-Python-Rock-Snakes always talk.

So he pulled, and the Elephant's Child pulled, and the Crocodile pulled; but the Elephant's Child and the Bi-Coloured-Python-Rock-Snake pulled hardest; and at last the

Crocodile let go of the Elephant's Child's nose with a plop that you could hear all up and down the Limpopo.

Then the Elephant's Child sat down most hard and sudden; but first he was careful to say "Thank you" to the Bi-Coloured-Python-Rock-Snake; and next he was kind to his poor pulled nose, and wrapped it all up in cool banana leaves, and hung it in the great gray-green, greasy Limpopo to cool.

"What are you doing that for?" said the Bi-Coloured-Python-Rock-Snake.

" 'Scuse me," said the Elephant's Child, "but my nose is badly out of shape, and I am waiting for it to shrink."

"Then you will have to wait a long time," said the Bi-Coloured-Python-Rock-Snake. "Some people do not know what is good for them."

The Elephant's Child sat there for three days waiting for his nose to shrink. But it never grew any shorter. . . . For, O Best Beloved, you will see and understand that the Crocodile had pulled it out into a really truly trunk same as all Elephants have to-day.

At the end of the third day a fly came and stung him on the shoulder, and before he knew what he was doing he lifted up his trunk and hit that fly dead with the end of it.

" 'Vantage number one!" said the Bi-Coloured-Python-Rock-Snake. "You couldn't have done that with a mere-smear nose. Try and eat a little, now."

Before he thought what he was doing the Elephant's Child put out his trunk and plucked a large bundle of grass, dusted it clean against his fore-legs, and stuffed it into his own mouth.

" 'Vantage number two!" said the Bi-Coloured-Python-Rock-Snake. "You couldn't have done that with a mere-smear nose. Don't you think the sun is very hot here?"

"It is," said the Elephant's Child, and before he thought what he was doing he schlooped up a schloop of mud from the banks of the great gray-green, greasy Limpopo, and slapped it on his head, where it made a cool schloopy-sloshy mud-cap all trickly behind his ears.

" 'Vantage number three!" said the Bi-Coloured-Python-Rock-Snake. "You couldn't have done that with a mere-smear nose. Now how do you feel about being spanked again?"

" 'Scuse me," said the Elephant's Child, "but I should not like it at all."

"How would you like to spank somebody?" said the Bi-Coloured-Python-Rock-Snake.

"I should like it very much indeed," said the Elephant's Child.

"Well," said the Bi-Coloured-Python-Rock-Snake, "you will find that new nose of yours very useful to spank people with."

"Thank you," said the Elephant's Child, "I'll remember that; and now I think I'll go home to all my dear families and try."

So the Elephant's Child went home across Africa frisking and whisking his trunk. . . . One dark evening he came back to all his dear families, and he coiled up his trunk and said, "How do you do?" They were very glad to see him, and immediately said, "Come here and be spanked for your 'satiable curtiosity."

"Pooh," said the Elephant's Child. "I don't think you peoples know anything about spanking; but *I* do, and I'll show you."

Then he uncurled his trunk and knocked two of his dear brothers head over heels.

"O Bananas!" said they, "where did you learn that trick, and what have you done to your nose?"

"I got a new one from the Crocodile on the banks of the great gray-green, greasy Limpopo River," said the Elephant's Child. "I asked him what he had for dinner, and he gave me this to keep."

Then that bad Elephant's Child spanked all his dear families for a long time, till they were very warm and greatly astonished. . . . At last things grew so exciting that his dear families went off . . . in a hurry . . . to borrow new noses from the Crocodile. When they came back nobody spanked anybody any more; and ever since that day, O Best Beloved, all the Elephants you will ever see, besides all those that you won't, have trunks precisely like the trunk of the 'satiable Elephant's Child.

# *Rootabaga Country*

*By Carl Sandburg*
*Illustrations by Peggy Bacon*

Rootabaga Stories *and* Rootabaga Country, *from which this selection comes, are nonsense tales by a famous American poet and folksinger. This is a funny story about eggs in all the wrong places.*

## SHUSH SHUSH, THE BIG BUFF BANTY HEN WHO LAID AN EGG IN THE POSTMASTER'S HAT

SHUSH SHUSH was a big buff banty hen. She lived in a coop. Sometimes she marched out of the coop and went away and laid eggs. But always she came back to the coop.

And whenever she went to the front door and laid an egg in the doorbell, she rang the bell once for one egg, twice for two eggs, and a dozen rings for a dozen eggs.

Once Shush Shush went into the house of the Sniggers family and laid an egg in the piano. Another time she climbed up in the clock and laid an egg in the clock. But always she came back to the coop.

One summer morning Shush Shush marched out through the front gate, up to the next corner and the next, till she came to the post office. There she walked into the office of the postmaster and laid an egg in the postmaster's hat.

The postmaster put on his hat, went to the hardware store and bought a keg of nails. He took off his hat and the egg dropped into the keg of nails.

The hardware man picked up the egg, put it in *his* hat, and went out to speak to a policeman. He took off his hat, speaking to the policeman, and the egg dropped on the sidewalk.

The policeman picked up the egg and put it in *his* police hat. The postmaster came past; the policeman took off his police hat and the egg dropped down on the sidewalk.

The postmaster said, "I lost that egg, it is my egg," picked it up, put it in his postmaster's hat, and forgot all about having an egg in his hat.

Then the postmaster, a long tall man, came to the door of the post office, a short small door. And the postmaster didn't stoop low, didn't bend under, so he bumped his hat and his head on the top of the doorway. And the egg *broke* and ran down over his face and neck.

And long before that happened, Shush Shush was home in her coop, standing in the door saying, "It is a big day for me because I laid one of my big buff banty eggs in the postmaster's hat."

There Shush Shush stays, living in a coop. Sometimes she marches out of the coop and goes away and lays eggs in pianos, clocks, hats. But she always comes back to the coop.

And whenever she goes to the front door and lays an egg in the doorbell, she rings the bell once for one egg, twice for two eggs, and a dozen rings for a dozen eggs.

# A Visit from St. Nicholas

*By Clement C. Moore*
*Illustrations by Boyd*

*Saint Nicholas, patron saint of children, was called* Sinterklass *by the Dutch who had settled in New York. From that name it was just a short step to Santa Claus. This poem, first printed in New York in 1823, helped create the jolly old Santa we know today.*

## VISIT FROM SANTA CLAUS

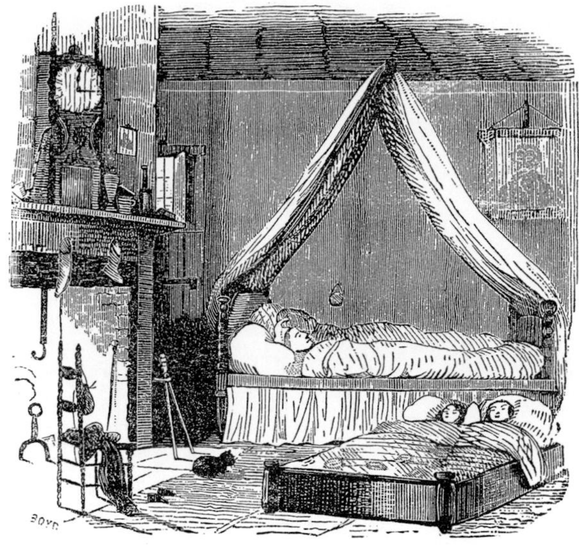

T was the night before Christmas,
when all through the house
Not a creature was stirring, not
even a mouse;
The stockings were hung by the
chimney with care,
In hopes that St. Nicholas soon
would be there;
The children were nestled all snug
in their beds,
While visions of sugar-plums danced in their
heads;
And Mamma in her 'kerchief, and I in my cap,
Had just settled our brains for a long winter's
nap;
When out on the lawn there arose such a
clatter,
I sprang from the bed to see what was the
matter.
Away to the window I flew like a flash,
Tore open the shutters and threw up the sash.
The moon on the breast of the new-fallen
snow,
Gave the lustre of mid-day to objects below,
When, what to my wondering eyes should
appear,
But a miniature sleigh, and eight tiny rein-
deer,
With a little old driver, so lively and quick,
I knew in a moment it must be St. Nick.
More rapid than eagles his coursers they came,
And he whistled, and shouted, and called them
by name;
"Now, *Dasher!* now, *Dancer!* now *Prancer*
and *Vixen!*
On, *Comet!* on, *Cupid!* on, *Donder* and
*Blitzen!*
To the top of the porch! to the top of the
wall!
Now dash away! dash away! dash away
all!"
As dry leaves that before the wild hurricane
fly,
When they meet with an obstacle, mount to
the sky;
So up to the house-top the coursers they flew,
With the sleigh full of Toys, and St. Nicholas
too.
And then in a twinkling, I heard on the roof,
The prancing and pawing of each little hoof—
As I drew in my head, and was turning
around,
Down the chimney St. Nicholas came with a
bound.
He was dressed all in fur, from his head to his
foot,
And his clothes were all tarnished with ashes
and soot;

A bundle of Toys he had flung on his back,
And he looked like a pedlar just opening his pack,
His eyes—how they twinkled! his dimples how merry!
His cheeks were like roses, his nose like a cherry!
His droll little mouth was drawn up like a bow,
And the beard of his chin was as white as the snow;
The stump of a pipe he held tight in his teeth,
And the smoke it encircled his head like a wreath;
He had a broad face and a little round belly,
That shook when he laughed like a bowlfull of jelly.
He was chubby and plump, a right jolly old elf,
And I laughed when I saw him, in spite of myself,
A wink of his eye and a twist of his head,
Soon gave me to know I had nothing to dread;
He spoke not a word, but went straight to his work,
And fill'd all the stockings; then turned with a jerk,
And laying his finger aside of his nose,
And giving a nod, up the chimney he rose;
He sprang to his sleigh, to his team gave a whistle,
And away they all flew like the down of a thistle.
But I heard him exclaim ere he drove out of sight,

# *My Own Treasury: A Gift Book for Boys and Girls*

*Edited by Mark Merriwell*

*This version of the story of the Ugly Duckling describes his adventures before he learned his true identity.*

## THE UGLY LITTLE DUCK

At last the egg burst. "Pee! pee!" said the little thing, as it scrambled out; but O, what a clumsy, ugly creature it was! The mother stared at it with amazement. "What a great big lump it is!" she said, "not one of the rest is at all like it. I wonder is it a turkey chick? Well, we shall soon see. Into the water it shall go, I will know for what."

The weather next day was as fine as heart could wish; the air was so clear and the sun shone so pleasantly on the green leaves. Mother duck now went down with all her family to the canal, and flop she went into the water. "Quack, quack," said she, and in tumbled the ducklings one after the other. The water closed over their heads but they were up again on the surface in a moment, and swam about in capital style; their legs went like paddles of their own accord, without the least apparent effort; and there they were, every one of them, even the ugly gray one, swimming away with the best of the brood.

"No," said the mother, "that is no turkey at all events! Only see how cleverly he uses his legs, how upright he sits! He is my own true child. And really now, if you consider him rightly, he is much prettier than you would fancy at first sight. Quack! quack! now come with me, and I will show you the world, and introduce you into the poultry-yard; but stay close to me, lest anyone tread on you, and be sure you keep clear of the cats!"

And so they came to the poultry-yard, which they found in a tremendous uproar, for two families were striving for the remains of an eel; but after all neither party triumphed, for the cats carried off the whole booty.

"Ah, my dears, just what is the way of the world," said the mother duck, licking her bill, for she, too, longed for a dainty morsel of eel. "Step out now, mind what you are about, and make a bow to the old lady duck yonder; she is the person of most consequence amongst us. She is of Spanish descent, as you may perceive by her dignified demeanour; and then you observe she has a strip of red cloth fastened round

her leg; that is an amazingly pretty thing, and the greatest mark of distinction that any duck can aspire to, for it signifies that she is not to be parted with, and that she is to be known and respected by birds, beasts, and men. Don't put your toes together in that manner. A well-bred duckling walks with its legs wide apart, just as father and mother do. Look at me. Now, bow your heads and say, Quack!"

They did as they were bid; but all the other ducks in the yard stared at them with no friendly looks, and some of them said aloud: "Pretty times these! As if there were not enough of us already, here comes a whole swarm to eat us out of house and home! and only look at that horrid ugly one; it is not to be endured!" and instantly a duck made a pounce upon it, and bit it in the neck.

"Let him alone, will you," said the mother, "he does no one any harm."

"Ay, but he is such a great awkward fright, he deserves to be pecked."

"Very nice children those the mother has got," said the old lady duck, with the red cloth on her leg. "Very pretty, indeed, all but one; she has not much to boast of there; I wish she could hatch it over again."

"That is not possible, please your ladyship," said the mother; "and, to be sure, the poor thing is not as handsome as it might be; but then it is such a dear good child, and it swims as well as any of the others, or may be a trifle better. I do hope it will turn out better looking as it grows up. It was an uncommonly long while in the egg, and that's why it is a little out of proportion." And then she fondled the duckling, scratched the back of its neck, and stroked it down with her bill. "Besides," she added, "it is a little drake, so its looks are not of so much consequence; bless its little heart it will be a fine strong fellow one of these days, and will make its way bravely in the world."

"The others are pretty little things, and very nicely behaved," said the old lady; "now, my dears, make yourselves quite at home, and if you pick up an eel's head, you may bring it to me."

And thenceforth they were quite at home.

But the poor young duck that was last hatched, and looked so ugly, was chased, and thumped, and pecked by ducks and hens. "Such a great awkward lout!" they all said; and the turkey cock that had come into the world with spurs on, and therefore imagined himself an emperor, spread himself out like a ship in full sail, made a rush at it, and gobbled till he was as red in the face as a pickled cabbage. The poor little duck hardly knew what to do with itself, and was sorely distressed at being so ugly, and finding itself the laughing-stock of the whole poultry-yard.

Thus passed the first day, and afterwards things grew worse and worse. The poor duckling was persecuted on all sides; and even its brothers and sisters were spiteful to it, and were always saying, "I wish the cat would take you, you nasty creature;" and its mother said, "Oh, I wish you were far away from here;" and the ducks bit it, and the hens pecked at it, and the girl that brought food to the poultry kicked it out of her way. So at last the poor duckling made a spring and flew over the hedge, and all the little birds in the bushes started back in a terrible fright. "That is because I am so ugly," said the duckling to itself, closing its eyes, but still continuing its flight. At last it came to a great marsh, where wild ducks lived, and there it lay all night, so weary and unhappy! In the morning the wild ducks got up and saw the newcomer.

"Hollo, who are you?" said they, and the duckling turned in every direction and saluted as mannerly as it could.

"Well, you're a precious fright; there's no denying that," said the wild ducks. "However, it is all the same to us, provided you don't marry into our family." Marry! The poor thing had certainly no thoughts of marrying; all it desired was leave to lie among the rushes and drink a little marsh water.

Two whole days it stayed in that place; on the third day came two wild geese, or rather goslings, that had not been a very long while out of the shell, and were, therefore, so much the more silly and conceited.

"Hark ye, old fellow," said one of them, "you are such a precious ugly quiz that I have taken a monstrous liking to you. What say you? Will you come with us and be a rover? In another marsh, not far from here, there are some charming young lady geese, the prettiest creatures you ever set eyes on. Now's your time to push your fortune, for all you are so ugly—"

Bang! bang! went two shots at that instant; both the wild geese lay dead in the rushes, and the water was blood-red. Bang! bang! it went again, and whole flocks of wild ducks flew up out of the sedges, and the firing was redoubled.

It was a great shooting party, and the sportsmen had posted themselves all round the marsh; the blue smoke spread like a cloud through the dark trees, and sank down upon the water; the dogs splashed about in the mud and slime, and the reeds and rushes were shaking on every side.

It was not until late in the day that the shooting ceased; but even then the poor little thing did not venture to stir. At last, after the lapse of several hours, it looked cautiously round, and then made off from the marsh as fast as it could, and flew and flew, but the wind was so strong it could scarcely make any way.

About nightfall it reached a miserable little cottage, that seemed as if it would rather tumble down than remain standing, but did not exactly know how to set about it. The wind was so violent that the unfortunate duckling was obliged to squat on its tail to resist it, and it grew worse and worse every minute. At last it perceived that the door hung aslant, having dropped out of one of the hinges; so it wriggled itself into the cottage through the gap.

The cottage was inhabited by an old woman, her tom-cat, and her hen. The cat could bend up its back like a horseshoe, and purr like a spinning wheel; nay, it could even crackle and sparkle, if any one stroked its back against the grain. The hen was a plump and rather fussy little person, with short legs. She laid an egg every day, and the old woman loved her as if she had been her own child.

Next morning the stranger was quickly

perceived, and the tom began to mew and the hen to cackle.

"What's the matter?" said the old woman, looking all round; but her sight was not good, and so she mistook the duckling for a good fat duck that had gone astray.

"I'm in luck this morning," said she, "I shall have duck eggs now, if it is not a drake. We must see how that may be. Time will tell."

And so the duck was taken on trial; but for three weeks no egg made its appearance. And the cat was master in the house, and the hen was mistress; and they always said, *"We and the rest of the world"*; for they thought they were themselves half the world, and that too by far the better half. The duck ventured to hint at a different opinion, but the hen fired up at him in a moment.

"Can you lay eggs?" she said.

"No."

"Then hold your tongue!"

And the cat said, "Can you bend up your back like a horseshoe, and purr like a spinning-wheel, and crackle and sparkle?"

"No."

"Then you should not presume to offer your opinions in presence of people that have more sense than yourself."...

"You don't understand me, I think I will go away into the wide, wide world," said the duckling.

"Well, go then," replied the hen.

So away went the duck; it swam on the water, and dived under it, but was disregarded by all creatures on account of its ugliness. November came at last, the leaves were yellow and brown, the wind caught hold of them and danced about with them, and the air was bleak and chilly; the clouds hung low, charged with snow or hail, and the raven sat on a bare branch, and croaked with cold—it was enough to freeze one, only to think of that bitter weather; you may be sure the poor duck had a very hard time of it.

One evening the sun set splendidly, and a great flock of beautiful large birds came out from among the bushes, on the waterside; the duck had never seen any thing to equal them; they were brilliantly white with long slender necks—they were swans. All at once they uttered a strange sound, spread their sailbroad wings, and flew away in search of warmer lands and opener lakes. They mounted up in the air so high, so high! and a most extraordinary feeling came over the ugly little duck; it spun round and round in the water like a wheel, stretched up its neck after the flock as high as ever it could, and sent forth a cry so loud and strange that it was itself quite astonished and frightened! Oh! it could never forget them, the noble birds! the happy birds! and as soon as they were no longer to be seen, it dived down to the bottom, and when it came up again it seemed almost beside itself. The duckling knew not the name of the birds; or whither they flew; but it loved them as it had never yet loved any living being. It did not envy them; O no! how could it ever dream of coveting such beauty? It could have been abundantly content if it might only be tolerated by the ducks in the poultry-yard, poor, little, ugly wretch that it was!

And then came the dreary, dreadful winter. The duck was obliged to swim about continually in order to keep the water open; but every night the opening in which it swam grew smaller and smaller; a thin sheet of ice gathered on the surface and crackled as the duck moved; the poor thing plied with its legs well; but at last its strength was exhausted, it remained motionless, and was frozen up fast in the ice.

Early next morning, a labouring man saw it as he was going to his work, broke the ice from about it, and carried it home to his wife.

The duck gradually recovered under the good woman's care. The children wanted to play with it; but not understanding their intentions, and supposing they wanted to torment it, it flew right into the milk dish, and spattered the milk all over the floor. The woman screamed and clapped her hands together; duckling then flew into the butter pan, and then into the flour tub and out again—you may guess what a pickle it was in! The woman bawled and struck at it with the tongs, and the

children tumbled one over the other laughing and shouting, and trying to catch the duck. Luckily the door was open, and the frightened creature darted out, flew through the bushes, and lighted in the new fallen snow, where it lay as if in a dream.

It would be too sad a tale to relate all the hardships and wretchedness it had to endure in that bitter winter. At last, as it lay among the sedges in the marsh, the sun began again to shine more warmly; the larks sang, and pleasant spring was come again.

Our duckling suddenly unfurled its wings; they whirred more strongly than formerly, and carried it onwards with more force; and before it well knew how, it found itself in a large garden, where the apple trees were in blossom, and the air was full of the perfume of lilac flowers, that hung down from the long green branches over a broad, winding expanse of water. Oh, it was beautiful! so full of the genial freshness of spring! And, behold, out came three fine white swans from the thicket, and swam so lightly along, with necks proudly arched, and wings partly spread, and feathers rustling. The duckling knew the magnificent birds, and was seized with a strange melancholy at sight of them.

"I will fly to them, to the kingly birds," it said; "they will kill me, for daring, ugly wretch that I am, to approach them. Well, be it so! It is better to be put to death by them than to be bitten by ducks, pecked by hens, kicked about by the girl that feeds the poultry, and compelled to endure such dreadful hardships in winter." With that it flew into the water, and swam towards the stately birds, that instantly shot forward to meet it with whirring pinions. "Kill me," said the poor creature, as it bent down its head towards the water to receive the death stroke—but, only think what it saw in the water as it stooped? Its own reflection; but it was no longer that of a dark gray fowl's, misshapen and ugly—it was a swan's!

What matters having been hatched in a duck's nest, if one has lain in a swan's egg!

# *The Farmyard Journal*

*Life in the countryside in the early nineteenth century could be pretty exciting, as described in this fictional journal published in 1828 in Cooperstown, New York.*

June 10th.—Last night we had a dreadful alarm. A violent scream was heard from the hen-roost, the geese all set up a cackle, and the dogs barked. Ned, the boy who lies over the stable, jumped up and ran into the yard, when he observed a fox galloping away with a chicken in his mouth, and the dogs in full chase after him. They could not overtake him, and soon returned. Upon further examination, the large white cock was found lying on the ground all bloody with his comb torn almost off, and his feathers all ruffled, and the speckled hen and three chickens lay dead beside him. The cock recovered, but appeared terribly frightened. It seems that the fox had jumped over the garden hedge, and then crossing part of the yard behind the straw, had crept into the hen-roost through a broken pale. John the carpenter was sent for, to make all fast, and prevent like mischief again.

Last night a poor old wandering beggar took his lodging in the barn; he appeared at the house this morning, and solicited our charity; we furnished him with better apparel and relieved his small necessities—while partaking of a hearty breakfast he entertained us with an interesting history of the many adventures and misfortunes he had undergone in the course of his life, and after returning us many thanks, he departed.

Early this morning, the brindled cow brought a fine calf—which is to be fattened by the butcher.

The duck-eggs that were sitten upon by the old black hen, were hatched this day, and the ducklings all directly ran into the pond, to the great terror of the hen, who went round and round, clucking with all her might in order to call them out, but they did not regard her. An old drake took the little ones under his care, and they swam about very merrily.

As Dolly this morning was milking the new cow that was bought yesterday, she kicked with her hind legs, and threw down the milkpail, at the same time knocking Dolly off her stool into the dirt. For this offence the cow was sentenced to have her head fastened to the rack, and her legs tied together.

A hawk was observed to hover a long while over the yard, with an intention of carrying off some of the young chickens; but the hens called their broods together under their wings, and the cocks put themselves in order of battle, so that the hawk was disappointed. At length, one chicken, not minding its mother, but straggling heedlessly to a distance, was descried by the hawk, who made a sudden swoop and seized it in his talons. The chicken cried out, and the cocks and hens all screamed; when Ralph, the farmer's son, who saw the attack, snatched up a loaded gun, and just as the hawk was flying off with his prey, fired and brought him dead to the ground, along with the poor chicken who was killed by the fall. The dead body of the hawk was nailed up against the fence, by way of warning to his wicked comrades.

In the forenoon we were alarmed with strange noises approaching us, and looking out we saw a number of people with frying pans, tongs, and shovels, beating, ringing, and making all possible din. We soon discovered them to be our neighbours of the next farm, in pursuit of a swarm of bees which was hovering in the air over their heads. The bees at length alighted on the tall pear tree in our orchard, and hung in a bunch from one of the boughs. A ladder was got, and a man ascending with gloves on his hands and an apron tied over his head, swept them into a hive which was rubbed on the inside with honey and sweet herbs. But, as he was descending, some bees which had got under his gloves, stung him in such a manner, that he hastily threw down the hive, upon which the greatest part of the bees fell out, and began in a rage to fly among the crowd, and sting all whom they lit upon. Away scampered the people, and women shrieking, the children roaring; and poor Adam, who had held the hive, was assailed so furiously, that he was obliged to throw himself on the ground and creep under the gooseberry bushes. At length the bees began to return to the hive, in which the queen bee had remained, and after a while, all being quietly settled, a cloth was thrown over it, and the swarm was carried home.

ÉTIENNE EST TROP PETIT : IL S'EFFORCE, IL HATE LE PAS. IL OUVRE TOUT GRAND SES COURTES JAMBES. IL AGITE SES BRAS PAR SURCROIT, MAIS IL EST TROP PETIT, IL NE PEUT PAS SUIVRE SES AMIS.
B.M.

# *Girls and Boys: Scenes from Town and Country*

*By Anatole France*
*Illustrations by Maurice Boutet de Monvel*

*This story shows that the small can sometimes outshine the big and strong.*

## THE BIG BOYS' MISTAKE

Off to visit their friend John went Roger, Marcel, Bernard, James, and Stephen. They set out on the highway that unrolled in the sunlight like a pretty yellow ribbon bordering the meadows and pastures.

You can see them here on their way, walking side by side, which is really the only way to walk. There is one problem with this formation, however; Stephen is much smaller than the others.

But he makes an effort to keep up; he quickens his step. He stretches his short legs as far as they will stretch, and he swings his arms as well, to increase his speed. But it's no use; he can't keep up. He remains behind because of his size, and there's nothing he can do about it.

The big boys, all of them older than he, ought, you might think, to wait for him and slow their pace to match his. They ought to do so, but they don't. "Forward!" say the big and strong everywhere in this world, leaving the weak behind. But just wait for the end of the story.

Suddenly our four big, strong boys stopped dead in their tracks. There on the ground, they saw a creature that jumped. The creature jumped because it was a frog, and it wanted to reach the meadow alongside the road. That meadow was its beloved home; there it had a pretty little house near a brook. It jumped. It was green. It looked like a living leaf. Bernard, Roger, James, and Marcel leapt after it in hot pursuit, and there they were in the meadow; soon they felt their feet plunge into the rich soil that nourished the thick grass. Several steps more and they were stuck up to their knees in mud. The grass had concealed a swamp.

With great difficulty, they struggled out of it. Their shoes, their socks, and the calves of their legs were black. It was the nymph of the green meadow who had put black mud "overshoes" on the four disobedient boys.

Stephen caught up with his friends, all out of breath. When he saw them booted in black mud, he didn't know whether he should laugh or cry. In his innocent soul he thought about the disasters that could strike even the big and strong. As for the four "muddy legs," they dolefully retraced their steps home, for how, I ask you, could they go to see their friend John in such attire?

When they got home, their mothers could read their mischief on their legs; meanwhile, the innocence of little Stephen shone from his sturdy clean calves.

# *Peter and Wendy*

*By James M. Barrie*
*Illustrations by F. D. Bedford*

*The creator of the famous children's play* Peter Pan *later retold the story in a book,* Peter and Wendy, *from which this scene is taken. Peter and the fairy Tinker Bell have flown off with the Darling children, Wendy, Michael, and John, to Neverland, where they will never have to grow up and Wendy can tell stories to the Lost Boys every night.*

## WENDY'S STORY

"Listen, then," said Wendy, settling down to her story, with Michael at her feet and seven boys in the bed. "There was once a gentleman—"

"I had rather he had been a lady," Curly said.

"I wish he had been a white rat," said Nibs.

"Quiet," their mother admonished them. "There was a lady also, and—"

"O mummy," cried the first twin, "you mean that there is a lady also, don't you? She is not dead, is she?"

"Oh no."

"I am awfully glad she isn't dead," said Tootles, "Are you glad, John?"

"Of course I am."

"Are you glad, Nibs?"

"Rather."

"Are you glad, Twins?"

"We are just glad."

"Oh dear," sighed Wendy.

"Little less noise there," Peter called out, determined that she would have fair play, however beastly a story it might be in his opinion.

"The gentleman's name," Wendy continued, "was Mr. Darling, and her name was Mrs. Darling."

"I knew them," John said, to annoy the others.

"I think I knew them," said Michael rather doubtfully.

"They were married, you know," explained Wendy, "and what do you think they had?"

"White rats," cried Nibs, inspired.

"No."

"It's awfully puzzling," said Tootles, who knew the story by heart.

"Quiet, Tootles. They had three descendants."

"What is descendants?"

"Well, you are one, Twin."

"Do you hear that, John? I am a descendant."

"Descendants are only children," said John.

"Oh dear, oh dear," sighed Wendy. "Now these three children had a faithful nurse called Nana; but Mr. Darling was angry with her and chained her up in the yard; and so all the children flew away."

"It's an awfully good story," said Nibs.

"They flew away," Wendy continued, "to the Neverland, where the lost children are."

"I just thought they did," Curly broke in excitedly. "I don't know how it is, but I just thought they did."

"O Wendy," cried Tootles, "was one of the lost children called Tootles?"

"Yes, he was."

"I am in a story. Hurrah, I am in a story, Nibs."

"Hush. Now I want you to consider the feelings of the unhappy parents with all their children flown away."

"Oo!" they all moaned, though they were not really considering the feelings of the unhappy parents one jot.

"Think of the empty beds!"

"Oo!"

"It's awfully sad," the first twin said cheerfully.

"I don't see how it can have a happy ending," said the second twin. "Do you, Nibs?"

"I'm frightfully anxious."

"If you knew how great is a mother's love," Wendy told them triumphantly, "you would have no fear." She had now come to the part that Peter hated.

"I do like a mother's love," said Tootles, hitting Nibs with a pillow. "Do you like a mother's love, Nibs?"

"I do just," said Nibs, hitting back.

"You see," Wendy said complacently, "our heroine knew that the mother would always leave the window open for her children to fly back by; so they stayed away for years and had a lovely time."

"Did they ever go back?"

"Let us now," said Wendy, bracing herself for her finest effort, "take a peep into the future"; and they all gave themselves the twist that makes peeps into the future easier. "Years have rolled by; and who is this elegant lady of uncertain age alighting at London Station?"

"O Wendy, who is she?" cried Nibs, every bit as excited as if he didn't know.

"Can it be—yes—no—it is—the fair Wendy!"

"Oh!"

"And who are the two noble portly figures accompanying her, now grown to man's estate? Can they be John and Michael? They are!"

"Oh!"

" 'See, dear brothers,' says Wendy, pointing upwards, 'there is the window still standing open. Ah, now we are rewarded for our sublime faith in a mother's love.' So up they flew to their mummy and daddy; and pen cannot describe that happy scene, over which we draw a veil."

That was the story, and they were as pleased with it as the fair narrator herself. Everything just as it should be, you see. Off we skip like the most heartless things in the world, which is what children are, but so attractive; and we have an entirely selfish time; and then when we have need of special attention we nobly return for it, confident that we shall be embraced instead of smacked.

So great indeed was their faith in a mother's love that they felt they could afford to be callous for a bit longer.

But there was one there who knew better; and when Wendy finished he uttered a hollow groan.

"What is it, Peter?" she cried, running to him, thinking he was ill. She felt him solicitously, lower down than his chest. "Where is it, Peter?"

"It isn't that kind of pain," Peter replied darkly.

"Then what kind is it?"

"Wendy, you are wrong about mothers."

They all gathered round him in affright, so alarming was his agitation; and with a fine candour he told them what he had hitherto concealed.

"Long ago," he said, "I thought like you that my mother would always keep the window open for me; so I stayed away for moons and moons and moons, and then flew back; but the window was barred, for mother had forgotten all about me, and there was another little boy sleeping in my bed."

I am not sure that this was true, but Peter thought it was true; and it scared them.

"Are you sure mothers are like that?"

"Yes."

So this was the truth about mothers. The toads!

Still it is best to be careful; and no one knows so quickly as a child when he should give in. "Wendy, let us go home," cried John and Michael together.

"Yes," she said, clutching them.

"Not to-night?" asked the lost boys bewildered. They knew in what they called their hearts that one can get on quite well without a mother, and that it is only the mothers who think you can't.

"At once," Wendy replied resolutely, for the horrible thought had come to her: "Perhaps mother is in half mourning by this time."

This dread made her forgetful of what must be Peter's feelings, and she said to him rather sharply, "Peter, will you make the necessary arrangements?"

"If you wish it," he replied, as coolly as if she had asked him to pass the nuts.

Not so much as a sorry-to-lose-you between them! If she did not mind the parting, he was going to show her, was Peter, that neither did he.

But of course he cared very much; and he was so full of wrath against grown-ups, who, as usual, were spoiling everything, that as soon as he got inside his tree he breathed intentionally quick short breaths at the rate of about five to a second. He did this because there is a saying in the Neverland that, every time you breathe, a grown-up dies; and Peter was killing them off vindictively as fast as possible.

Then having given the necessary instructions to the redskins he returned to the home, where an unworthy scene had been enacted in his absence. Panic-stricken at the thought of losing Wendy, the lost boys had advanced upon her threateningly.

"It will be worse than before she came," they cried.

"We shan't let her go."

"Let's keep her prisoner."

"Ay, chain her up."

In her extremity an instinct told her to which of them to turn.

"Tootles," she cried, "I appeal to you."

Was it not strange? she appealed to Tootles, quite the silliest one.

Grandly, however, did Tootles respond. For that one moment he dropped his silliness and spoke with dignity.

"I am just Tootles," he said, "and nobody minds me. But the first who does not behave to Wendy like an English gentleman I will blood him severely."

He drew his hanger; and for that instant his sun was at noon. The others held back uneasily. Then Peter returned, and they saw at once that they would get no support from him. He would keep no girl in the Neverland against her will.

"Wendy," he said, striding up and down, "I have asked the redskins to guide you through the wood, as flying tires you so."

"Thank you, Peter."

"Then," he continued, in the short sharp voice of one accustomed to be obeyed, "Tinker Bell will take you across the sea. Wake her, Nibs."

Nibs had to knock twice before he got an answer, though Tink had really been sitting up in bed listening for some time.

"Who are you? How dare you? Go away," she cried.

"You are to get up, Tink," Nibs called, "and take Wendy on a journey."

Of course Tink had been delighted to hear that Wendy was going; but she was jolly well determined not to be her courier, and she said so in still more offensive language. Then she pretended to be asleep again.

"She says she won't," Nibs exclaimed, aghast at such insubordination, whereupon Peter went sternly toward the young lady's chamber.

"Tink," he rapped out, "if you don't get up and dress at once I will open the curtains, and then we shall all see you in your negligee."

This made her leap to the floor. "Who said I wasn't getting up?" she cried.

In the meantime the boys were gazing very

WENDY'S STORY

forlornly at Wendy, now equipped with John and Michael for the journey. By this time they were dejected, not merely because they were about to lose her, but also because they felt that she was going off to something nice to which they had not been invited. Novelty was beckoning to them as usual.

Crediting them with a nobler feeling, Wendy melted.

"Dear ones," she said, "if you will all come with me I feel almost sure I can get my father and mother to adopt you."

The invitation was meant specially for Peter; but each of the boys was thinking exclusively of himself, and at once they jumped with joy.

"But won't they think us rather a handful?" Nibs asked in the middle of his jump.

"Oh no," said Wendy, rapidly thinking it

out, "it will only mean having a few beds in the drawing-room; they can be hidden behind screens on first Thursdays."

"Peter, can we go?" they all cried imploringly. They took it for granted that if they went he would go also, but really they scarcely cared. Thus children are ever ready, when novelty knocks, to desert their dearest ones.

"All right," Peter replied with a bitter smile; and immediately they rushed to get their things.

"And now, Peter," Wendy said, thinking she had put everything right, "I am going to give you your medicine before you go." She loved to give them medicine, and undoubtedly gave them too much. Of course it was only water, but it was out of a calabash, and she always shook the calabash and counted the drops, which gave it a certain medicinal quality. On this occasion, however, she did not give Peter his draught, for just as she had prepared it, she saw a look on his face that made her heart sink.

"Get your things, Peter," she cried, shaking.

"No," he answered, pretending indifference, "I am not going with you, Wendy."

"Yes, Peter."

"No."

To show that her departure would leave him unmoved, he skipped up and down the room, playing gaily on his heartless pipes. She had to run about after him, though it was rather undignified.

"To find your mother," she coaxed.

Now, if Peter had ever quite had a mother, he no longer missed her. He could do very well without one. He had thought them out, and remembered only their bad points.

"No, no," he told Wendy decisively; "perhaps she would say I was old, and I just want always to be a little boy and to have fun."

"But, Peter—"

"No."

And so the others had to be told.

"Peter isn't coming."

Peter not coming! They gazed blankly at him, their sticks over their backs, and on each stick a bundle. Their first thought was that if Peter was not going he had probably changed his mind about letting them go.

But he was far too proud for that. "If you find your mothers," he said darkly, "I hope you will like them."

The awful cynicism of this made an uncomfortable impression, and most of them began to look rather doubtful. After all, their faces said, were they not noodles to want to go?

"Now then," cried Peter, "no fuss, no blubbering; good-bye, Wendy," and he held out his hand cheerily, quite as if they must really go now, for he had something important to do.

She had to take his hand, as there was no indication that he would prefer a thimble.*

"You will remember about changing your flannels, Peter?" she said, lingering over him. She was always so particular about their flannels.

"Yes."

"And you will take your medicine?"

"Yes."

That seemed to be everything; and an awkward pause followed. Peter, however, was not the kind that breaks down before people. "Are you ready, Tinker Bell?" he called out.

"Ay, ay."

"Then lead the way."

Tink darted up the nearest tree; but no one followed her, for it was at this moment that the pirates made their dreadful attack upon the redskins. Above, where all had been so still, the air was rent with shrieks and the clash of steel. Below, there was dead silence. Mouths opened and remained open. Wendy fell on her knees, but her arms were extended toward Peter. All arms were extended to him, as if suddenly blown in his direction; they were beseeching him mutely not to desert them. As for Peter, he seized his sword, the same he thought he had slain Barbecue with; and the lust of battle was in his eye.

*Peter Pan's word for a kiss.

# *Billy Bounce*

*By W. W. Denslow and Dudley A. Bragdon*
*Illustrations by W. W. Denslow*

*The artist who illustrated* The Wizard of Oz *later wrote and illustrated his own book. The story is about a messenger, Billy, who is sent off by Nickel Plate "the polished villain" and his partner Bumbus to find Bogie Man. In this chapter Billy meets a witch with thirteen black cats.*

## THE WISHING BOTTLE

"I can't understand why Bumbus wanted to take that note away from me," Billy said to himself as he floated along. "First he and Nickel Plate employed me to carry it and now he tries to hinder me. Why of course—I know—he is aware that Princess Honey Girl has told me her story and fears that when once I do find Bogie Man I will vanquish him—so I shall, too. I wonder what the future will bring."

"Won't you have your fortune told sir?" and Billy looked up to see sailing along at his side a very old, very withered woman sitting on a broom.

"Why it's a witch," said Billy.

"I'm not a which, I'm a Was," said the old woman.

"Oh! I beg your pardon, ma'am," said Billy, "I saw that you were riding a broom."

"Well what of it—the broom's willing."

"I didn't mean it that way," began Billy.

"Oh! you mean you meant it any way. But this is not having your fortune told," interrupted the old woman. "Come right into the house."

And sure enough Billy discovered that he was standing in front of a little old house, as

wrinkled and ugly and out of repair as the old woman.

"What town is this?" he asked.

"Superstitionburg—don't bump into the ladder."

"What is it for?"

"Oh! we all have ladders over our doors here for bad luck. Sit down and I'll get the cards and tell your fortune."

"Thank you," said Billy, "will it be true?"

"No, of course not. Ah—h! you have lately had serious trouble."

"That's true," said Billy.

"Then I've made a mistake. You will marry a tall, short, blonde, dark complected man."

"Hold on," said Billy, "I'm a boy—how can I marry a man?"

"There I knew something was wrong. I have the deck of cards that I tell ladies' fortunes with—shall I try it over again?"

"No, I think not," said Billy, "I must be going."

"Purr-r-r-r-r, Purr-r-r-r," and a great black, hump-backed cat with glaring green eyes and nine long black tails rubbed against his leg.

"Oh!" he cried, "what a large cat."

"Yes," said the old woman, "that's my black cat-o'-nine-tails. I'm very proud of him, he's the unluckiest cat of the entire thirteen in Superstitionburg."

"Unlucky?"

"Yes, the cats always sit thirteen at table for bad luck. As there never is more than enough for twelve and as he always gets his share he brings bad luck to one of the cats every meal. Isn't that nice?"

"But isn't that hard on the extra cat?"

"Oh! no they don't mind at all—it's so good for the digestion."

"Won't you have a cup of poison before you go?"

"Poison?" said Billy, edging toward the door.

"Yes. I have some lovely poison, I brewed it myself; *do* have some."

"No thank you, I—I really am not thirsty, and I *must* go."

"I don't see how you are going to get away now, the town guard knows you are here and is bound to arrest you if your eyes are not crossed."

"What have I done?" asked Billy.

"Nothing, only it's not bad luck to meet a straight-eyed person, and if you can't bring somebody bad luck you're not allowed in the city."

"But how do they know I am here?"

"Their noses are itching because a stranger has come to call. Their noses are very sensitive to strangers. It makes them such careful guards."

"Have they guns?" asked Billy.

"Oh! yes, they all have guns that are not loaded."

"Oh! well, then, they can't shoot me."

"I guess you don't know much about guns—because it is always guns that are not loaded that shoot people."

"That's so, I had forgotten," said Billy. "But as you are a witch, can't you—"

"I am a Was, remember."

"I mean as you are a Was—can't you help me?"

"I can lend you my invisible cloak," said the old woman, going to a closet and taking nothing out of it. "Here it is," handing Billy nothing at all very carefully.

"But where is it?" asked Billy.

"I just gave it to you."

"I don't see it."

"Of course not—it's invisible."

"Then if I put it on will it make me invisible?"

"Certainly not—it's the cloak that's invisible."

"Have you anything else?" asked Billy.

"Yes, I have a wishing bottle."

"Shall I be able to see that?"

"Oh! yes—here it is."

"Why that's hair dye, it says on the label."

"Sh-h—don't speak so loud—that's all it is, but you see it turns hair so black that it almost makes it invisible. It's the best I can do for you."

"Thank you very much for the wishing bottle," said Billy. "I don't know that I shall need it, but I'll take it anyway."

"Bad luck to you," called the old woman. "By the way where are you going now?"

"To Bogie Man's House," answered Billy.

"What have I done—what have I done—I'll have to stop him—if I only hadn't been a Was I might have guessed this was the boy," said the old woman, wringing her hands.... "My cats," cried she, "I'll send them after him," and opening an inner door she called:

"Stingaree, Stangaree,
Whollop and Whim,
Mizzle and Muzzle,
Luckety, Limb,
Niddle and Noddle
And Puzzlecat too,
Roly and Poly,
I need all of you."

As each name was called, out ran a great black hump-backed cat-o'-nine-tails, and by the time she was done the thirteen of them were standing in front of her, their 117 tails swishing back and forth with a noise like a hurricane. "Run and catch that boy for me," said she, pointing to Billy. And off they scampered.

"What a wind is coming up," said Billy to himself when he heard the cats behind him.

"Meow-w-w—"

And turning round he saw the great cats bounding after him.

"They're after me—I'm sure," he said to himself, "but I can jump."

Alas for Billy, he was standing under a ladder when he spoke, and when he jumped, "bump" he hit his head on the topmost rung.

Quick as a flash he reached out his hand and caught the ladder—and there he hung, dangling in mid air with thirteen great cats meowing and spitting and yowling on the ground just out of reach of his feet.

"This won't do—they will climb the ladder in a moment. The wishing bottle: maybe I can blind them with the dye." Holding on tight with one hand, he fished the bottle out of his pocket. "If only I had something to turn them into white cats," he said, staring at the bottle, "maybe they would become harmless."

And just at that minute a thought struck him so hard that it almost knocked loose his hold on the ladder.

"This is black dye," said he; "perhaps if I reverse the label, it will become white dye. I'll try it anyway."

And quick as thought he had loosened the label and turned it upside down. Certain it is that the contents of the bottle changed to a snow-white on the instant.

Out came the cork. "Blub—blub—gog—gurgle, splash," and the cats were drenched with the liquid. "Pouf," and where Billy had seen thirteen black cats appeared thirteen snow-white ones.

The cats looked at one another in astonishment for a moment, and then forgetting all about Billy, began to flog one another with their nine tails.

"White ca-a-a-a-at—meow—flog him out of town," and off they went flogging each other mercilessly, each one thinking that he was the only black cat in the whole town and determined to beat the strangers out of Superstitionburg.

"There's some good in hair dye after all," laughed Billy, and dropping to the ground, he stepped from under the ladder, leaped into the air, and bade farewell to Superstitionburg for ever and ever.

# *The Lost Zoo (A Rhyme for the Young, but Not Too Young)*

*By Christopher Cat and Countee Cullen*

*This creature liked to sleep so much that he missed the boat—and a very important one at that.*

## THE SLEEPAMITEMORE

This sign was always on the door
Behind which slept the Sleepamitemore:

"Just one more wink, one little nap,
Another dip in the slumber stream;
I'm such a sleepy, sleepy chap;
I'm having such a pleasant dream.
Please do not shake me,
Please, please, don't wake me
With whistle, bell, or silver chime,
And please return some other time."

Within, a round and fuzzy ball,
No matter what the hour might be,
The laziest animal of all
Continued sleeping endlessly.

He had no friends, which was no wonder;
For louder than a clap of thunder
There issued forth his mighty snore
That shook the world from shore to shore;
And not a beast was there so brave
Who dared come near that dreadful cave.

Strange tales were told of his aspect,
But these were not at all correct,
Since not a soul, for real and true,
Was speaking from a point of *view*!

Some said, "The lion's tame to *him*!"
Said some, "He's like a dragon grim;
He's rivers wide and mountains high,
And flames shoot out from mouth and eye."

(But all he was was Laziness,
And nothing was he more, nor less.)

Each week for minutes just a score,
The latch was lifted from his door,
As out on fat and shuffling feet,
The lazy beast came forth to eat.

Thus once in passing Noah spied
Him munching on a tender herb;
"Our dragon's toothless," Noah cried,
"There's not a mouse he could disturb.
This gentle creature must not perish;
Into my Ark I must ensnare him;
My duty is this beast to cherish,
And from the flood's destruction spare him."

Brave Noah, with no hesitation,
Knocked loudly on the bolted door,—
Unanswered, shoved his invitation
Beneath a cranny in the floor.
The drowsy one was furious,
But till his visitor departed
Lay quietly, then curious
Arose, and at the letter darted.
At what he read he was delighted.
His eyes grew wider more and more,
For he had never been invited
To take an ocean trip before.

He read that letter many times,
Until its meaning rang like chimes
Within his fastly nodding head;
And as he nodded, still he read.
The nods grew fewer, weaker, stopped;
His head upon his bosom dropped,
And soon he was asleep once more,
And as he slept a great ship bore
Him (dreaming still) far into space
To many a strange and foreign place.

It was a lovely dream he had,
An ideal dream. *It was too bad*
*He thought he must continue dreaming!*
He never heard the water streaming
In torrents on the forest floor,
Nor heard the Ark shove off from shore.

Perhaps he still is there, asleep,
In spite of currents cool and deep;
Perhaps that warning, as before,
Still dangles from his cavern door:
"Just one more wink, one little nap,
Another dip in the slumber stream;
I'm such a sleepy, sleepy chap.
I'm having such a pleasant dream."

# *Susan and Edward; or, A Visit to Fulton Market*

*The famous old New York City market, described here more than 150 years ago, survives today at the South Street Seaport Museum.*

Fulton Market is a large building, filling up a whole square, and is erected near the East River, opposite the town of Brooklyn, and close to the ferry that crosses over to that thriving village.

Now the first object that caught the sight of the children, were the Butchers' Stalls, hung full of beef, pork, veal, mutton, all for sale for ready pay to whoever will step up to buy. The little visitors saw the men and boys busy whetting their long knives, and cutting and sawing up the meat in suitable pieces for the buyers. The noise was something like a company of mowers whetting their scythes, and their voices and motion might be compared to a hive of bees.

Their mother having got of the butcher, her supply of meat, they next visited the fish stalls.—"O mother! mother!" said the lively little boy, "see the fish all jumping alive. O look there! there!" Sure enough, here were fish, just out of the river, where the fishermen keep them in wooden cars or boxes, under water, till wanted to be put on the stall. See here is a picture of a Salmon.

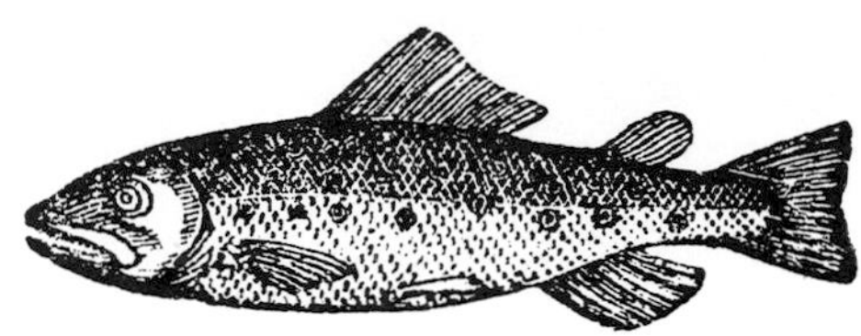

The children took a walk around, to see the different kinds of fish, displayed on the stalls. Here were to be seen the Sea-Bass, Blackfish, the Sheep's-Head, the Pike, the Flounder, and a number of others, so many that it would fill a good part of this little book, just to print pictures of them all. But we will give them one;

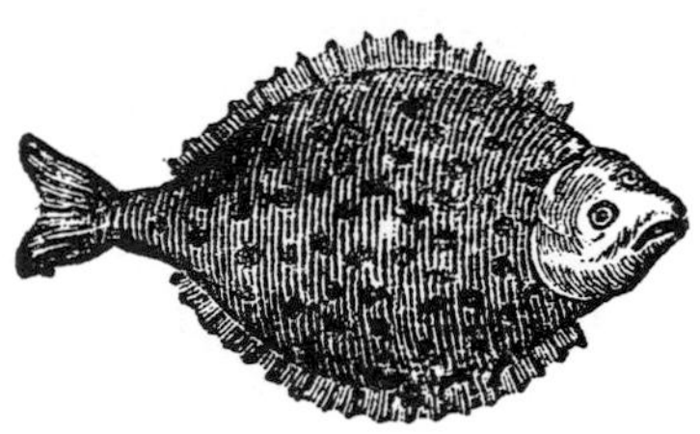

this is the Flounder. Then passing along they came to the Oyster and Clam stands. "Mother, I do want *one* oyster," said little modest Susan. "Only look what a big pile. Mother, may I have a clam?" said the boy. The men would quickly wait on them, by giving each what they asked for as a taste, and then add fifty or a hundred more to fill the tin kettle, for the family's supply. We will now print a picture of an Oyster opened. A large curious animal laid under one

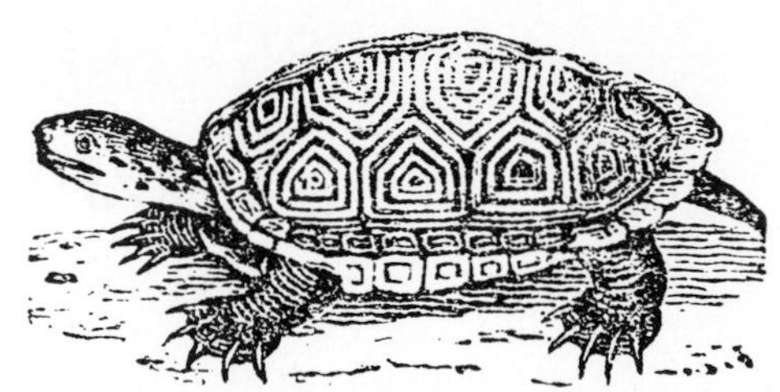

of the stalls. The children's attention was drawn to it. "Do see, mother, what is that!" "It is a Turtle," replied their mother. So they went and looked at it near by. It [was] laid on its back to prevent its crawling away. The fisherman was kind enough to let the young visitors look at it till they were tired—and then away they went to another part of the market. But we will first show them a picture of a Turtle: see there he is on the next page, almost big enough to frighten any body.

These turtles were esteemed a great delicacy. People bring them all the way from the West Indies, and sell them for a high price to the keepers of hotels, who make soup of them; the signs may be seen hanging at the doors, in large capital letters; "TURTLE SOUP AT ELEVEN O'CLOCK, THIS DAY—FAMILIES SUPPLIED."

After this they went to another part of the building called the Country Market. Here they were delighted with what they saw; and a great many sights there were for such little prattlers. "O see, here is a Rabbit with a white tail! see, see, Susan—do come this way." But Susan had her fine blue eyes also engaged in viewing a cage of Pigeons, some of which had their tails spread like a fan. They saw also a great many baskets of Peaches, Apples, Potatoes, and Pumpkins, Watermelons, Cantaleupes, pile upon pile, enough to make one ask, "Where are all these to go? Who will buy them?" But we must remember, that there are more than 200,000 mouths to eat three or four times a day in New-York, enough to make way with the loads of vegetables that are brought here every day for sale.

# *The Woodcutter's Dog*

*By Charles Nodier*
*Illustrations by Claud Lovat Fraser*

*The author was a librarian in nineteenth-century France; he wrote this story to remind us of the loyalty of dogs to their owners.*

In the Forest of Lions, not far from the village of La Goupilière and close to a fine well which belongs to St. Mathurin's Chapel, lived a kindly soul, a woodcutter by trade, who was called Brisquet, or, as often as not, the Man with the Trusty Axe.

He and his wife, whose name was Brisquette, lived poorly enough on the sale of his faggots. God had given them two pretty children—a seven year old boy, who was dark and was called Biscotin, and Biscotine, a girl of six who was very fair.

They had, besides, a dog, a curly-haired mongrel, which was all black except for its nose, and that was red as fire. They called it Bichonne.

You may remember the time when such numbers of wolves swarmed in the Forest of Lions. It was a year of the Great Snow, when the poor folk found it so hard to keep alive. The misery in the country was dreadful.

Brisquet, who never shirked his work, and, thanks to his good axe, had no fear of wolves, said to his wife one morning: "Oh, do not let either Biscotin or Biscotine run about outside until the master of the wolf-hounds arrives. It will be dangerous if they do. There is room enough for them to play between the mound and the pond, now that I have put stakes along the water to prevent any accident happening to

them. And do not let Bichonne out either; she is always wanting to be on the run."

Morning after morning he cautioned Brisquette in the same way.

One evening Brisquet did not reach home at his usual time. Brisquette went to the doorstep, returned, went back again, and "Oh, dear; oh dear!" she said, wringing her hands, "how late he is!" Then she ran out of doors, shouting, "Oh, Brisquet, Brisquet!"

And Bichonne leaped as high as her shoulders, as if she were asking, "Shall *I* not go?"

"Be quiet!" said Brisquette; then turning to the children, "Listen, Biscotine, run as far as the mound and see if your father is not coming. And you, Biscotin, take the path along the pond, and be careful lest some of the stakes should be missing. And shout out loud, 'Brisquet! Brisquet!'

"Be quiet, Bichonne!"

The children went on and on, and when they met at the place where the path by the pond and path by the mound crossed, Biscotin exclaimed excitedly, "I shall find my father, I will find him, or the wolves shall eat me up!"

"And they shall eat me up too!" said Biscotine.

All this while Brisquet was returning by the Puchay high road, passing the Asses' Cross at Mortemer Abbey, because he had a bundle of faggots to leave at Jean Paquiér's.

"Have you seen the children?" Brisquette asked him.

"The children," said Brisquet, "the children! Oh mercy, have they gone out?"

"I sent them out as far as the mound and the pond to meet you, but you had taken another road."

Brisquet gripped his good axe and set off running towards the mound.

"Won't you take Bichonne with you?" his wife called after him.

But Bichonne was already far ahead—so far that Brisquet immediately lost sight of her.

In vain he shouted, "Biscotin! Biscotine!" There was no answer.

Then he burst into tears for he believed that the children were lost.

When he had run a great way he thought he heard Bichonne's bark. With his good axe above his head he dashed through the thicket in the direction of the sound.

Bichonne had reached the spot at the very moment a huge wolf was about to spring upon the children. She had flung herself between, barking furiously so that she might warn Brisquet. With one stroke of his good axe the woodman laid the wolf lifeless, but it was too late to save Bichonne. She was already dead.

Brisquet, Biscotin and Biscotine returned home to Brisquette. There was great joy, but they were all weeping. There was not a look that was not turned towards Bichonne.

Brisquet buried Bichonne at the foot of the little garden, under a great stone on which the schoolmaster wrote in Latin:

HERE LIES BICHONNE,
BRISQUET'S POOR DOG.

Ever since that time we have had the saying, "Unlucky as Brisquet's dog which went to the wood once, and the wolf ate him."

# *Picture Riddler*

*Riddles have amused people for centuries; these from the last century offer you a hint to the solution.*

**1.**

For vigilance and courage true
I've no superiors—equals few;
Which makes me by the industrious prized,
But by the indolent despised;
Bold and alert I meet the foe;
In all engagements valor show;
And if he prove too proud to yield,
One falls before we quit the field.

**2.**

Your praise in letters *two*, will serve to show,
The *figure* they've long made all scholars know.

**3.**

Why is a bee-hive like a spectator?

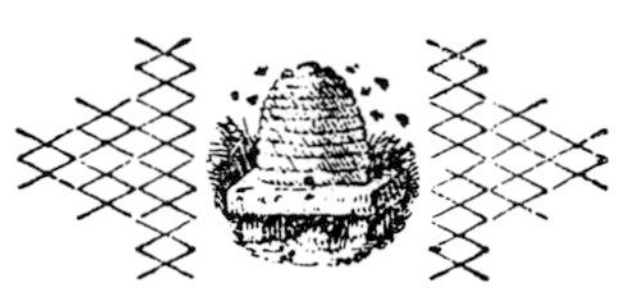

SOLUTIONS:

**1.**
A rooster.
**2.**
XL, excel.
**3.**
It is a beholder.

# *The Book of Riddles*

*By The Editress of "The Lady's Library"*

*Just how far back riddles go is shown by the first of these, which was known to the ancient Greeks and was thought to be the riddle asked by the Egyptian sphinx.*

**1.** What animal is it that goes on four legs in the morning, on two at noon, and on three at night?

**2.** What is that which was to-morrow, and will be yesterday?

**3.** What must you add to nine to make it six?

**4.** What is the numerical difference between three and two, and two and three?

**5.** What must you subtract from fifty-nine to leave sixty?

**6.** If a person suffering from hydrophobia [fear of water] were asked to describe the symptoms of his disorder, what summer dainties would he name?

## SOLUTIONS:

**1.** Man—as he goes on hands and knees in childhood (or the morning of life); on his feet in his prime (or noon); and with a crutch in old age (or at night).

**2.** To-day.

**3.** The letter S; for as IX are nine, SIX make six.

**4.** Nine; for whilst three and two are 32, two and three are only 23.

**5.** One; LIX is fifty-nine, LX sixty.

**6.** Water ices; ice creams. (Water I sees; I screams).

# *The Young Visiters; or, Mr. Salteenas Plan*

*By Daisy Ashford*

*This story was written (in fact, handwritten) by a sharp-eyed nine-year-old girl who had some difficulties with her spelling. Published twenty-nine years later, in 1919, it was so popular that it had eight printings in a month.*

CHAPTER 1

## QUITE A YOUNG GIRL

Mr. Salteena was an elderly man of 42 and was fond of asking peaple to stay with him. He had quite a young girl staying with him of 17 named Ethel Monticue. Mr. Salteena had dark short hair and mustache and wiskers which were very black and twisty. He was middle sized and he had very pale blue eyes. He had a pale brown suit but on Sundays he had a black one and he had a topper every day as he thought it more becoming. Ethel Monticue had fair hair done on the top and blue eyes. She had a blue velvit frock which had grown rather short in the sleeves. She had a black straw hat and kid gloves.

One morning Mr. Salteena came down to brekfast and found Ethel had come down first which was strange. Is the tea made Ethel he said rubbing his hands. Yes said Ethel and such a quear shaped parcel has come for you. Yes indeed it was a quear shape parcel it was a hat box tied down very tight and a letter stuffed between the string. Well well said Mr. Salteena parcels do turn quear I will read the letter first and so saying he tore open the letter and this is what it said

My Dear Alfred.

I want you to come for a stop with me so I have sent you a top hat wraped up in tishu paper inside the box. Will you wear it staying with me because it is very uncommon. Please bring one of your young ladies whichever is the prettiest in the face.

I remain Yours truely
Bernard Clark.

Well said Mr. Salteena I shall take you to stay Ethel and fancy him sending me a top hat. Then Mr S. opened the box and there lay the most splendid top hat of a lovly rich tone rarther like grapes with a ribbon round compleat.

Well said Mr Salteena peevishly I dont know if I shall like it the bow of the ribbon is too flighty for my age. Then he sat down and eat the egg which Ethel had so kindly laid for him. After he had finished his meal he got down and began to write to Bernard Clark he ran up stairs on his fat legs and took out his blotter with a loud sniff and this is what he wrote

My Dear Bernard

Certinly I shall come and stay with you next Monday I will bring Ethel Monticue commonly called Miss M. She is very active and pretty. I do hope I shall enjoy myself with you. I am fond of digging in the garden and I am parshial to ladies if they are nice I suppose it is my nature. I am not quite a gentleman but you would hardly notice it but cant be helped anyhow. We will come by the 3-15.

Your old and valud friend
Alfred Salteena.

Perhaps my readers will be wondering why Bernard Clark had asked Mr. Salteena to stay with him. He was a lonely man in a remote spot and he liked peaple and partys but he did not know many. What rot muttered Bernard Clark as he read Mr Salteenas letter. He was rarther a presumshious man.

CHAPTER 2

## STARTING GAILY

When the great morning came Mr Salteena did not have an egg for his brekfast in case he should be sick on the jorney.

What top hat will you wear asked Ethel.

I shall wear my best black and my white alpacka coat to keep off the dust and flies replied Mr Salteena.

I shall put some red ruge on my face said Ethel because I am very pale owing to the drains in this house.

You will look very silly said Mr Salteena with a dry laugh.

Well so will you said Ethel in a snappy tone and she ran out of the room with a very superier run throwing out her legs behind and her arms swinging in rithum.

Well said the owner of the house she has a most idiotick run.

Presently Ethel came back in her best hat and a lovly velvit coat of royal blue. Do I look nice in my get up she asked.

Mr Salteena survayed her. You look rarther rash my dear your colors dont quite match your face but never mind I am just going up to say goodbye to Rosalind the housemaid.

Well dont be long said Ethel. Mr S. skipped upstairs to Rosalinds room. Goodbye Rosalind he said I shall be back soon and I hope I shall enjoy myself.

I make no doubt of that sir said Rosalind with a blush as Mr Salteena silently put 2/6 on the dirty toilet cover.

Take care of your bronkitis said Mr S. rarther bashfully and he hastilly left the room waving his hand carelessly to the housemaid.

Come along cried Ethel powdering her nose in the hall let us get into the cab. Mr Salteena did not care for powder but he was an unselfish man so he dashed into the cab. Sit down said Ethel as the cabman waved his whip you are standing on my luggage. Well I am paying for the cab said Mr S. so I might be allowed to put my feet were I like.

They traveled 2nd class in the train and Ethel was longing to go first but thought perhaps least said soonest mended. Mr Salteena got very excited in the train about his visit. Ethel was calm but she felt excited inside. Bernard has a big house said Mr S. gazing at Ethel he is inclined to be rich.

Oh indeed said Ethel looking at some cows flashing past the window. Mr. S. felt rarther disheartened so he read the paper till the train stopped and the porters shouted Rickamere station. We had better collect our traps said Mr Salteena and just then a very exalted footman in a cocked hat and olive green uniform put his head in at the window. Are you for Rickamere Hall he said in impressive tones.

Well yes I am said Mr Salteena and so is this lady.

Very good sir said the noble footman if you will alight I will see to your luggage there is a convayance awaiting you.

Oh thankyou thankyou said Mr. S. and he and Ethel stepped along the platform. Outside they found a lovely cariage lined with olive green cushons to match the footman and the horses had green bridles and bows on their manes and tails. They got gingerly in. Will he bring our luggage asked Ethel nervously.

I expect so said Mr Salteena lighting a very long cigar.

Do we tip him asked Ethel quietly.

Well no I dont think so not yet we had better just thank him perlitely.

Just then the footman staggered out with the baggage. Ethel bowed gracefully over the door of the cariage and Mr S. waved his hand as each bit of luggage was hoisted up to make sure it was all there. Then he said thankyou my good fellow very politely. Not at all sir said the footman and touching his cocked hat he jumped actively to the box.

I was right not to tip him whispered Mr Salteena the thing to do is to leave 2/6 on your dressing table when your stay is over.

Does he find it asked Ethel who did not really know at all how to go on at a visit. I beleeve so replied Mr Salteena anyhow it is quite the custom and we cant help it if he does not. Now my dear what do you think of the sceenery.

Very nice said Ethel gazing at the rich fur rug on her knees. Just then the cariage rolled into a beautifull drive with tall trees and big red flowers growing amid shiny dark leaves. Presently the haughty coachman pulled up with a great clatter at a huge front door with tall pillers each side a big iron bell and two very clean scrapers. The doors flung open as if by majic causing Ethel to jump and a portly butler appeared on the scene with a very shiny shirt front and a huge pale face. Welcome sir he exclaimed good naturedly as Mr Salteena alighted rarther quickly from the viacle and please to step inside.

Mr Salteena stepped in as bid followed by Ethel. The footman again struggled with the luggage and the butler Francis Minnit by name kindly lent a hand. The hall was very big and hung round with guns and mats and ancesters giving it a gloomy but a grand air. The butler then showed them down a winding corridoor till he came to a door which he flung open shouting Mr Salteena and a lady sir.

A tall man of 29 rose from the sofa. He was rarther bent in the middle with very nice long legs fairish hair and blue eyes. Hullo Alf old boy he cried so you have got here all safe and no limbs broken.

None thankyou Bernard replied Mr Salteena shaking hands and let me introduce Miss Monticue she is very pleased to come for this visit. Oh yes gasped Ethel blushing through her red ruge. Bernard looked at her keenly and turned a dark red. I am glad to see you he said I hope you will enjoy it but I have not arranged any partys yet as I dont know anybody.

Dont worry murmered Ethel I dont mix much in Socierty and she gave him a dainty smile.

I expect you would like some tea said Bernard I will ring.

Yes indeed we should said Mr Salteena egerly. Bernard pealed on the bell and the butler came in with a stately walk.

Tea please Minnit crid Bernard Clark. With pleshure sir replied Minnit with a deep bow. A glorious tea then came in on a gold tray two kinds of bread and butter a lovly jam role and lots of sugar cakes. Ethels eyes began to sparkle and she made several remarks during the meal. I expect you would now like to unpack said Bernard when it was over.

Well yes that is rarther an idear said Mr Salteena.

I have given the best spare room to Miss Monticue said Bernard with a gallant bow and yours turning to Mr Salteena opens out of it so you will be nice and friendly both the rooms have big windows and a handsome view.

How charming said Ethel. Yes well let us go up replied Bernard and he led the way up many a winding stairway till they came to an oak door with some lovly swans and bull rushes painted on it. Here we are he cried gaily. Ethels room was indeed a handsome compartment with purple silk curtains and a 4 post bed draped with the same shade. The toilit set was white and mouve and there were some violets in a costly varse. Oh I say cried Ethel in surprise. I am glad you like it said Bernard and here we have yours Alf. He opened the dividing doors and portrayed a smaller but dainty room all in pale yellow and wild primroses. My own room is next the bath room said Bernard it is decerated dark red as I have somber tastes. The bath room has got a tip up bason and a hose thing for washing your head.

A good notion said Mr Salteena who was secretly getting jellus.

Here we will leave our friends to unpack and end this Chapter.

# *The Stories That Little Breeches Told*

*Written and illustrated by Charles Bennett*

*This story might better be called "Mouse Bites Cat." Like many tales written for Victorian children, it teaches a little lesson.*

## CAT'S-EYES

Once there lived a very clever Cat. She was so sharp at finding the mice, that they called her Cat's-eyes. She caught them, too, when she had found them, which was a sad thing for the poor mice, as you may well suppose.

Now, there were two little Tinies who lived quietly together in a dark little corner under the floor, and if they sometimes took a small piece of bread, and then again a crumb or two of cheese, it was not much that they ate altogether; and so they hoped to lead a quiet life, and keep out of the way of the terrible Cat's-eyes; but one day when they had been out for a walk, and were coming back home in the cool of the evening, who should fly at them but the Cat. Caught they would have been in a trice, had not one little Tiny, as bold as a Briton, run at her tail, and given it such a sharp bite, that she turned round to see what it was, and so let them scamper away to their dark little corner under the floor.

"Come, come," said they, when they had calmed down, and had finished their suppers, "let us lay a plot." They were as cunning as they were bold, and had made up their minds to serve out the Cat for her cruelty.

The plot was just this. Says one little Tiny to the other:

"Pussy is very clever and very sharp; but she is as vain as a peacock. She can see so many things, that she thinks she can see behind her; but that I'm sure she cannot: so we will get on to the top of the high house when Cat's-eyes is there. She'll jump at you in front; then I'll squeak out behind. Pussy will jump backwards, and there will be an end of her."

So it happened.

Pussy could not see behind, although she thought she could. She did jump backwards; she fell off the high house; and that is what became of her.

## WHAT LITTLE POLLY SAID ABOUT CAT'S-EYES

"Well," said Polly, "I don't think I should ever be so silly as to think I could see behind me."

"No, my dear," said Mamma; "but you might think too much of yourself all the same. Don't you see?"

CATS EYES
HOW PUSSY CAUGHT SO MANY MICE
THAT THESE LITTLE TINIES
WERE NEARLY CAUGHT TOO
HOW THEY LAID A PLOT
TO CATCH THE CAT
AND WHAT BECAME OF HER

# *Griset's Grotesques*

*Rhymes by Tom Hood*
*Illustrations by Ernest Griset*

*It is possible to describe this animal more briefly and with greater scientific accuracy—but it would be nowhere near the fun.*

## HIGH ART

Long necks,
  Queer shanks,
Brown specks,
  Quaint pranks,
Large eyes,
  Wisp tails,
Huge size,
  No nails,
Cloven hoofs,
  Horned head;
Ample proofs—
  Quadruped!
Timid heart,
  Soon fright,
Give a start—
  Swift flight.
Long strides—
  Awful quite!
Soon glides
  Out of sight.
Would you view?
  Don't laugh!
Visit Zoo—
  See giraffe.

Vast plain,
  Sultry sky,
No rain,
  Very dry;
Thirst begins,
  Distant springs—
Long pins
  Useful things!

Lone man
  Come to sketch—
His plan
  Not to catch.
"Sky-scraper,
  Oh, law!
Long paper
  If I draw!"

Progress slow,
  By degrees!
"Tishoo!" Oh
  What a sneeze!
On the sly,
  Paper peppered.
Good bye,
  Camelopard!

# *The Wind in the Willows*

*By Kenneth Grahame*
*Illustrations by Ernest H. Shephard*

*Toad of Toad Hall has escaped from prison disguised as a laundress, and we join him here on his first glorious morning of freedom.*

## THE FURTHER ADVENTURES OF TOAD

The front door of the hollow tree faced eastwards, so Toad was called at an early hour; partly by the bright sunlight streaming in on him, partly by the exceeding coldness of his toes, which made him dream that he was at home in bed in his own handsome room with the Tudor window, on a cold winter's night, and his bedclothes had got up, grumbling and protesting they couldn't stand the cold any longer, and had run downstairs to the kitchen fire to warm themselves; and he had followed, on bare feet, along miles and miles of icy stone-paved passages, arguing and beseeching them to be reasonable. He would probably have been aroused much earlier, had he not slept for some weeks on straw over stone flags, and almost forgotten the friendly feeling of thick blankets pulled well up round the chin.

Sitting up, he rubbed his eyes first and his complaining toes next, wondered for a moment where he was, looking round for familiar stone wall and little barred window; then, with a leap of the heart, remembered everything—his escape, his flight, his pursuit; remembered, first and best thing of all, that he was free!

Free! The word and the thought alone were worth fifty blankets. He was warm from end to end as he thought of the jolly world outside, waiting eagerly for him to make his triumphal entrance, ready to serve him and play up to him, anxious to help him and to keep him company, as it always had been in days of old before misfortune fell upon him. He shook himself and combed the dry leaves out of his hair with his fingers; and, his toilet complete, marched forth into the comfortable morning sun, cold but confident, hungry but hopeful, all nervous terrors of yesterday dispelled by rest and sleep and frank and heartening sunshine.

He had the world all to himself, that early summer morning. The dewy woodland, as he threaded it, was solitary and still; the green fields that succeeded the trees were his own to do as he liked with; the road itself, when he reached it, in that loneliness that was everywhere, seemed, like a stray dog, to be looking anxiously for company. Toad, however, was looking for something that could talk, and tell him clearly which way he ought to go. It is all very well, when you have a light heart, and a clear conscience, and money in your pocket, and nobody scouring the country for you to drag you off to prison again, to follow where the road beckons and points, not caring whither. The practical Toad cared very much indeed, and he could have kicked the road for its helpless silence when every minute was of importance to him.

The reserved rustic road was presently joined by a shy little brother in the shape of a

canal, which took its hand and ambled along by its side in perfect confidence, but with the same tongue-tied, uncommunicative attitude towards strangers. "Bother them!" said Toad to himself. "But, anyhow, one thing's clear. They must both be coming *from* somewhere, and going *to* somewhere. You can't get over that, Toad, my boy!" So he marched on patiently by the water's edge.

Round a bend in the canal came plodding a solitary horse, stooping forward as if in anxious thought. From rope traces attached to his collar stretched a long line, taut, but dipping with its stride, the further part of it dripping pearly drops. Toad let the horse pass, and stood waiting for what the fates were sending him.

With a pleasant swirl of quiet water at its blunt bow the barge slid up alongside of him, its gaily painted gunwale level with the towing-path, its sole occupant a big stout woman wearing a linen sun-bonnet, one brawny arm laid along the tiller.

"A nice morning, ma'am!" she remarked to Toad, as she drew up level with him.

"I dare say it is, ma'am!" responded Toad politely, as he walked along the tow-path abreast of her. "I dare [say] it *is* a nice morning to them that's not in sore trouble, like what I am. Here's my married daughter, she sends off to me post-haste to come to her at once; so off I comes, not knowing what may be happening or going to happen, but fearing the worst, as you will understand, ma'am, if you're a mother, too. And I've left my business to look after itself—I'm in the washing and laundering line, you must know, ma'am—and I've left my young children to look after themselves, and a more mischievous and troublesome set of young imps doesn't exist, ma'am; and I've lost all my money, and lost my way, and as for what may be happening to my married daughter, why, I don't like to think of it, ma'am!"

"Where might your married daughter be living, ma'am?" asked the barge-woman.

"She lives near to the river, ma'am," replied Toad. "Close to a fine house called Toad Hall, that's somewheres hereabouts in these parts. Perhaps you may have heard of it."

"Toad Hall? Why, I'm going that way myself," replied the barge-woman. "This canal joins the river some miles further on, a little above Toad Hall; and then it's an easy walk. You come along in the barge with me, and I'll give you a lift."

She steered the barge close to the bank, and Toad, with many humble and grateful acknowledgments, stepped lightly on board and sat down with great satisfaction. "Toad's luck again!" thought he. "I always come out on top!"

# *Raggedy Andy Stories*

*Written and illustrated by Johnny Gruelle*

*Making taffy candy can be difficult enough; but if you are a rag doll, it can be a real problem.*

## THE TAFFY-PULL

"I know how we can have a whole lot of fun!" Raggedy Andy said to the other dolls. "We'll have a taffy pull!"

"Do you mean crack the whip, Raggedy Andy?" asked the French doll.

"He means a tug of war, don't you, Raggedy Andy?" asked Henny.

"No," Raggedy Andy replied, "I mean a taffy pull!"

"If it's lots of fun, then show us how to play the game!" Uncle Clem said. "We like to have fun, don't we?" And Uncle Clem turned to all the other dolls as he asked the question.

"It really is not a game," Raggedy Andy explained. "You see, it is only a taffy pull.

"We take sugar and water and butter and a little vinegar and put it all on the stove to cook. When it has cooked until it strings 'way out when you dip some up in a spoon, or gets hard when you drop some of it in a cup of water, then it is candy.

"Then it must be placed upon buttered plates until it has cooled a little, and then each one takes some of the candy and pulls and pulls until it gets real white. Then it is called 'Taffy.' "

"That will be loads of fun!" "Show us how to begin!"

"Let's have a taffy pull!" "Come on, everybody!" the dolls cried.

"Just one moment!" Raggedy Ann said. She had remained quiet before, for she had been thinking very hard, so hard, in fact, that two stitches had burst in the back of her rag head. The dolls, in their eagerness to have the taffy pull, were dancing about Raggedy Andy, but when Raggedy Ann spoke, in her soft cottony voice, they all quieted down and waited for her to speak again.

"I was just thinking," Raggedy Ann said, "that it would be very nice to have the taffy pull, but suppose some of the folks smell the candy while it is cooking."

"There is no one at home!" Raggedy Andy said. "I thought of that, Raggedy Ann. They have all gone over to Cousin Jenny's house and will not be back until day after tomorrow. I heard Mama tell Marcella."

"If that is the case, we can have the taffy pull and all the fun that goes with it!" Raggedy Ann cried, as she started for the nursery door.

After her ran all the dollies, their little feet pitter-patting across the floor and down the hall.

When they came to the stairway Raggedy Ann, Raggedy Andy, Uncle Clem and Henny threw themselves down the stairs, turning over and over as they fell.

The other dolls, having china heads, had to be much more careful; so they slid down the banisters, or jumped from one step to another.

Raggedy Ann, Raggedy Andy, Uncle Clem and Henny piled in a heap at the bottom of the steps, and by the time they had untangled themselves and helped each other up, the other dolls were down the stairs.

To the kitchen they all raced. There they found the fire in the stove still burning.

Raggedy Andy brought a small stew kettle, while the others brought the sugar and water

JOHNNY GRUELLE.

and a large spoon. They could not find the vinegar and decided not to use it, anyway.

Raggedy Andy stood upon the stove and watched the candy, dipping into it every once in a while to see if it had cooked long enough, and stirring it with the large spoon.

At last the candy began to string out from the spoon when it was held above the stew kettle, and after trying a few drops in a cup of cold water, Raggedy Andy pronounced it "done."

Uncle Clem pulled out a large platter from the pantry, and Raggedy Ann dipped her rag hand into the butter jar and buttered the platter.

The candy, when it was poured into the platter, was a lovely golden color and smelled delicious to the dolls. Henny could not wait until it cooled; so he put one of his chamois skin hands into the hot candy.

Of course it did not burn Henny, but when he pulled his hand out again, it was covered with a great ball of candy, which strung out all over the kitchen floor and got upon his clothes.

Then too, the candy cooled quickly, and in a very short time Henny's hand was encased in a hard ball of candy. Henny couldn't wiggle any of his fingers on that hand and he was sorry he had been so hasty.

While waiting for the candy to cool, Raggedy Andy said, "We must rub butter upon our hands before we pull the candy, or else it will stick to our hands as it has done to Henny's hands and have to wear off!"

"Will this hard ball of candy have to wear off of my hand?" Henny asked. "It is so hard, I cannot wiggle any of my fingers!"

"It will either have to wear off, or you will have to soak your hand in water for a long time, until the candy on it melts!" said Raggedy Andy.

"Dear me!" said Henny.

Uncle Clem brought the poker then and, asking Henny to put his hand upon the stove leg, he gave the hard candy a few sharp taps with the poker and chipped the candy from Henny's hand.

"Thank you, Uncle Clem!" Henny said, as he wiggled his fingers. "That feels much better!"

Raggedy Andy told all the dolls to rub butter upon their hands.

"The candy is getting cool enough to pull!" he said.

Then, when all the dolls had their hands nice and buttery, Raggedy Andy cut them each a nice piece of candy and showed them how to pull it.

"Take it in one hand this way," he said, "and pull it with the other hand, like this!"

When all the dolls were supplied with candy they sat about and pulled it, watching it grow whiter and more silvery the longer they pulled.

Then, when the taffy was real white, it began to grow harder and harder, so the smaller dolls could scarcely pull it any more.

When this happened, Raggedy Andy, Raggedy Ann, Uncle Clem and Henny, who were larger, took the little dolls' candy and mixed it with what they had been pulling until all the taffy was snow white.

Then Raggedy Andy pulled it out into a long rope and held it while Uncle Clem hit the ends a sharp tap with the edge of the spoon.

This snipped the taffy into small pieces, just as easily as you might break icicles with a few sharp taps of a stick.

The small pieces of white taffy were placed upon the buttered platter again and the dolls all danced about it, singing and laughing, for this had been the most fun they had had for a long, long time.

"But what shall we do with it?" Raggedy Ann asked.

"Yes, what shall we do with it!" Uncle Clem said. "We can't let it remain in the platter here upon the kitchen floor! We must hide it, or do something with it!"

"While we are trying to think of a way to dispose of it, let us be washing the stew kettle and the spoon!" said practical Raggedy Ann.

"That is a very happy thought, Raggedy Ann!" said Raggedy Andy. "For it will clean the butter and candy from our hands while we are doing it!"

So the stew kettle was dragged to the sink and filled with water, the dolls all taking turns scraping the candy from the sides of the kettle, and scrubbing the inside with a cloth.

When the kettle was nice and clean and had been wiped dry, Raggedy Andy found a roll of waxed paper in the pantry upon one of the shelves.

"We'll wrap each piece of taffy in a nice little piece of paper," he said, "then we'll find a nice paper bag, and put all the pieces inside the bag, and throw it from the upstairs window when someone passes the house so that someone may have the candy!"

All the dolls gathered about the platter on the floor, and while Raggedy Andy cut the paper into neat squares, the dolls wrapped the taffy in the papers.

Then the taffy was put into a large bag, and with much pulling and tugging it was finally dragged up into the nursery, where a window faced out toward the street.

Then, just as a little boy and a little girl, who looked as though they did not ever have much candy, passed the house, the dolls all gave a push and sent the bag tumbling to the sidewalk.

The two children laughed and shouted, "Thank you," when they saw that the bag contained candy, and the dolls, peeping from behind the lace curtains, watched the two happy-faced children eating the taffy as they skipped down the street.

When the children had passed out of sight, the dolls climbed down from the window.

"That was lots of fun!" said the French doll, as she smoothed her skirts and sat down beside Raggedy Andy.

"I believe Raggedy Andy must have a candy heart too, like Raggedy Ann!" said Uncle Clem.

"No!" Raggedy Andy answered, "I'm just stuffed with white cotton and I have no candy heart, but some day perhaps I shall have!"

"A candy heart is very nice!" Raggedy Ann said. (You know, she had one.) "But one can be just as nice and happy and full of sunshine without a candy heart."

"I almost forgot to tell you," said Raggedy Andy, "that when pieces of taffy are wrapped in little pieces of paper, just as we wrapped them, they are called 'Kisses.' "

# *The Water-Babies: A Fairy Tale for a Land-Baby*

*By the Reverend Charles Kingsley*
*Illustrations by J. Noel Paton*

*Tom, an orphan boy mistreated by his master, flees to the river, where he turns into a water baby less than four inches long. He finds he is able to live underwater with all the river creatures, with whom he shares many strange adventures. This is one of them.*

BUT what became of little Tom? He slipt away off the rocks into the water, as I said before.... And here is the account of what happened to him as it was published next morning in the "Water-proof Gazette," on the finest watered paper, for the use of the great fairy Mrs. Bedonebyasyoudid, who reads the news very carefully every morning, and especially the police cases, as you will hear very soon.

He was going along the rocks in three-fathom water, watching the pollock catch prawns, and the wrasses nibble barnacles off the rocks, shells and all, when he saw a round cage of green withes; and inside it, looking very much ashamed of himself, sat his friend the lobster, twiddling his horns, instead of thumbs.

"What! have you been naughty, and have they put you in the lock-up?" asked Tom.

The lobster felt a little indignant at such a

notion, but he was too much depressed in spirits to argue; so he only said, "I can't get out."

"Why did you get in?"

"After that nasty piece of dead fish." He had thought it looked and smelt very nice when he was outside, and so it did, for a lobster; but now he turned round and abused it because he was angry with himself.

"Where did you get in?"

"Through that round hole at the top."

"Then why don't you get out through it?"

"Because I can't"; and the lobster twiddled his horns more fiercely than ever, but he was forced to confess.

"I have jumped upwards, downwards, backwards, and sideways, at least four thousand times; and I can't get out: I always get up underneath there, and can't find the hole."

Tom looked at the trap, and having more wit than the lobster, he saw plainly enough what was the matter; as you may if you will look at a lobster-pot.

"Stop a bit," said Tom. "Turn your tail up to me, and I'll pull you through hindforemost, and then you won't stick in the spikes."

But the lobster was so stupid and clumsy that he couldn't hit the hole. Like a great many fox-hunters, he was very sharp as long as he was in his own country; but as soon as they get out of it they lose their heads; and so the lobster, so to speak, lost his tail.

Tom reached and clawed down the hole after him, till he caught hold of him; and then, as was to be expected, the clumsy lobster pulled him in head foremost.

"Hullo! here is a pretty business," said Tom. "Now take your great claws, and break the points off those spikes, and then we shall both get out easily."

"Dear me, I never thought of that," said the lobster; "and after all the experience of life that I have had!"

You see, experience is of very little good unless a man, or a lobster, has wit enough to make use of it. For a good many people . . . have seen all the world, and yet remain little better than children after all.

But they had not got half the spikes away, when they saw a great dark cloud over them; and lo and behold, it was the otter.

How she did grin and grin when she saw Tom. "Yar!" said she, "you little meddlesome wretch, I have you now! I will serve you out for telling the salmon where I was!" And she crawled all over the pot to get in.

Tom was horribly frightened, and still more frightened when she found the hole in the top, and squeezed herself right down through it, all eyes and teeth. But no sooner was her head inside than valiant Mr. Lobster caught her by the nose, and held on.

And there they were all three in the pot, rolling over and over, and very tight packing it was. And the lobster tore at the otter, and the otter tore at the lobster, and both squeezed and thumped poor Tom till he had no breath left in his body; and I don't know what would have happened to him if he had not at last got on the otter's back, and safe out of the hole.

He was right glad when he got out: but he would not desert his friend who had saved him; and the first time he saw his tail uppermost he caught hold of it, and pulled with all his might.

But the lobster would not let go.

"Come along," said Tom; "don't you see she is dead?" And so she was, quite drowned and dead.

And that was the end of the wicked otter.

F. Mazzanti

# *Pinocchio: The Adventures of a Marionette*

*By Carlo Collodi*

*This world-famous story first appeared as a serial in an Italian children's magazine over a hundred years ago. This excerpt from the first installment tells how the mischievous Pinocchio was created from a piece of ordinary wood that turned out to have extraordinary powers.*

## CHAPTER 1

Once upon a time there was—

"A king?" my little readers will immediately say.

No, children, you are mistaken. Once upon a time there was a piece of wood. It was not fine wood, but a simple piece of wood from the wood yard—the kind we put in the stoves and fireplaces so as to make a fire and heat the rooms.

I do not know how it happened, but one beautiful day a certain old woodcutter found a piece of this kind of wood in his shop. The name of the old man was Antonio, but everybody called him Master Cherry on account of the point of his nose, which was always shiny and purplish, just like a ripe cherry.

As soon as Master Cherry saw that piece of wood he was overjoyed; and rubbing his hands contentedly, he mumbled to himself, "This has come in very good time. I will make it into a table leg."

No sooner said than done. He quickly took a sharpened ax to raise the bark and shape the wood; but when he was on the point of striking it he stopped with his arm in the air, because he heard a tiny, thin little voice say, "Do not strike so hard!"

Just imagine how surprised good old Master Cherry was! He turned his bewildered eyes around the room in order to see whence that little voice came; but he saw no one. He looked under the bench, and no one was there; he looked in a sideboard which was always closed; he looked in the basket of chips and shavings; he opened the door in order to glance around his house; still he could see no one. What then?

"I understand," he said, laughing and scratching his wig; "I imagined I heard that little voice. I will begin to work again."

He took up the ax and gave the piece of wood another hard blow.

"Oh! you have hurt me!" cried the little voice, as if in pain.

This time Master Cherry was dumb. His eyes were nearly popping out of his head; his mouth was opened wide, and his tongue hung down on his chin, like that of a gorgon head on a fountain.

As soon as he could speak he said, trembling and stammering from fright, "But where does that little voice come from that says 'Oh'? There is nothing alive in this room. Can it be that this piece of wood has learned to cry and scream like a baby? I cannot believe it. This is an ordinary piece of wood for the fireplace, like all other pieces with which we boil a pot of beans. What next? What if there is some one hidden inside? If there is, so much the worse for him. I will settle him." And saying this, he seized with both hands the poor piece of wood and knocked it against the wall.

Then he stopped to listen, so as to hear if any voice complained. He waited two minutes, and heard nothing; five minutes, and nothing; ten minutes, and nothing.

"I understand," he said, forcing a laugh and rubbing his wig; "I imagined that I heard a voice cry 'Oh!' I will begin to work again." And because he was somewhat frightened, he tried to hum an air so as to make himself courageous.

At the same time he stopped working with the ax and took up a plane to make the wood even and clean; but while he planed he heard again the little voice, this time in a laughing tone, "Stop! you are taking the skin off my body."

This time poor Master Cherry fell down as if shot. When he opened his eyes he found himself sitting on the ground. His face expressed utter amazement, and the end of his nose, which was always purple, became blue from great fear.

CHAPTER 2

At this moment there was a knock at the door.

"Come in," said the woodcutter, without having strength enough to arise.

Then a lively old man called Geppetto entered the room.

"Good morning, Master Antonio," said Geppetto. "What are you doing on the ground?"

"I am teaching the ants their ABC's. What has brought you here, brother Geppetto?"

"I have come to ask a favor of you, Master Antonio."

"Here I am, prompt to serve you!" replied the woodcutter, raising himself on his knees.

"This morning I had an idea."

"Let me hear it."

"I thought that I would make a pretty marionette; I mean a wonderful marionette, one that can dance, walk, and jump. With this marionette I wish to travel through the world and earn myself a little bread."

"What then, brother Geppetto, can I do for you?"

"I should like a piece of wood to make a marionette. Will you give it to me?"

Master Antonio gladly took up the piece of wood that had frightened him so. But when he was about to hand it to Geppetto the piece of wood gave a spring, and, slipping violently from his hands, fell and struck the shins of poor Geppetto.

"Ah! you are very polite when you give presents! Truly, Master Antonio, you have nearly lamed me."

"I swear to you that I did not do it."

"Surely it was you who threw the piece of wood at my legs."

"I did not throw it. The fault is all in this wood."

"Truly?"

"Truly!"

Upon that Geppetto took the piece of wood in his arms and, thanking Master Antonio, went home, limping all the way.

CHAPTER 3

Geppetto's home consisted of one room on the ground floor. It received light from a window under a staircase. The furniture could not have been more simple—a broken chair, a hard bed, and a dilapidated table. On one side of the room there was a fireplace with wood burning; but the fire was painted, and above it there was also painted a boiling pot with clouds of steam all around it that made it quite real.

As soon as he entered Geppetto began to make a marionette. "What name shall I give him?" he said to himself. "I think I will call him Pinocchio. That name will bring with it good fortune. I have known a whole family called Pinocchio. Pinocchio was the father, Pinocchio was the mother, and the children were called little Pinocchios, and everybody lived well. It was a happy family."

When he had found the name for the marionette he began to work with a will. He quickly made the forehead, then the hair, and then the eyes. After he had made the eyes, just imagine how surprised he was to see them look around, and finally gaze at him fixedly! Geppetto, seeing himself looked at by two eyes of wood, said to the head, "Why do you look at me so, eyes of wood?"

No response.

After he had made the eyes, he made the nose; but the nose began to grow, and it grew, grew, grew, until it became a great big nose, and Geppetto thought it would never stop. He tried hard to stop it, but the more he cut at it the longer that impertinent nose became.

After the nose he made the mouth. The mouth was hardly finished when it commenced to sing and laugh. "Stop laughing," said Geppetto, vexed; but it was like talking to the wall. "Stop laughing, I tell you," he said again in a loud tone. Then the features began to make grimaces.

Geppetto feigned not to see this impertinence and continued to work. After the mouth he made the chin, then the neck, then the shoulders, then the body, then the arms and hands.

Hardly had he finished the hands when Geppetto felt his wig pulled off. He turned quickly, and what do you think he saw?—his yellow wig in the hands of the marionette! "Pinocchio! give me back my wig immediately," said the old man. But Pinocchio, instead of giving back the wig, put it on his own head, making himself look half smothered.

# *First Landscapes*

*By Maurice Denis*

*These pages are from a drawing and coloring book created especially for children by a French artist in the early part of this century.*

It isn't difficult to draw houses, especially if one doesn't put in each and every window.

Nor is it difficult to draw trees, especially if one doesn't try to draw each and every leaf.

Here is a market square and a beautiful cathedral, a pretty French town.

Here is a meadow with cows.

In winter mothers tell you that you should run around to keep yourself warm. That's no fun.

In summer, as soon as you start running around, mothers tell you that it's too hot to run and you will catch a cold.

# *Jack Huckaback*

*Written and illustrated by Wilhelm Busch*

*This is part of a very old story about one tough raven.*

Here squats young Fred, with sack and pack,
And there's the raven, Huckaback.

And Fred, like so many a lad,
To have a raven would be glad.

Along the bough, he glides most fine; —
The raven fears some bad design.

Bang! little Fred, of his great cap,
Cunnigly makes a raven trap.

He nearly has him, but, oh woe!
The bough breaks off, he falls below.

In juicy bilberries sits young Fred;
The raven his cap has on his head.

Fred's sprinkled black; oh what a sight!
The raven hops in sad affright.

The silly bird is caught at last.
His head in the lining sits full fast.

So, now I have you, Huckaback!
How glad Aunt Jane, when I come back.

Out comes Aunt Jane — her nose is red —
"Oh, what a pretty bird!" she said.

Scarce had she his beauty praised;—
Snap! he has her finger seized.

"Ah!" cried she, "he's not so good,
For he has basely drawn my blood."

Here in the pot, lurks Huckaback;
His mind is dark, his coat is black.

From Pincher he had stol'n a bone,
But he comes now, to claim his own.

Look! there they pull with growl and croak,—
You see in their faces, 'tis no joke.

"I've won," thought Pincher, in his mind,
But the raven picks him from behind.

Oh woe! he jumps upon his back;
His hair he'll tear, Jack Huckaback.

But Pincher, now with rage doth burn;
Fleeces the raven in his turn.

# *The Brownies: Their Book*

*Written and illustrated by Palmer Cox*

*The Brownies are now almost one hundred years old, but the magic of these good-natured sprites still enchants.*

## THE BROWNIES ON SKATES

One night, when the cold moon hung low
And winter wrapped the world in snow
And bridged the streams in wood and field
With ice as smooth as shining shield,
Some skaters swept in graceful style
The glistening surface, file on file.
For hours the Brownies viewed the show,
Commenting on the groups below;
Said one: "That pleasure might be ours—
We have the feet and motive powers;
No mortal need us Brownies teach,
If skates were but within our reach."
Another answered: "Then, my friend,
To hear my plan let all attend.
I have a building in my mind
That we within an hour can find.
Three golden balls hang by the door,
Like oranges from Cuba's shore;
Behind the dusty counter stands
A native of queer, far-off lands;
The place is filled with various things,
From baby-carts to banjo-strings;
Here hangs a gun without a lock
Some pilgrim bore to Plymouth Rock;
And there a pair of goggles lie,
That saw the red-coats marching by;
While piles of club and rocker skates
Of every shape the buyer waits!
Though second-hand, I'm sure they'll do,
And serve our wants as well as new.
That place we'll enter as we may,
To-morrow night, and bear away
A pair, the best that come to hand,

PALMER COX

For every member of the band."
At once, the enterprise so bold
Received support from young and old.
A place to muster near the town,
And meeting hour they noted down;
And then retiring for the night,
They soon were lost to sound and sight.

When evening next her visit paid
To fold the earth in robes of shade,
From out the woods across the mead,
The Brownies gathered as agreed,
To venture boldly and procure
The skates that would their fun insure.
As mice can get to cake and cheese
Without a key whene'er they please,
So, cunning Brownies can proceed
And help themselves to what they need.
For bolts and bars they little care
If but a nail is wanting there!...
So rushed the eager band away
To fields of ice without delay.

Though far too large at heel and toe,
The skates were somehow made to go.
But out behind and out before,
Like spurs, they stuck a span or more,
Alike afflicting foe and friend
In bringing journeys to an end.
They had their slips and sudden spreads,
Where heels flew higher than their heads,
As people do, however nice,
When venturing first upon the ice.
But soon they learned to curve and wheel
And cut fine scrolls with scoring steel,
To race in clusters to and fro,
To jump and turn and backward go,
Until a rest on bed so cool,
Was more the wonder than the rule.
But from the lake they all withdrew
Some hours before the night was through,
And hastened back with lively feet
Through narrow lane and silent street,
Until they reached the broker's door
With every skate that left the store.
And, ere the first faint gleam of day,
The skates were safely stowed away;
Of their brief absence not a trace
Was left within the dusty place.

# *Once in Puerto Rico*

*By Pura Belpré White*
*Illustrations by Christine Price*

*The librarian who has retold this Puerto Rican Indian legend was among the first to explore the rich traditions of Hispanic folklore with the children who use the New York Public Library's branches.*

## THE LEGEND OF THE ROYAL PALM

Among the Taino Indians on the Island of Boriquen there was once a man named Milomaki. He was tall, brave and handsome, and he had a wonderful singing voice, a voice possessed of strange power. If you were sick, his singing made you well. If you were sad, it made you happy. His fame spread all over the island, and people came from far away to see and hear him. But his popularity and his power over the people soon angered the Indian gods. They became jealous and plotted against him.

One afternoon, as the Indians were returning with their catch of fresh fish from the river, they came upon Milomaki.

"Sing for us," they said, "for we have been working since dawn and we are tired."

Milomaki began to sing songs that had the coolness of a soft breeze, and the Indians forgot their weariness and were refreshed. Then Milomaki sang heroic songs, and the Indians felt like fishermen no longer but like Indian chiefs performing mighty deeds in war. As they listened, caught by the spell of the music, the hot sun shone down on them and on the fish they had caught.

After a while the songs ended. The Indians thanked Milomaki, picked up their fish and went home.

When they arrived, their wives prepared the fish and they all sat down to enjoy the delicious meal. But after dinner a terrible thing happened. Everyone who had eaten the fish became ill.

"It is Milomaki's fault!" said the fishermen. "He made us forget the fish while he sang, and the hot sun has spoiled them."

All their happiness turned to anger. Only the Indian gods were happy. They had been waiting for just such an incident to occur. Now they stirred up the men against Milomaki, filling their hearts with evil thoughts. The Indians decided that Milomaki must die.

"Burn him at the stake!" they shouted. Their anger made them forget their illness, and off they went in search of Milomaki. They searched all night. It was not until dawn that they caught up with him. They pounced on

him and bound him, and he gave in without a struggle. He felt no anger toward them, only wonder and surprise. Were these the same men who only the day before had quietly listened to his singing?

The Indians tied him to a heavy log. Then they gathered firewood and built a great fire. Milomaki understood what they were going to do and he became very sad. When everything was ready they lifted him up to stand above the fire.

Suddenly he began to sing. His song was more beautiful than any they had ever heard. He sang and sang. He was still singing when a soft rain began to fall. It clung to the leaves of the trees, moistened the grass and moss underfoot and touched with coolness the face of Milomaki as he sang.

His voice rose and fell under the spell of its own music. The Indians listened in awe and the spell of the music swept away their evil thoughts. Suddenly they were horrified at what they were about to do. Gone was their anger. A feeling of remorse surged through their bodies.

"Milomaki, Milomaki!" they cried, and they rushed to untie him. But they were too late. Right before their eyes Milomaki's form began to disappear. Where he had been standing there was now a tall regal-looking palm tree, its crown of leafy fronds spread out toward the sky. A gust of wind blew through its branches and they stirred with a soft rustling sound. The Indians had never seen such a tree before, and because it had a royal look and stood so tall and straight, they called it Royal Palm. Whenever they heard the wind blowing through its branches, they imagined it was Milomaki singing to them, and they would stop to listen with delight and wonder.

They told their children and their children's children the tale of Milomaki, and when more palm trees grew on the island, as straight and tall and beautiful as the first of the Royal Palms, the voice of the great singer could be heard in all of them.

# *Wanda Ga'g's Story Book*

*Written and illustrated by Wanda Ga'g.*

*A love of cats can sometimes get out of hand, as this tale from a popular story book shows.*

## MILLIONS OF CATS

Once upon a time there was a very old man and a very old woman. They lived in a nice clean house which had flowers all around it, except where the door was. But they couldn't be happy because they were so very lonely.

"If we only had a cat!" sighed the very old woman.

"A cat?" asked the very old man.

"Yes, a sweet little fluffy cat," said the very old woman.

"I will get you a cat, my dear," said the very old man.

And he set out over the hills to look for one. He climbed over the sunny hills. He trudged through the cool valleys. He walked a long, long time and at last he came to a hill which was quite covered with cats.

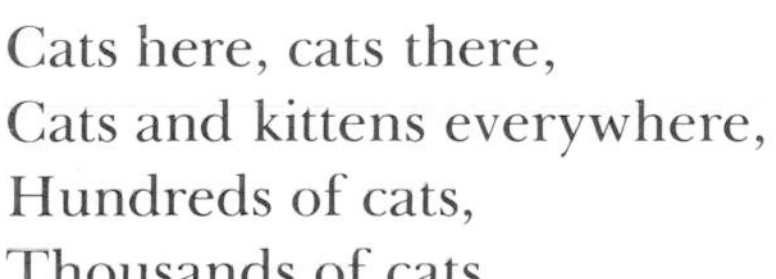

Cats here, cats there,
Cats and kittens everywhere,
Hundreds of cats,
Thousands of cats,
Millions and billions and trillions of cats.

"Oh," cried the old man joyfully. "Now I can choose the prettiest cat and take it home with me!" So he chose one. It was white.

But just as he was about to leave, he saw another one all black and white and it seemed just as pretty as the first. So he took this one also.

But then he saw a fuzzy grey kitten way over here which was every bit as pretty as the others so he took it too.

And now he saw one way down in a corner which he thought too lovely to leave so he took this too.

And just then, over here, the very old man found a kitten which was black and very beautiful.

"It would be a shame to leave that one," said the very old man. So he took it.

And now, over there, he saw a cat which had brown and yellow stripes like a baby tiger.

"I simply must take it!" cried the very old man, and he did.

So it happened that every time the very old man looked up, he saw another cat which was so pretty he could not bear to leave it, and before he knew it, he had chosen them all.

# *Andy and the Lion*

*Written and illustrated*
*by James Daugherty*

*This book was dedicated "To Lady Astor and Lord Lenox, the library lions who have so long sat in front of the New York Public Library."*

It was a bright day with just enough wind to float a flag. Andy started down to the library to get a book about lions. He took the book home and read and read. Andy read all through supper and he read all evening and just before bedtime his grandfather told him some tall stories about hunting lions in Africa. Every story ended with "And then I gave him both BAR-R-R-E-L-L-S!" That night Andy dreamed all night long that he was in Africa hunting lions. When at last morning came Andy woke up. The sun was looking in at the window and Prince was tugging at the bedclothes. The lions had left but Andy kept thinking about them.

Andy thought lions on the back porch and his father had to remind him to wash behind his ears. Andy was still thinking lions after breakfast when his mother gave his hair a final brush and Andy started off to school. Andy walked along swinging his books and whistling a tune. As he came to the turn in the road he noticed something sticking out from behind the big rock just at the bend. It looked very queer so Andy and Prince crept up cautiously to investigate. It moved!

It was a lion! At this moment Andy thought he'd better be going and the lion thought so too. They ran and ran around the rock. Whichever way that Andy ran—there was the lion. Whichever way the lion ran—there was Andy. At last they both stopped for breath. The lion held out his paw to show Andy what was the matter. It was a big thorn stuck in his

paw. But Andy had an idea. He told the lion to just be patient and they'd have that thorn out in no time. Fortunately Andy always carried his pliers in the back pocket of his overalls. He took them out and got a tight grip. Then Andy braced one foot against the lion's paw and pulled with all his might until the thorn came out.

The grateful lion licked Andy's face to show how pleased he was. But it was time to part. So they waved good-by. Andy went on to school and the lion went off about the business of being a lion.

In the Spring the circus came to town. Of course Andy went. He wanted to see the famous lion act. Right in the middle of the act the biggest lion jumped out of the high steel cage and with a terrible roar dashed straight toward the people. They ran for their lives and in the scramble Andy found himself right in the lion's path. He thought his last moment had come. But then who should it be but Andy's own lion. They recognized each other and danced for joy. When the crowd came back ready to fight the lion and capture him Andy stood in front of the lion and shouted to the angry people: "Do not hurt this lion. He's a friend of mine."

Then the next day Andy led the lion and all the people in a grand parade down Main Street to the City Hall. There the mayor presented Andy with a medal for bravery. And the lion was very much pleased. And the next day Andy took the book back to the library.

# *The Wonderful Wizard of Oz*

*By L. Frank Baum*
*Illustrations by W. W. Denslow*

*Dorothy and her dog, Toto, have been carried by a cyclone from a farm in Kansas to the Land of Oz. There they meet the Scarecrow and the Tin Woodman, who join them on their way to see the Wizard. In this first adventure they make a new friend.*

All this time Dorothy and her companions had been walking through the thick woods. The road was still paved with yellow brick, but these were much covered by dried branches and dead leaves from the trees, and the walking was not at all good.

There were few birds in this part of the forest, for birds love the open country where there is plenty of sunshine; but now and then there came a deep growl from some wild animal hidden among the trees. These sounds made the little girl's heart beat fast, for she did not know what made them; but Toto knew, and he walked close to Dorothy's side, and did not even bark in return.

"How long will it be," the child asked of the

Tin Woodman, "before we are out of the forest?"

"I cannot tell," was the answer, "for I have never been to the Emerald City. But my father went there once, when I was a boy, and he said it was a long journey through a dangerous country, although nearer to the city where Oz dwells the country is beautiful. But I am not afraid so long as I have my oil-can, and nothing can hurt the Scarecrow, while you bear upon your forehead the mark of the good Witch's kiss, and that will protect you from harm."

"But Toto!" said the girl, anxiously; "what will protect him?"

"We must protect him ourselves, if he is in danger," replied the Tin Woodman.

Just as he spoke there came from the forest a terrible roar, and the next moment a great lion bounded into the road. With one blow of his paw he sent the Scarecrow spinning over and over to the edge of the road, and then he struck at the Tin Woodman with his sharp claws. But, to the Lion's surprise, he could make no impression on the tin, although the Woodman fell over in the road and lay still.

Little Toto, now that he had an enemy to face, ran barking toward the Lion, and the great beast had opened his mouth to bite the dog, when Dorothy, fearing Toto would be killed, and heedless of danger, rushed forward and slapped the Lion upon his nose as hard as she could, while she cried out:

"Don't you dare to bite Toto! You ought to be ashamed of yourself, a big beast like you, to bite a poor little dog!"

"I didn't bite him," said the Lion, as he rubbed his nose with his paw where Dorothy had hit it.

"No, but you tried to," she retorted. "You are nothing but a big coward."

"I know it," said the Lion, hanging his head in shame; "I've always known it. But how can I help it?"

"I don't know, I'm sure. To think of your striking a stuffed man, like the poor Scarecrow!"

"Is he stuffed?" asked the Lion, in surprise, as he watched her pick up the Scarecrow and set him upon his feet, while she patted him into shape again.

"Of course he's stuffed," replied Dorothy, who was still angry.

"That's why he went over so easily," remarked the Lion. "It astonished me to see him whirl around so. Is the other one stuffed, also?"

"No," said Dorothy, "he's made of tin." And she helped the Woodman up again.

"That's why he nearly blunted my claws," said the Lion. "When they scratched against the tin it made a cold shiver run down my back. What is that little animal you are so tender of?"

"He is my dog, Toto," answered Dorothy.

"Is he made of tin, or stuffed?" asked the Lion.

"Neither. He's a—a—a meat dog," said the girl.

"Oh. He's a curious animal, and seems remarkably small, now that I look at him. No one would think of biting such a little thing except a coward like me," continued the Lion, sadly.

"What makes you a coward?" asked Dorothy, looking at the great beast in wonder, for he was as big as a small horse.

"It's a mystery," replied the Lion. "I suppose I was born that way. All the other animals in the forest naturally expect me to be brave, for the Lion is everywhere thought to be the King of Beasts. I learned that if I roared very loudly every living thing was frightened and got out of my way. Whenever I've met a man I've been awfully scared; but I just roared at him, and he has always run away as fast as he could go. If the elephants and the tigers and the bears had ever tried to fight me, I should have run myself—I'm such a coward; but just as soon as they hear me roar they all try to get away from me, and of course I let them go."

"But that isn't right. The King of Beasts shouldn't be a coward," said the Scarecrow.

"I know it," returned the Lion, wiping a tear from his eye with the tip of his tail; "it is my great sorrow, and makes my life very unhappy. But whenever there is danger my heart begins to beat fast."

# LAND OF OZ

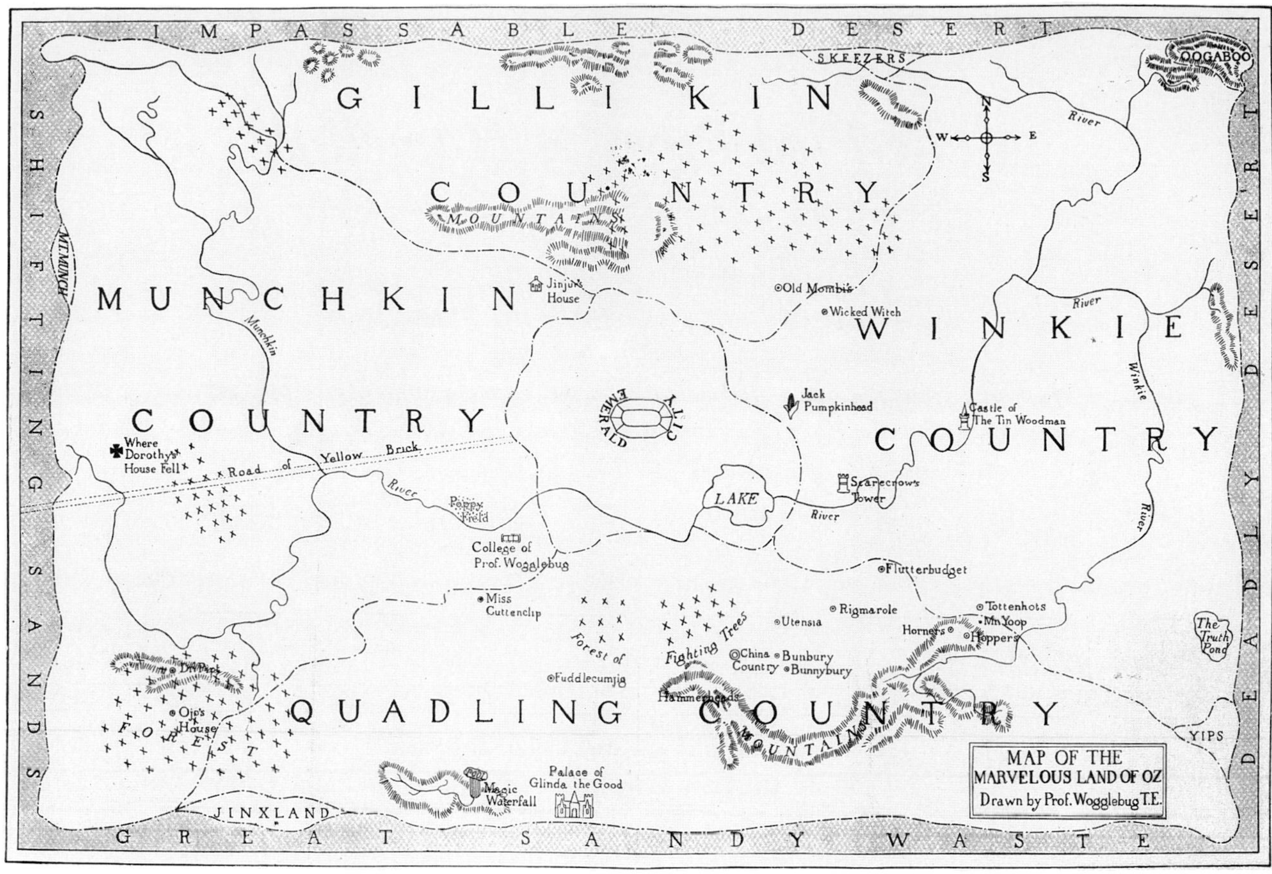


"Perhaps you have heart disease," said the Tin Woodman.

"It may be," said the Lion.

"If you have," continued the Tin Woodman, "you ought to be glad, for it proves you have a heart. For my part, I have no heart; so I cannot have heart disease."

"Perhaps," said the Lion, thoughtfully, "if I had no heart I should not be a coward."

"Have you brains?" asked the Scarecrow.

"I suppose so. I've never looked to see," replied the Lion.

"I am going to the great Oz to ask him to give me some," remarked the Scarecrow, "for my head is stuffed with straw."

"And I am going to ask him to give me a heart," said the Woodman.

"And I am going to ask him to send Toto and me back to Kansas," added Dorothy.

"Do you think Oz could give me courage?" asked the cowardly Lion.

"Just as easily as he could give me brains," said the Scarecrow.

"Or give me a heart," said the Tin Woodman.

"Or send me back to Kansas," said Dorothy.

"Then, if you don't mind, I'll go with you," said the Lion, "for my life is simply unbearable without a bit of courage."...

So once more the little company set off upon the journey, the Lion walking with stately strides at Dorothy's side.

# *The Pied Piper of Hamelin*

*By Robert Browning*
*Illustrations by Arthur Rackham*

*Just how annoying rats can be is shown in this segment of the famous poem, where we meet the Pied Piper for the first time when he comes to offer his services to the town of Hamelin.*

Rats!
They fought the dogs and killed the cats,
  And bit the babies in the cradles,
And ate the cheeses out of the vats,
  And licked the soup from the cooks'
    own ladles,
Split open the kegs of salted sprats,
Made nests inside men's Sunday hats,
And even spoiled the women's chats
  By drowning their speaking
  With shrieking and squeaking
In fifty different sharps and flats.
At last the people in a body
  To the Town Hall came flocking:
" 'Tis clear," cried they, "our Mayor's a
    noddy;
  And as for our Corporation—shocking
To think we buy gowns lined with ermine
For dolts that can't or won't determine
What's best to rid us of our vermin!...
Rouse up, sirs! Give your brains a racking
To find the remedy we're lacking,
Or, sure as fate, we'll send you packing!"
At this the Mayor and Corporation
Quaked with a mighty consternation.
An hour they sat in council;
  At length the Mayor broke silence:

ILLUSTRATED·BY
ARTHUR·RACKHAM

"For a guilder I'd my ermine gown sell,
I wish I were a mile hence!
It's easy to bid one rack one's brain—
I'm sure my poor head aches again,
I've scratched it so, and all in vain.

Oh for a trap, a trap, a trap!"
Just as he said this, what should hap
At the chamber door but a gentle tap?
"Bless us," cried the Mayor, "what's that?...
Only a scraping of shoes on the mat?
Anything like the sound of a rat
Makes my heart go pit-a-pat!"

"Come in!"—the Mayor cried, looking
bigger:
And in did come the strangest figure!
His queer long coat from heel to head
Was half of yellow and half of red,
And he himself was tall and thin,
With sharp blue eyes, each like a pin,
And light loose hair, yet swarthy skin,
No tuft on cheek nor beard on chin,
But lips where smiles went out and in;
There was no guessing his kith and kin:
And nobody could enough admire
The tall man and his quaint attire.
Quoth one: "It's as my great-grandsire,
Starting up at the Trump of Doom's tone,
Had walked this way from his painted
tombstone!"

He advanced to the council-table:
And, "Please your honours," said he, "I'm
able,
By means of a secret charm, to draw
All creatures living beneath the sun,
That creep or swim or fly or run,
After me so as you never saw!
And I chiefly use my charm
On creatures that do people harm,
The mole and toad and newt and viper;
And people call me the Pied Piper."
(And here they noticed round his neck
A scarf of red and yellow stripe,
To match with his coat of the selfsame
check;
And at the scarf's end hung a pipe;
And his fingers, they noticed, were ever
straying
As if impatient to be playing
Upon this pipe, as low it dangled
Over his vesture so old-fangled.)
"Yet," said he, "poor piper as I am,
In Tartary I freed the Cham,
Last June, from his huge swarms of
gnats;
I eased in Asia the Nizam
Of a monstrous brood of vampire-bats:
And as for what your brain bewilders,
If I can rid your town of rats
Will you give me a thousand guilders?"
"One? fifty thousand!"—was the exclamation
Of the astonished Mayor and Corporation.
Into the street the Piper stept,
Smiling first a little smile,
As if he knew what magic slept
In his quiet pipe the while;
Then, like a musical adept,
To blow the pipe his lips he wrinkled,
And green and blue his sharp eyes
twinkled,
Like a candle-flame where salt is sprinkled;
And ere three shrill notes the pipe uttered,
You heard as if an army muttered;
And the muttering grew to a grumbling;
And the grumbling grew to a mighty
rumbling;
And out of the houses the rats came
tumbling.
Great rats, small rats, lean rats, brawny
rats,
Brown rats, black rats, grey rats, tawny
rats,
Grave old plodders, gay young friskers,
Fathers, mothers, uncles, cousins,
Cocking tails and pricking whiskers,
Families by tens and dozens,
Brothers, sisters, husbands, wives—
Followed the Piper for their lives.
From street to street he piped advancing,
And step for step they followed dancing,
Until they came to the river Weser,
Wherein all plunged and perished!

# *Peacock Pie: A Book of Rhymes*

*By Walter De la Mare*
*Illustrations by W. Heath Robinson*

*The English poet presents us here with a view of the past, a dream, and a fantasy.*

## THEN

Twenty, forty, sixty, eighty,
  A hundred years ago,
All through the night with lantern bright
  The Watch trudged to and fro.
And little boys tucked snug abed
  Would wake from dreams to hear—
"Two o' the morning by the clock,
  And the stars a-shining clear!"
Or, when across the chimney-tops
  Screamed shrill a North-East gale,
A faint and shaken voice would shout,
  "Three! and a storm of hail!"

## FULL MOON

One night as Dick lay half asleep,
Into his drowsy eyes
A great still light began to creep
From out the silent skies.
It was the lovely moon's, for when
He raised his dreamy head,
Her surge of silver filled the pane
And streamed across his bed.
So, for awhile, each gazed at each—
Dick and the solemn moon—
Till, climbing slowly on her way,
She vanished, and was gone.

# THE PIGS AND THE CHARCOAL-BURNER

The old Pig said to the little pigs,
  "In the forest is truffles and mast,
Follow me then, all ye little pigs,
  Follow me fast!"
The Charcoal-burner sat in the shade
  With his chin on his thumb,
And saw the big Pig and the little pigs,
  Chuffling come.
He watched 'neath a green and giant bough,
  And the pigs in the ground
Made a wonderful grisling and gruzzling
  And greedy sound.
And when, full-fed, they were gone, and Night
  Walked her starry ways,
He stared with his cheeks in his hands
  At his sullen blaze.

# *In Wink-A-Way Land*

*By Eugene Field*

*In this curious land some particularly strange birds sing their songs.*

## THE DINKEY-BIRD

In an ocean way out yonder
  (As all sapient people know)
Is the land of Wonder-Wander,
  Whither children love to go;
It's their playing, romping, swinging,
  That giveth joy to me,
While the Dinkey-Bird goes singing
  In the amfalula tree!

There the gumdrops grow like cherries
  And taffy's thick as peas—
Caramels you pick like berries
  When and where and how you please;
Big red sugar plums are clinging
  To the cliffs beside that sea
Where the Dinkey-Bird is singing
  In the amfalula tree!

So when the children shout and scamper
  And make merry all the day,
When there's naught to put a damper
  On the ardor of their play;
When I hear their laughter ringing,
  Then I'm sure as sure can be
That the Dinkey-Bird is singing
  In the amfalula tree.

For the Dinkey-Bird's bravuras
  And the staccatos are so sweet—
His roulades, appoggiaturas
  and robustos so complete,
That the youth of every nation—
  Be they near or far away—
Have especial delectation
  In that gladsome roundelay.

Their eyes grow bright and brighter,
  Their lungs begin to crow,
Their hearts get light and lighter
  And their cheeks are all aglow;
For an echo cometh bringing
  The news to all and me
That the Dinkey-Bird is singing
  In the amfalula tree!

Yes, I'm sure you'd like to go there
  To see your feathered friend—
And so many goodies grow there
  You would like to comprehend!
*Speed, little dreams, your winging*
  *To that land across the sea*
*Where the Dinkey-Bird is singing*
  *In the amfalula tree!*

# FIDDLE-DEE-DEE

There once was a bird that lived up in a tree,
And all he could whistle was "Fiddle-dee-dee"—
A very provoking, unmusical song
For one to be whistling the summer day long!
Yet always contented and busy was he
With that vocal recurrence of "Fiddle-dee-dee."

Hardby lived a brave little soldier of four
That weird iteration repented him sore;
"I pri'thee, Dear-Mother-Mine! fetch me my gun,
For, by our St. Didy! the deed must be done
That shall presently rid all creation and me
Of that ominous bird and his 'Fiddle-dee-dee!' "

Then out came Dear-Mother-Mine, bringing her son
His awfully truculent little red gun;
The stock was of pine and the barrel of tin,
The "bang" it came out where the bullet went
  in—
The right kind of weapon, I think you'll agree,
For slaying all fowl that go "Fiddle-dee-dee!"

The brave little soldier quoth never a word,
But he up and he drew a straight bead on that
  bird;
And, while that vain creature provokingly sang,
Then loud laughed the youth—"By my Bottle,"
  cried he,
"I've put a quietus on 'Fiddle-dee-dee'!"
Out came then Dear-Mother-Mine, saying: "My
  son,
Right well have you wrought with your little red
  gun!
Hereafter no evil at all need I fear,
With such a brave soldier as You-My-Love here!"
She kissed the dear boy. (The bird in the tree
Continued to whistle his "Fiddle-dee-dee!")

# At the Back of the North Wind

*By George MacDonald*
*Illustrations by Jessie Willcox Smith*

*Having found the North Wind way up in the icy Arctic, the boy in this story goes traveling with her, and at her back he discovers a content "better than mere happiness."*

After a little while Diamond went out and sat on the edge of his floating island, and looked down into the ocean beneath him. The white sides of the berg reflected so much light below the water, that he could see far down into the green abyss. Sometimes he fancied he saw the eyes of North Wind looking up at him from below, but the fancy never lasted beyond the moment of its birth. And the time passed he did not know how, for he felt as if he were in a dream. When he got tired of the green water, he went into the blue cave; and when he got tired of the blue cave he went out and gazed all about him on the blue sea, ever sparkling in the sun, which kept wheeling about the sky, never going below the horizon. But he chiefly gazed northwards, to see whether any land were appearing. All this time he never wanted to eat. He broke off little bits of the berg now and then and sucked them, and he thought them very nice.

At length, one time he came out of his cave, he spied, far off upon the horizon, a shining peak that rose into the sky like the top of some tremendous iceberg; and his vessel was bearing him straight towards it. As it went on the peak rose and rose higher and higher above the horizon; and other peaks rose after it, with sharp edges and jagged ridges connecting them. Diamond thought this must be the place he was going to; and he was right; for the mountains rose and rose, till he saw the line of the coast at their feet, and at length the iceberg drove into a little bay, all round which were lofty precipices with snow on their tops, and streaks of ice down their sides. The berg floated slowly up to a projecting rock. Diamond stepped on shore, and without looking behind him began to follow a natural path which led windingly towards the top of the precipice.

When he reached it, he found himself on a broad table of ice, along which he could walk without much difficulty. Before him, at a considerable distance, rose a lofty ridge of ice, which shot up into fantastic pinnacles and towers and battlements. The air was very cold, and seemed somehow dead, for there was not the slightest breath of wind.

In the centre of the ridge before him appeared a gap like the opening of a valley. But as he walked towards it, gazing, and wondering whether that could be the way he had to take, he saw that what had appeared a gap was the form of a woman seated against the ice front of the ridge, leaning forward with her hands in her lap, and her hair hanging down to the ground.

"It is North Wind on her doorstep," said Diamond joyfully, and hurried on.

He soon came up to the place, and there the form sat, like one of the great figures at the door of an Egyptian temple, motionless, with drooping arms and head. Then Diamond grew frightened, because she did not move nor speak. He was sure it was North Wind, but he thought she must be dead at last. Her face was white as the snow, her eyes were blue as the air in the ice-cave, and her hair hung down straight, like icicles. She had on a greenish robe, like the color in the hollows of a glacier seen from far off.

He stood up before her, and gazed fearfully into her face for a few minutes before he ventured to speak. At length, with a great effort and a trembling voice, he faltered out—

"North Wind!"

"Well, child?" said the form, without lifting its head.

"Are you ill, dear North Wind?"

"No. I am waiting."

"What for?"

"Till I'm wanted."

"You don't care for me any more," said Diamond, almost crying now.

"Yes, I do. Only I can't show it. All my love is down at the bottom of my heart. But I feel it bubbling there."

"What do you want me to do next, dear North Wind?" said Diamond, wishing to show his love by being obedient.

"What do you want to do yourself?"

"I want to go into the country at your back."

"Then you must go through me."

"I don't know what you mean."

"I mean just what I say. You must walk on as if I were an open door, and go right through me."

"But that will hurt you."

"Not in the least. It will hurt you, though."

"I don't mind that, if you tell me to do it."

"Do it," said North Wind.

Diamond walked towards her instantly. When he reached her knees, he put out his hand to lay it on her, but nothing was there save an intense cold. He walked on. Then all grew white about him; and the cold stung him like fire. He walked on still, groping through the whiteness. It thickened about him. At last, it got into his heart, and he lost all sense. I would say that he fainted—only whereas in common faints all grows black about you, he felt swallowed up in whiteness. It was when he reached North Wind's heart that he fainted and fell. But as he fell, he rolled over the threshold, and it was thus that Diamond got to the back of the north wind.

# *The Boy Who Drew Cats*

*Rendered into English*
*by Lafcadio Hearn*

*This Japanese fairy tale tells us of the powerful magic to be found in a work of art.*

A long, long time ago, in a small country village in Japan, there lived a poor farmer and his wife, who were very good people. They had a number of children, and found it very hard to feed them all. The elder son was strong enough when only fourteen years old to help his father; and the little girls learned to help their mother almost as soon as they could walk.

But the youngest child, a little boy, did not seem to be fit for hard work. He was very clever,—cleverer than all his brothers and sisters; but he was quite weak and small, and people said he could never grow very big. So his parents thought it would be better for him to become a priest than to become a farmer. They took him with them to the village temple one day, and asked the good old priest who lived there if he would have their little boy for his acolyte and teach him all that a priest ought to know.

The old man spoke kindly to the lad, and asked him some hard questions. So clever were the answers that the priest agreed to take the little fellow into the temple as an acolyte, and to educate him for the priesthood.

The boy learned quickly what the old priest taught him, and was very obedient in most things. But he had one fault. He liked to draw cats during study-hours, and to draw cats even where cats ought not to have been drawn at all.

Whenever he found himself alone, he drew cats. He drew them on the margins of the priest's books, and on all the screens of the temple, and on the walls, and on the pillars. Several times the priest told him this was not right; but he did not stop drawing cats. He drew them because he could not really help it. He had what is called "the genius of an *artist*," and just for that reason he was not quite fit to be an acolyte;—a good acolyte should study books.

One day after he had drawn some very clever pictures of cats upon a paper screen, the old priest said to him severely, "My boy, you must go away from this temple at once. You will never make a good priest, but perhaps you will become a great artist. Now let me give you a last piece of advice, and be sure you never forget it. *Avoid large places at night;—keep to small!*"

The boy did not know what the priest meant by saying, *"Avoid large places;—keep to small."* He thought and thought, while he was tying up his little bundle of clothes to go away; but he could not understand those words, and he was afraid to speak to the priest any more, except to say goodbye.

He left the temple very sorrowfully, and began to wonder what he should do. If he went straight home he felt sure his father would punish him for having been disobedient to the priest: so he was afraid to go home. All at once he remembered that at the next village, twelve miles away, there was a very big temple. He had heard there were several priests at that temple; and he made up his mind to go to them and ask them to take him for their acolyte.

Now the big temple was closed up but the boy did not know this fact. The reason it had been closed up was that a goblin had frightened the priests away, and had taken possession of the place. Some brave warriors had afterward gone to the temple at night to kill the goblin; but they had never been seen alive again. Nobody had ever told these things to the boy;—so he walked all the way to the village hoping to be kindly treated by the priests.

When he got to the village it was already dark, and all the people were in bed; but he saw the big temple on a hill at the other end of the principal street, and he saw there was a light in the temple. People who tell the story say the goblin used to make that light, in order to tempt lonely travellers to ask for shelter. The boy went at once to the temple, and knocked. There was no sound inside. He knocked and knocked again; but still nobody came. At last he pushed gently at the door, and was quite glad to find that it had not been fastened. So he went in, and saw a lamp burning,—but no priest.

He thought some priest would be sure to come very soon, and he sat down and waited. Then he noticed that everything in the temple was grey with dust, and thickly spun over with cobwebs. So he thought to himself that the priests would certainly like to have an acolyte, to keep the place clean. He wondered why they had allowed everything to get so dusty. What most pleased him, however, were some big white screens, good to paint cats upon. Though he was tired, he looked at once for a writing-box, and found one, and ground some ink, and began to paint cats.

He painted a great many cats upon the screens; and then he began to feel very, very sleepy. He was just on the point of lying down to sleep beside one of the screens, when he suddenly remembered the words: *"Avoid large places;—keep to small!"*

The temple was very large; he was all alone; and as he thought of these words,—though he could not quite understand them—he began to feel for the first time a little afraid; and he resolved to look for a *small place* in which to sleep. He found a little cabinet, with a sliding door, and went into it, and shut himself up. Then he lay down and fell fast asleep.

Very late in the night he was awakened by a most terrible noise,—a noise of fighting and screaming. It was so dreadful that he was afraid even to look through a chink of the little cabinet: he lay very still, holding his breath for fright.

The light that had been in the temple went out; but the awful sounds continued, and became more awful, and all the temple shook. After a long time silence came; but the boy was still afraid to move. He did not move until the light of the morning sun shone into the cabinet through the chinks of the little door.

Then he got out of his hiding-place very cautiously, and looked about. The first thing he saw was that all the floor of the temple was covered with blood. And then he saw, lying dead in the middle of it, an enormous, monstrous rat—a goblin-rat—bigger than a cow!

But who or what could have killed it? There was no man or other creature to be seen. Suddenly the boy observed that the mouths of all the cats he had drawn the night before, were red and wet with blood. Then he knew that the goblin had been killed by the cats which he had drawn. And then also, for the first time, he understood why the wise old priest had said to him: *"Avoid large places at night;—keep to small."*. . .

Afterward that boy became a very famous artist. Some of the cats which he drew are still shown to travellers in Japan.

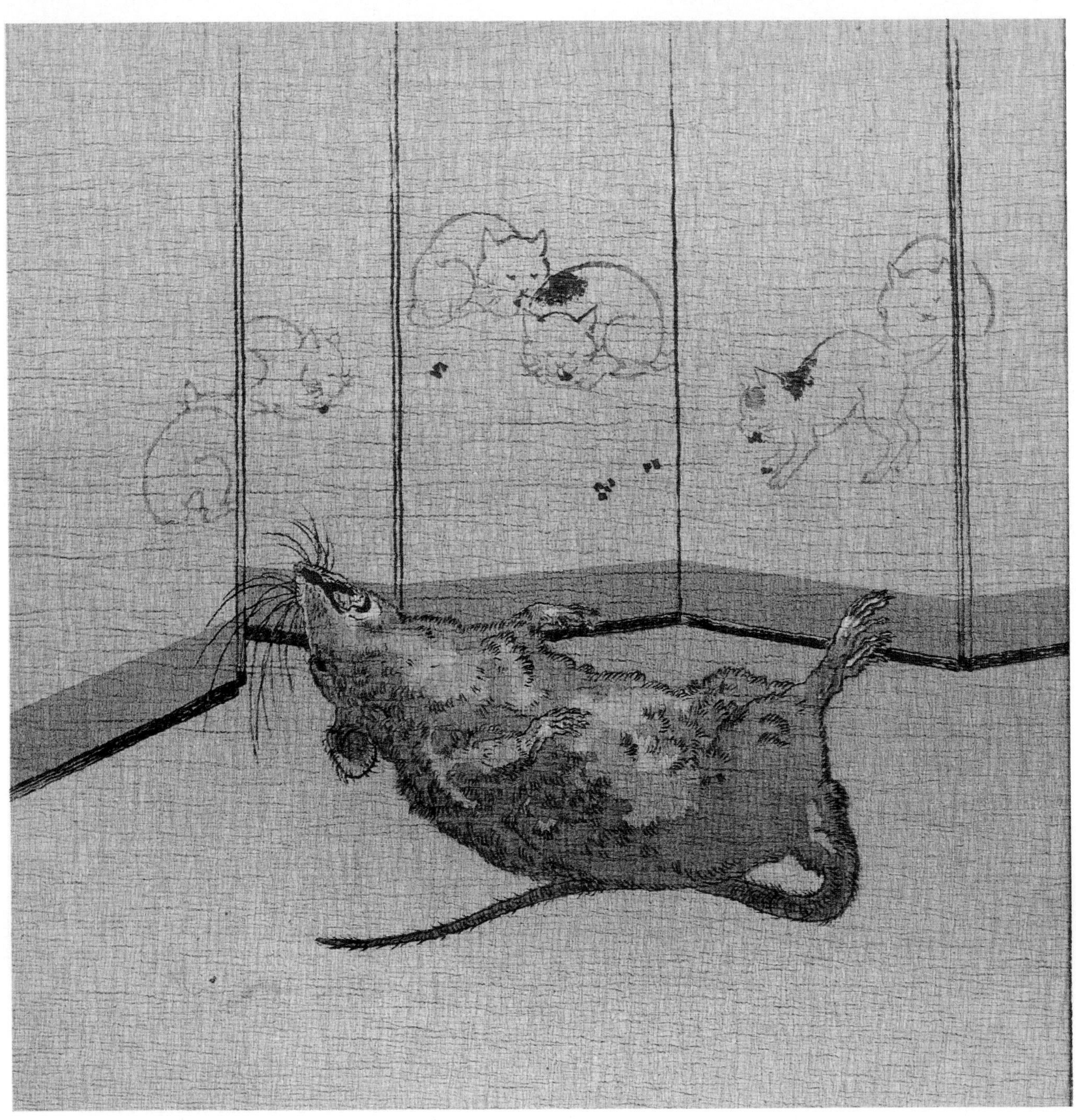

# *Fables and Fairy Tales for Little Folk; or, Uncle Remus in Hausaland*

*By Mary and Newman Tremearne*

*In this tale set in Africa early in this century, the devotion of an elder sister to a younger one is vividly described.*

## WHY HAWA PREVENTED THE BEASTS FROM DRINKING

ow I am going to tell you a story about a girl who was very fond of her little sister. She was named Hawa, while the little one was called Zainabu. The whole family worked on a farm.

When the father and mother started out in the morning with Hawa, they used to hide little Zainabu in a pot of grease! It was not a very nice place, but Zainabu was a dear little girl and never complained. Perhaps this is why Hawa was so fond of her? I wonder! Of course they had to put the pot of grease away in a safe place, too, in case anything should upset it, and it should be spilt.

All went well for some time, and every evening Zainabu was delighted when her sister came home, and she could come out of her hiding place. What games they had together! You would think she would have been quite tired of hiding, but no! "hide and seek" was one of their favourite games.

Her father and mother were looking forward to the time when Zainabu would be big enough to go to the farm with them. There was no school time for these little girls, as soon as ever they were strong and big enough, they had to do their share of hard work.

But alas! one day they forgot to wake as early as they usually did, and were rather late at starting, and so Hawa, like the dear little helpful soul she was, offered to hide her little sister. But when she had hidden her, she was unable to lift the pot into its accustomed place, and in their hurry to be off, the parents forgot that part of the arrangement for Zainabu's safety.

As ill-luck would have it, no sooner had they all gone, than wicked Mrs. Hyaena chanced to come sniffing round the house, to see what she could pick up. Now Hyaenas, as everybody knows, are very fond of all kinds of grease, and what do you think? Why this horrible old Hyaena just swallowed the pot of grease at a mouthful, with poor little Zainabu in it! Then she scurried away back to her den as fast as ever her legs could take her.

You can fancy what a terrible state the poor father and mother were in when they reached home that night. The pot of grease had disappeared as if it had never been there—it left no traces behind. "Where is our darling Zainabu? Whatever could have become of her?" they asked each other. But their sorrow was as nothing compared with Hawa's, for she blamed herself so bitterly for not having tried to lift the pot up into a safer place. "I shall never be happy again," she wailed. "Oh! my sister, my sister."

Now Hawa was a clever little girl, and while she was walking up and down and round the house, she saw the marks of foot-prints, and she wondered whose they could be. Of course *we* know it was wicked Mrs. Hyaena who had been prowling round, but Hawa did not know this, and so she had to examine the marks very carefully. Even then she could not decide, but she thought out a plan, and now you will see what a very clever, persevering little girl she was.

On their way to the farm there was a stream called "Let-me-Run," and Hawa had noticed how all the beasts of the forest came there to drink every evening when their day's hunting was over. So she got a big calabash (or bowl) and scooped up all the water into it! There was nothing but mud left. Then she climbed up into the Baobab tree and waited till evening came. In the evening all the beasts came, as was their custom. When Hawa looked, she saw the first was a Lion! But she was not a bit frightened, and began singing softly:—

> *"Oh! Mr. Lion, where have you been?*
> *Have you my dear little sister seen?"*

And the Lion answered, "I am going to 'Let-me-Run,' for my evening drink."

So Hawa said, "You cannot, for I have taken up all the water. If you will give me back my sister, I will give you some water to drink," and then she went on singing:—

> *"If you my sister will restore to me*
> *I'll give you water which I have, you see."*

Then the Lion coughed, "Hakk, hakk," and said, "You can see *I* have only eaten grass."

Now the Baobab is a magical tree, and when Hawa heard the Lion's reply, she said, "Good Mrs. Tree grow up higher," and it was as well, for the Lion began roaring and growling. However, he soon calmed down for he did not want to keep all the other beasts away. So the tree had grown a little taller, and taken Hawa up with it. Presently the Hedgehog came and Hawa sang again:—

> *"O Mr. Hedgehog where have you been?*
> *Have you my dear little sister seen?"*

And the Hedgehog said he had not seen Zainabu, and that he wanted a drink, but he could not find the stream "Let-me-Run." So Hawa sang on:—

> *"If you my sister will restore to me,*
> *I'll give you water, which I have, you see."*

But of course the Hedgehog did not know any more about it than the Lion.

So Hawa said, "Good Mrs. Tree, grow up higher."

Now when the Giraffe came, Hawa was glad she had gone up a good way, for you know that the Giraffe is so tall he can easily eat even the higher branches of some trees, and so it was as well to be out of reach, or she herself might have shared little Zainabu's fate and been swallowed with a bunch of leaves!

All the animals came, and one by one Hawa asked them the same question, and they all coughed "Hakk, hakk," in turn, and assured her that they had only eaten grass.

But Hawa had no pity. She was determined to find her sister, and now the thought of seeing her again filled her with such joy that she forgot to be very miserable, for she began to feel sure Zainabu was alive, and would soon be with her again. So she said each time, "Good Mrs. Tree grow up a little higher"—and the kind tree grew up.

Now we know that only the wicked old Hyaena was guilty, so all the other poor animals had to suffer until she came. Soon the forest resounded with their groans. They were nearly dead with thirst. The day had been a hot, trying one, and their poor throats were parched and dry.

Still Hawa thought only of her sister. Perhaps little Zainabu, too, was suffering agonies of thirst and hunger. Perhaps she was as miserable at being parted from her parents, as they were at losing their dear little girl. And she hardened her heart and would not come down. She was very, very high up by this time, for she had asked all the animals, and as we know, they could none of them give up her sister, and so she had risen higher and higher with the tree.

At last the Hyaena came. She was late, for after swallowing the pot of grease, she had had a nap, and it was long past her usual time. Sang Hawa again:

*"Mrs. Hyaena, where have you been?*
*Have you my dear little sister seen?"*

"Not I!" said the wicked beast. "I don't know and I don't care as long as I get my evening drink." (Can you imagine anyone as wicked as the Hyaena?) Then Hawa guessed that it was the Hyaena, and so she sang on quite calmly—

*"Mrs. Hyaena, what do you think."*
*The Animals all are waiting to drink."*

The Hyaena growled back, "Well, *I'm* not going to wait," but she found the stream quite dry.

How frightened she must have been, knowing how wicked she was. Hawa's song came softly down—she was up so high now, her voice sounded quite faint and dim—

*"Oh! sister Zainabu, never you fear,*
*I'll not give them drink till you appear."*

This was too much for the Hyaena, and in her excitement she coughed, "Hakk, hakk," and up came the pot of grease with little Zainabu in it!

"Oh dear, Mrs. Tree, put me down, put me down," cried Hawa, and the Tree, who loved all good children, put her down so quickly that she upset the calabash, and the stream was quite full again, and all the poor animals were able to drink.

However, they could not forgive the wicked Hyaena, and they beat her and drove her off into the forest, where she perished of thirst. And I think you will agree with me that she was well punished.

And to return to Hawa and Zainabu, their joy was too great for me to describe, you must try and imagine it. But I must tell you that like good little girls, they ran home as quickly as ever they could. Hawa had not told anyone of her plan, and the poor parents were nearly frantic with grief when evening came, and neither of their children was to be found. They thought of course that the same fate had befallen Hawa that had robbed them of Zainabu. So their joy knew no bounds. I don't think they ever left Zainabu alone in the house any more.

# *Lulu's Library*

*By Louisa May Alcott*

*In this story by the author of* Little Women, *we see that a bad dream can have a good outcome.*

## THE PIGGY GIRL

"I won't be washed! I won't be washed!" screamed little Betty, kicking and slapping the maid who undressed her one night.

"You'd better go and live with the pigs, dirty child," said Maria, scrubbing away at two very grubby hands.

"I wish I could! I love to be dirty,—I *will* be dirty!" roared Betty, throwing the sponge out of the window and the soap under the table.

Maria could do nothing with her; so she bundled her into bed half wiped, telling her to go to sleep right away.

"I won't! I'll go and live with Mrs. Gleason's pigs, and have nothing to do but eat and sleep, and roll in the dirt, and never, never be washed any more," said Betty to herself.

She lay thinking about it and blinking at the moon for a while; then she got up very softly, and crept down the back stairs, through the garden, to the sty where the two nice little pigs were fast asleep among the straw in their small house. They only grunted when Betty crept into a corner, laughing at the fun it would be to play piggy and live here with no Maria to wash her and no careful mamma to keep saying,—

"Put on a clean apron, dear!"

Next morning she was waked up by hearing Mrs. Gleason pour milk into the trough. She lay very still till the woman was gone; then she crept out and drank all she wanted, and took the best bits of cold potato and bread for her breakfast, and the lazy pigs did not get up till she was done. While they ate and rooted in the dirt, Betty slept as long as she liked, with no school, no errands, no patchwork to do. She liked it, and kept hidden till night; then she went home, and opened the little window in the store closet, and got in and took as many good things to eat and carry away as she liked. She had a fine walk in her nightgown, and saw the flowers asleep, heard the little birds chirp in the nest, and watched the fireflies and moths at their pretty play. No one saw her but the cats; and they played with her, and hopped at her toes, in the moonlight, and had great fun.

When she was tired she went to sleep with the pigs, and dozed all the next day, only coming out to eat and drink when the milk was brought and the cold bits; for Mrs. Gleason took good care of her pigs, and gave them clean straw often, and kept them as nice as she could.

Betty lived in this queer way a long time, and soon looked more like a pig than a little girl; for her nightgown got dirty, her hair was never combed, her face was never washed, and she loved to dig in the mud till her hands looked like paws. She never talked, but began to grunt as the pigs did, and burrowed into the straw to sleep, and squealed when they crowded her, and quarrelled over the food, eating with her nose in the trough like a real pig. At first she used to play about at night, and steal things to eat; and people set traps to catch the thief in their gardens, and the cook in her own house scolded about the rats that carried off the cake and pies out of her pantry. But by and by she got too lazy and fat to care for anything but sleeping and eating, and never left the sty. She went on her hands and knees now, and began to wonder if a little tail wouldn't grow and her nose change to a snout.

All summer she played being a pig, and thought it good fun; but when the autumn came it was cold, and she longed for her nice warm flannel nightgown, and got tired of cold victuals, and began to wish she had a fire to sit by and good buckwheat cakes to eat. She was ashamed to go home, and wondered what she should do after this silly frolic. She asked the pigs how they managed in winter; but they only grunted, and she could not remember what became of them, for the sty was always empty in cold weather.

One dreadful night she found out. She was snuggled down between the great fat piggies to keep warm; but her toes were cold, and she was trying to pull the straw over them when she heard Mr. Gleason say to his boy,—"We must kill those pigs to-morrow. They are fat enough; so come and help me sharpen the big knife."

"Oh, dear, what will become of *me*?" thought Betty, as she heard the grindstone go round and round as the knife got sharper and sharper. "I look so like a pig they will kill me too, and make me into sausages if I don't run away. I'm tired of playing piggy, and I'd rather be washed a hundred times a day than be put in a pork barrel."

So she lay trembling till morning; then she ran through the garden and found the back door open. It was very early, and no one saw her, for the cook was in the shed getting wood to make her fire; so Betty slipped upstairs to the nursery and was going to whisk into bed, when she saw in the glass an ugly black creature, all rags and dirt, with rumpled hair, and a little round nose covered with mud.

"Can it be me?" she said. "How horrid I am!"And she could not spoil her nice white bed, but hopped into the bathtub and had a good scrubbing. Next she got a clean nightgown, and brushed her hair, and cut her long nails, and looked like a tidy little girl again.

Then she lay down in her cosy crib with the pink cover and the lace curtains, and fell fast asleep, glad to have clean sheets, soft blankets, and her own little pillow once more.

"Come, darling, wake up and see the new frock I have got for you, and the nice ruffled apron. It's Thanksgiving day, and all the cousins are coming to dinner," said her mamma, with a soft kiss on the rosy cheek.

Betty started up, screaming,—

"Don't kill me! Oh, please don't! I'm not a truly pig, I'm a little girl; and if you'll let me run home, I'll never fret when I'm washed again."

"What is the dear child afraid of?" said mamma, cuddling her close, and laughing to see Betty stare wildly about for the fat pigs and the stuffy sty.

She told her mother all about the queer time she had had, and was much surprised to hear mamma say,—

"It was all a dream, dear; you have been safely asleep in your little bed ever since you slapped poor Maria last night."

"Well, I'm glad I dreamed it, for it has made me love to be clean. Come, Maria, soap and scrub as much as you like, I won't kick and scream ever any more," cried Betty, skipping about, glad to be safe in her pleasant home and no longer a dirty, lazy piggy girl.

# *The Tales of Perrault*

*By Charles Perrault*
*Illustrations by Gustave Doré*

*In this French fairy tale about a young man and his cat, just who is the master and who the dependent is clearly set out.*

## PUSS IN BOOTS

A miller died and left his three sons his only belongings: his mill, his donkey, and his cat. The eldest received the mill, the middle son received the donkey, and the youngest got only the cat.

The youngest son was unhappy and lamented his pitiful inheritance: "My brothers can make a good living by working together; but, as for me, after I have eaten the cat and made a fur muff from its skin, I will have nothing and I will die of hunger."

The Cat, who overheard him but pretended that he hadn't, said with a calm air: "Don't distress yourself, master, you have only to give me a sack, and have a pair of boots made for me so I can walk easily through the underbrush, and you will see that your inheritance is not half so bad as it seems." The Cat's new owner didn't think too much of this idea, but he had seen so many of the animal's cunning tricks for catching rats and mice, such as hanging by his feet or hiding himself in the flour to play dead, that he thought the Cat might find him a way out of his predicament.

As soon as the Cat got what he had asked for, he boldly pulled on his boots, flung his sack over his shoulder (he held it there with his fore-paws), and went out into a field where he knew there were a lot of rabbits. He put some bran and vegetables in the sack. Then he lay down, pretending to be dead, while he waited for a young rabbit, inexperienced in the tricks of the world, to poke his nose into the sack so he could eat what was in it.

Scarcely had the cat lay down when a foolish young rabbit crawled into the sack. In a wink Master Cat pulled the cords tightly shut and, showing no mercy, killed the rabbit.

Proud of his booty, the Cat set off to the King's castle and demanded to speak to him. When he was introduced, he made a sweeping bow, and he said to the King: "Here, your Majesty, is a rabbit that my master, the Marquis de Carabas (for this was the name he decided to give to the miller's son), has asked me to present to you." "Say thank you to your master for me," said the King, "and tell him that his present pleases me."

Another time the Cat caught a brace of partridges, and he brought them to the King as well. Again, the King received the gift with pleasure, and this time gave him a tip.

The Cat continued thus for several months, presenting the King with game from his master's hunting. Then one day he learned that the King was going to take a drive along the river with his daughter, the most beautiful princess in the world. So he went to his master and said, "If you follow my advice, your fortune is made. Go down to the river and take a swim at a spot that I will show you. Leave the rest to me."

The Marquis de Carabas did as he was told. While he was swimming, the King's carriage passed by, and the Cat cried out with all his might: "Help! Help! My master, the Marquis de Carabas, is drowning." At this the King stuck his head out of his carriage window and, recognizing the cat who had often brought him gifts of game, he ordered his guards to quickly help the Marquis de Carabas.

While the guards were rescuing the poor Marquis, the Cat, approaching the carriage, told the King that while his master was swimming, thieves had made off with his clothes. (Actually, the rascal had hidden them under a large rock.) So the King ordered the officers of his wardrobe to fetch one of his handsomest robes for the Marquis de Carabas. The fine clothes set off his handsome face (for he was a good-looking and well-built young man), and the King's daughter found him much to her liking. The Marquis de Carabas had only to glance at her two or three times, very respectfully but with tenderness, for her to fall head over heels in love.

The King invited the Marquis into his carriage and continued his ride. The Cat meanwhile, delighted to see his plan beginning to succeed, ran on ahead, and meeting some peasants who were mowing the fields, he told them, "My good people, if you don't tell the King that the field you are mowing belongs to the Marquis de Carabas, I will chop you up like mincemeat."

The King, sure enough, asked the mowers whose field they were working. "It belongs to the Marquis de Carabas," they stated, for the Cat's threat had filled them with fear. "You have a fine estate here," the King said to the Marquis de Carabas. "You see, sire," the Marquis answered, "it is a field that yields abundantly every year."

Master Cat, always running on ahead, encountered some peasants reaping. "Good people, if you don't say that all this wheat belongs to the Marquis de Carabas, I will chop you up like mincemeat." The King, passing by a moment later, wanted to know who owned all the wheat that he saw. "It belongs to the Marquis de Carabas," the reapers replied, and again the King complimented the Marquis.

The Cat, running well ahead of the carriage, gave the same instructions to everyone he met, and the King was astonished at the great wealth of the Marquis de Carabas. Master Cat arrived at last at a beautiful castle belonging to an ogre, the richest in the world, for all the land through which the King had passed was the property of this castle. The Cat inquired about the ogre and asked to speak to him, saying that he didn't want to pass so close to his castle without having the honor of paying his respects.

The ogre received him politely—as politely as an ogre can—and asked him to stay a while. "I hear," said the Cat, "that you have the gift of transforming yourself into all kinds of animals, a lion or an elephant, for example." "That's true," answered the ogre brusquely, "and I'll show you how I can become a lion." The Cat was so terrified to see a lion suddenly appear before him that he leapt up to the roof, not without some trouble because of his boots.

Later, when the Cat saw the ogre assume his own form again, he climbed back down. "I have also heard," said the Cat, "but I can scarcely believe it, that you have as well the power to take the form of the smallest animals, that you can change yourself, for example, into a rat or a mouse. I must tell you that I find that absolutely impossible." "Impossible!" replied the ogre. "You will see," and at the same moment he changed himself into a little mouse running across the floor. The Cat did not see it for long, for he leapt upon the mouse and ate it.

When the Cat heard the King's carriage wheels rumbling on the drawbridge, he ran before it and said to the King, "Your Majesty is welcome to the castle of the Marquis de Carabas."

"What, Marquis," cried the King, "this château also belongs to you? It is so handsome, let us go inside."

The Marquis gave his hand to the young princess and, following the King, they all went in. There they found a magnificent feast that had been prepared for the ogre.

The King, charmed by the good qualities of the Marquis de Carabas, as was his lovestruck daughter, and seeing the great wealth that he possessed, said to him, after drinking five or six cups of wine, "It is up to you, Marquis, if you would be my son-in-law." The Marquis, making a deep bow, accepted the honor, and that very same day he married the princess.

The Cat became a great lord and chased after mice only when he got bored.

# *The Jewish Fairy Book*

*By Gerald Friedlander*

*There is a story about the Danish king Canute, who tried—and failed—to make the sea obey him. In this story, the order comes from a higher power.*

## THE REBELLIOUS WATERS

On the third day of the week of creation the mighty waters covered the face of all the earth. Then the Holy One commanded the waters to be gathered together so that the dry land might appear. The prince of the sea forced back the rolling waves, whereupon the mountains and hills scattered over the surface of all the earth rose beneath the blue sky. Now the prince of the sea brought the waters into the deep oceans. When the waters saw this they became proud and attempted once again to cover the face of the earth. The prince of the sea rebuked them and warned them not to disobey the great Creator. They refused to listen and were about to submerge the earth when the Holy One blamed them for being disobedient. He at once subdued them and placed them beneath the level of the earth. In order to restrain the sea He put the sand as their boundary. Whenever the water is tempted to rebel and to pass over its bounds, it sees the sand and returns to its proper place.

When the sea saw the sand for the first time it said: "What need have I to be afraid of the sand? Is it likely that its tiny grains can hold me in check?"

The tiny grains of sand heard these proud words of the sea. They whispered to one another: "Let us not be frightened by the big talk of the waves. It is quite true that each one of us is very small. What of that? If we be friendly to one another and remain united we shall be able to do what the good Creator intends us to do. We all know what that is. We were made to hold the great sea in check. This we certainly shall not be able to do if we quarrel and stand apart. Then each one of us will be very easily washed away by the waves. Now let us all promise one another to remain always united. Union is strength. Then we need have no fear of the raging waters. Their roaring and foam will not frighten us."

The Holy One blessed their union and to this day the golden sand holds the proud waves in check.

Chapters of Rabbi Eliezer, v.

# *The Golden Cockerel*

*By Alexander Pushkin*
*Illustrations by Ivan Bilibin*

*The opera and ballet entitled* Le Coq d'Or *are based upon this Russian poem about a magical golden bird who long ago watched over the Tsar's country, warning if enemies approached.*

Now he's sent upon the double
To his sorcerer and sage,
A eunuch far advanced in age,
A messenger requesting aid.
The ancient wise man's not delayed,
He stands before the Tsar, behold,
Presents him with a cock of gold.
"But place this bird, my lord and sire,"
He says, "upon your highest spire,
And he, the golden cockerel
Will prove your faithful sentinel.
If peace be certain all around
He'll utter not a single sound,
But should a threatening foe appear
From any side, or should there near
An army with hostile intent
Or raiders on some mischief bent,
Immediately his comb will rise,
He'll flap his wings, give mighty cries,
And turn to face the place from whence

There comes the enemy's offense."
The Tsar gives thanks unto his sage,
"A sack of gold shall be your wage,
And when you make your first wish known
It shall be granted as my own."
Once perched aloft the Tsar's domain
The cock watched like a weather vane;
No sooner danger rumored when
He'd rouse as though from sleep and then
He'd flap and turn in that direction
Crowing news of his detection.
"Cock-a-doodle-doo," he said,
"Rule on like any sleepy-head.
Thou shan't be harmed nor hide nor hair
While I am here to shout beware."
The neighboring countries when they heard
Were humbled by the magic bird,
And Tsar Dadon in such a way
Kept all his enemies at bay.

# *The Red Fairy Book*

*By Andrew Lang*
*Illustrations by Lancelot Speed*

*An encounter between a little girl and a wolf is a familiar story; this version shows us a lucky little girl.*

## THE TRUE HISTORY OF LITTLE GOLDEN-HOOD

You know the tale of poor Little Red Riding-hood, that the wolf deceived and devoured, with her cake, her little butter can, and her Grandmother; well, the true story happened quite differently, as we know now. And first of all the little girl was called and is still called Little Golden-hood; secondly, it was not she, nor the good grand-dame, but the wicked Wolf who was, in the end, caught and devoured.

Only listen.

The story begins something like the tale.

There was once a little peasant girl, pretty and nice as a star in its season. Her real name was Blanchette, but she was more often called Little Golden-hood, on account of a wonderful little cloak with a hood, gold- and fire-coloured, which she always had on. This little hood was given her by her Grandmother, who was so old that she did not know her age; it ought to bring her good luck, for it was made of a ray of sunshine, she said. And as the good old woman was considered something of a witch, everyone thought the little hood rather bewitched too.

And so it was, as you will see.

One day the mother said to the child: "Let us see, my Little Golden-hood, if you know how to find your way by yourself. You shall take this good piece of cake to your Grandmother for a Sunday treat to-morrow. You will ask her how she is, and come back at once, without stopping to chatter on the way with people you don't know. Do you quite understand?"

"I quite understand," replied Blanchette gaily. And off she went with the cake, quite proud of her errand.

But the Grandmother lived in another village, and there was a big wood to cross before getting there. At a turn of the road under the trees, suddenly "Who goes there?"

"Friend Wolf."

He had seen the child start alone, and the villain was waiting to devour her; when at the same moment he perceived some wood-cutters who might observe him, and he changed his mind. Instead of falling upon Blanchette he came frisking up to her like a good dog.

"'Tis you! my nice Little Golden-hood," said he. So the little girl stops to talk with the Wolf, who, for all that, she did not know in the least.

"You know me, then!" said she; "what is your name?"

"My name is friend Wolf. And where are you going thus, my pretty one, with your little basket on your arm?"

"I am going to my Grandmother, to take her a good piece of cake for her Sunday treat to-morrow."

"And where does she live, your Grandmother?"

"She lives at the other side of the wood, in the first house in the village, near the windmill, you know."

"Ah! yes! I know now," said the Wolf. "Well, that's just where I'm going; I shall get there before you, no doubt, with your little bits of legs, and I'll tell her you're coming to see her; then she'll wait for you."

Thereupon the Wolf cuts across the wood, and in five minutes arrives at the Grandmother's house.

He knocks at the door: toc, toc.

No answer.

He knocks louder.

Nobody.

Then he stands up on end, puts his two fore-paws on the latch and the door opens.

Not a soul in the house.

The old woman had risen early to sell herbs in the town, and she had gone off in such haste that she had left her bed unmade, with her great night-cap on the pillow.

"Good!" said the Wolf to himself, "I know what I'll do."

He shuts the door, pulls on the Grandmother's night-cap down to his eyes, then he lies down all his length in the bed and draws the curtains.

In the meantime the good Blanchette went quietly on her way, as little girls do, amusing herself here and there by picking Easter daisies, watching the little birds making their nests, and running after the butterflies which fluttered in the sunshine.

At last she arrives at the door.

Knock, knock.

"Who is there?" says the Wolf, softening his rough voice as best he can.

"It's me, Granny, your Little Golden-hood. I'm bringing you a big piece of cake for your Sunday treat to-morrow."

"Press your finger on the latch, then push and the door opens."

"Why, you've got a cold, Granny," said she, coming in.

"Ahem! a little, a little . . ." replies the Wolf, pretending to cough. "Shut the door well, my little lamb. Put your basket on the table, and then take off your frock and come lie down by me: you shall rest a little."

The good child undresses, but observe this! She kept her little hood upon her head. When she saw what a figure her Granny cut in bed, the poor little thing was much surprised.

"Oh!" cries she, "how like you are to friend Wolf, Grandmother!"

"That's on account of my night-cap, child," replies the Wolf.

"Oh! what hairy arms you've got, Grandmother!"

"All the better to hug you, my child."

"Oh! what a big tongue you've got, Grandmother!"

"All the better for answering, child."

"Oh! what a mouthful of great white teeth you have, Grandmother!"

"That's for crunching little children with!" And the Wolf opened his jaws wide to swallow Blanchette.

But she put down her head crying:

"Mamma! Mamma!" and the Wolf only caught her little hood.

Thereupon, oh dear! oh dear! he draws back, crying and shaking his jaw as if he had swallowed red-hot coals.

It was the little fire-coloured hood that had burnt his tongue right down his throat.

The little hood, you see, was one of those magic caps that they used to have in former times, in the stories, for making oneself invisible or invulnerable.

So there was the Wolf with his throat burnt, jumping off the bed and trying to find the door, howling and howling as if all the dogs in the country were at his heels.

Just at this moment the Grandmother arrives, returning from the town with her long sack empty on her shoulder.

"Ah, brigand!" she cries, "wait a bit!" Quickly she opens her sack wide across the door, and the maddened Wolf springs in head downwards.

It is he now that is caught, swallowed like a letter in the post.

For the brave old dame shuts her sack, so; and she runs and empties it in the well, where the vagabond, still howling, tumbles in and is drowned.

"Ah, scoundrel! you thought you would crunch my little grandchild! Well, to-morrow we will make her a muff of your skin, and you yourself shall be crunched, for we will give your carcass to the dogs."

Thereupon the Grandmother hastened to dress poor Blanchette, who was still trembling with fear in the bed.

"Well," she said to her, "without my little hood where would you be now, darling?" And, to restore heart and legs to the child, she made her eat a good piece of her cake, and drink a good draught of wine, after which she took her by the hand and led her back to the house.

And then, who was it who scolded her when she knew all that had happened?

It was the mother.

But Blanchette promised over and over again that she would never more stop to listen to a Wolf, so that at last the mother forgave her.

And Blanchette, the Little Golden-hood, kept her word. And in fine weather, she may still be seen in the fields with her pretty little hood, the colour of the sun.

But to see her you must rise early.

# *The Fairy Tales of the Brothers Grimm*

*Illustrations by Arthur Rackham*

*Jacob and Wilhelm Grimm did not make up this story but retold in vivid detail their version of a popular legend.*

## TOM THUMB

A poor Peasant sat one evening at his hearth and poked the fire, while his Wife sat opposite spinning. He said: "What a sad thing it is that we have no children; our home is so quiet, while other folk's houses are noisy and cheerful."

"Yes," answered his Wife, and she sighed; "even if it were an only one, and if it were no bigger than my thumb, I should be quite content; we would love it with all our hearts."

Now, some time after this, she had a little boy who was strong and healthy, but was no bigger than a thumb. Then they said: "Well, our wish is fulfilled, and, small as he is, we will love him dearly"; and because of his tiny stature they called him Tom Thumb. They let him want for nothing, yet still the child grew no bigger, but remained the same size as when he was born. Still, he looked out on the world with intelligent eyes, and soon showed himself a clever and agile creature, who was lucky in all he attempted.

One day, when the Peasant was preparing to go into the forest to cut wood, he said to him-

self: "I wish I had some one to bring the cart after me."

"O Father!" said Tom Thumb, "I will soon bring it. You leave it to me; it shall be there at the appointed time."

Then the Peasant laughed, and said: "How can that be? You are much too small even to hold the reins."

"That doesn't matter, if only Mother will harness the horse," answered Tom. "I will sit in his ear and tell him where to go."

"Very well," said the Father; "we will try it for once."

When the time came, the Mother harnessed the horse, set Tom in his ear, and then the little creature called out "Gee-up" and "Whoa" in turn, and directed it where to go. It went quite well, just as though it were being driven by its master; and they went the right way to the wood. Now it happened that while the cart was turning a corner, and Tom was calling to the horse, two strange men appeared on the scene.

"My goodness," said one, "what is this? There goes a cart, and a driver is calling to the horse, but there is nothing to be seen."

"There is something queer about this," said the other; "we will follow the cart and see where it stops."

The cart went on deep into the forest, and arrived quite safely at the place where the wood was cut.

When Tom spied his Father, he said: "You see, Father, here I am with the cart; now lift me down." The Father held the horse with his left hand, and took his little son out of its ear with the right. Then Tom sat down quite happily on a straw.

When the two strangers noticed him, they did not know what to say for astonishment.

Then one drew the other aside, and said: "Listen, that little creature might make our fortune if we were to show him in the town for money. We will buy him."

So they went up to the Peasant, and said: "Sell us the little man; he shall be well looked after with us."

"No," said the Peasant; "he is the delight of my eyes, and I will not sell him for all the gold in the world."

But Tom Thumb, when he heard the bargain, crept up by the folds of his father's coat, placed himself on his shoulder, and whispered in his ear: "Father, let me go; I will soon come back again."

Then his Father gave him to the two men for a fine piece of gold.

"Where will you sit?" they asked him.

"Oh, put me on the brim of your hat, then I can walk up and down and observe the neighbourhood without falling down."

They did as he wished, and when Tom had said good-bye to his Father, they went away with him.

They walked on till it was twilight, when

the little man said: "You must lift me down."

"Stay where you are," answered the Man on whose head he sat.

"No," said Tom; "I will come down. Lift me down immediately."

The Man took off his hat and set the little creature in a field by the wayside. He jumped and crept about for a time, here and there among the sods, then slipped suddenly into a mouse-hole which he had discovered.

"Good evening, gentlemen, just you go home without me," he called out to them in mockery.

They ran about and poked with sticks into the mouse-hole, but all in vain. Tom crept further and further back, and, as it soon got quite dark, they were forced to go home, full of anger, and with empty purses.

When Tom noticed they were gone, he crept out of his underground hiding-place again. "It is dangerous walking in this field in the dark," he said; "one might easily break one's leg or one's neck." Luckily, he came to an empty snail shell. "Thank goodness," he said; "I can pass the night in safety here," and he sat down.

Not long after, just when he was about to go to sleep, he heard two men pass by. One said: "How shall we set about stealing the rich parson's gold and silver?"

"I can tell you," interrupted Tom.

"What was that?" said one robber in a fright. "I heard some one speak."

They remained standing and listened.

Then Tom spoke again: "Take me with you and I will help you."

"Where are you?" they asked.

"Just look on the ground and see where the voice comes from," he answered.

At last the thieves found him, and lifted him up. "You little urchin, are *you* going to help us?"

"Yes," he said; "I will creep between the iron bars in the Pastor's room, and will hand out to you what you want."

"All right," they said, "we will see what you can do."

When they came to the Parsonage, Tom crept into the room, but called out immediately with all his strength to the others: "Do you want everything that is here?"

The thieves were frightened, and said: "Do speak softly, and don't wake any one."

But Tom pretended not to understand, and called out again: "What do you want? Everything?"

The Cook, who slept above, heard him and sat up in bed and listened. But the thieves were so frightened that they retreated a little way. At last they summoned up courage again, and thought to themselves, "The little rogue wants to tease us." So they came back and whispered to him: "Now, do be serious, and hand us out something."

Then Tom called out again, as loud as he could, "I will give you everything if only you will hold out your hands."

The Maid, who was listening intently, heard him quite distinctly, jumped out of bed, and stumbled to the door. The thieves turned and fled, running as though wild huntsmen were after them. But the Maid, seeing nothing, went to get a light. When she came back with it, Tom, without being seen, slipped out into the barn, and the Maid, after she had searched every corner and found nothing, went to bed again, thinking she had been dreaming with her eyes and ears open.

Tom Thumb climbed about in the hay, and found a splendid place to sleep. There he determined to rest till day came, and then to go home to his parents. But he had other experiences to go through first. This world is full of trouble and sorrow!

The Maid got up in the grey dawn to feed the cows. First she went into the barn, where she piled up an armful of hay, the very bundle in which poor Tom was asleep. But he slept so soundly that he knew nothing till he was almost in the mouth of the cow, who was eating him up with the hay.

"Heavens!" he said, "however did I get into this mill?" but he soon saw where he was, and the great thing was to avoid being crushed between the cow's teeth. At last, whether he liked it or not he had to go down the cow's throat.

"The windows have been forgotten in this house," he said. "The sun does not shine into it, and no light has been provided."

Altogether he was very ill-pleased with his quarters, and, worst of all, more and more hay came in at the door, and the space grew narrower and narrower. At last he called out, in his fear, as loud as he could, "Don't give me any more food. Don't give me any more food."

The Maid was just milking the cow, and when she heard the same voice as in the night, without seeing any one, she was frightened, and slipped from her stool and spilt the milk. Then, in the greatest haste, she ran to her master, and said: "Oh, your Reverence, the cow has spoken!"

"You are mad," he answered; but he went into the stable himself to see what was happening.

Scarcely had he set foot in the cow-shed before Tom began again, "Don't bring me any more food."

Then the Pastor was terrified too, and thought that the cow must be bewitched; so he ordered it to be killed. It was accordingly slaughtered, but the stomach, in which Tom was hidden, was thrown into the manure heap. Tom had the greatest trouble in working his way out. Just as he stuck out his head, a hungry Wolf ran by and snapped up the whole stomach with one bite. But still Tom did not lose courage. "Perhaps the Wolf will listen to reason," he said. So he called out, "Dear Wolf, I know where you would find a magnificent meal."

"Where is it to be had?" asked the Wolf.

"Why, in such and such a house," answered Tom. "You must squeeze through the grating of the store-room window, and there you will find cakes, bacon, and sausages, as many as you can possibly eat"; and he went on to describe his father's house.

The Wolf did not wait to hear this twice, and at night forced himself in through the grating, and ate to his heart's content. When he was satisfied, he wanted to go away again; but he had grown so fat that he could not get out the same way. Tom had reckoned on this, and began to make a great commotion inside the Wolf's body, struggling and screaming with all his might.

"Be quiet," said the Wolf; "you will wake up the people of the house."

"All very fine," answered Tom. "You have eaten your fill, and now I am going to make merry"; and he began to scream again with all his might.

At last his Father and Mother woke up, ran to the room, and looked through the crack of the door. When they saw a Wolf, they went away, and the husband fetched his axe, and the wife a scythe.

"You stay behind," said the man, as they came into the room. "If my blow does not kill him, you must attack him and rip up his body."

When Tom Thumb heard his Father's voice, he called out: "Dear Father, I am here, inside the Wolf's body."

Full of joy, his Father cried, "Heaven be praised! our dear child is found again," and he bade his wife throw aside the scythe that it might not injure Tom.

Then he gathered himself together, and struck the Wolf a blow on the head, so that it fell down lifeless. Then with knives and shears they ripped up the body, and took their little boy out.

"Ah," said his Father, "what trouble we have been in about you."

"Yes, Father, I have travelled about the world, and I am thankful to breathe fresh air again."

"Wherever have you been?" they asked.

"Down a mouse-hole, in a Cow's stomach, and in a Wolf's maw," he answered; "and now I shall stay with you."

"And we will never sell you again, for all the riches in the world," they said, kissing and fondling their dear child.

Then they gave him food and drink, and had new clothes made for him, as his own had been spoilt in his travels.

# *Hop-o'my-Thumb and the Seven-League Boots*

*Edited and illustrated by George Cruikshank*

*In this story from George Cruikshank's* Fairy Library, *six brothers have been abandoned by their poor parents in the woods, and the smartest (and smallest) of them tries to lead them home. Here they meet an ogre who will, in spite of himself, provide them and their parents with money.*

So, after a tiresome walk over the rough ground, and being terrified by the howling of the wolves, who now came out of their dens, they at last came to a very large house; and after they had knocked several times on the great gate with a large stone, it was opened by a great big woman, a sort of Giantess, who was very much surprised at seeing the children, and asked them what they wanted. Upon which Hop-o'my-Thumb told her that they were the six sons of a Count, and having lost their way, they had to beg for a little food and a night's lodging, upon which she said,—

"You may be the sons of a Count, but I can only count five of you; so I think you must have lost your wits as well as your way."

So little Hop replied,—

"Oh, yes, ma'am, there are six of us; but I am so small that, perhaps, you can't see me."

"See you!" she cried; "why, where are you?"

"On my brother's shoulder, ma'am."

So the Giantess was curious to see the little body from which the little voice came, and she said,—

"Dear me! come into the light, and let me

have a look at you." So they all went into the house, and then they put Hop-o'my-Thumb on the table. O, such a big table! And then the Giantess took the lamp and had a good look at little Hop, and seemed very much pleased with him; so, without any ceremony, Hop begged she would be so kind as to give them something to eat, for that they were all dying with hunger. Now she was a very good-natured lady, as most of those Giantesses are, and gave them some food directly, and told them to make haste and eat it up,—which they would have done without being told, for if they were hungry before they came in, they were more so afterwards, as they could smell that meat was being roasted.

So soon as the boys had eaten up the victuals, the Giantess took Hop off the table and gave him to his eldest brother, saying, "Now, my little men, you had better run away, for you must not stop here any longer." Upon which little Hop begged very hard that they might be allowed to stop until the morning, if it was only in an outhouse or barn, as they were afraid of the wolves. Upon which she began to sigh, and said, "Ah, my little dears, you little think what kind of house you are in; but I must tell you that my husband is a Giant-Ogre; and if he does not come home tipsy, he is sure to get tipsy after his supper, and then he'll be *sure* to kill you and eat you up; whereas if you go away, you may by chance escape from the wolves." But all the boys were so afraid to go out into the dark forest where the wolves were, and felt so warm and comfortable where they were, that they all begged and prayed of her to let them stay. So, as she was such a good-natured Giant-woman, she at last consented, as she thought she might be able to hide the children from her husband, who, she thought, would not perhaps smell them out in consequence of the smell of the meat which she was cooking for his supper. So she took them into the kitchen, where they were surprised to see a whole sheep roasting; and showed them a box that stood in a corner of the kitchen, and told them, when they heard a knock at the door, to run and hide themselves behind the box. They looked about, but as they could not see anything that looked like a box, little Hop asked her where it was; upon which she showed them a great square wooden thing that looked almost as big as their father's hut: but you must understand that everything in the house,—tables, stools, plates, dishes, and so on,—were of a very large size; even too big for the Giantess, who was obliged to use a small ladder herself to get the plates off the shelf; and the dish she had to put the sheep in was as much as she could lift, and the gravy-spoon was as big as a shovel. While she was busy getting all ready for the Giant's return, the boys looked about in wonder. By-and-by they heard a confused, rumbling sound, and then something like the roaring of a lion:—it was the Giant singing!—he was coming home merry!

"Ah!" said the Giantess, "he has had something to drink. Run and hide yourselves!" And they had no sooner got behind the great box than a knock came at the door, so loud that it quite stunned them; and when the door was opened, and the Giant-Ogre walked in, and every step he took shook the house, big and strong as it was, it made all the little fellows tremble. As soon as he came in he said, in a loud, frightful voice,—

"Well, wife, what have you got for supper? Something nice? It smells nice!"

"Here it is," she said; "it's a fine large sheep!"

"Ah! is there nothing else?" he asked. "I smell fresh meat!"

"Oh!" replied his wife, "it's the calf I've just killed."

With this answer he seemed satisfied, and sat himself down to supper. By this time, what with being over tired, having had a hearty full meal, and being very warm, Hop's five brothers had dropped off to sleep; but little Hop, although very sleepy himself, was curious to see a Giant-Ogre eat. The sharpening of his knife, which was as big as a sword, was something fearful to behold. He then cut off a shoulder of the mutton, and gave it to his wife for her supper, and then took the other shoulder himself, which he devoured in a very short time; and

George Cruikshank

then one leg, and then the other; and then ate the neck, the ribs, and the loin, giving his wife some of the bones to pick. When he had finished eating, he filled out a cup that would hold about two gallons, from a great bottle that he had been drinking from every now and then whilst he was eating. He then leaned with his elbows on the table, and began picking his teeth with a fork, by which Hop-o'my-Thumb judged that the Giant was not a gentleman. Hop's father and mother, of course, knew good manners, and had taught them to their children.

As the wife was clearing away the supper things, the Giant-Ogre kept on drinking; and just as little Hop was falling asleep, he heard the Giant taking long sniffs, and at last he cried out,—

"Wife, I know there is something else in the house besides the calf. I smell fresh *meat*—something delicate."

"Ah, it is the veal, you may be sure: it *is* very delicate!"

But without noticing what she said, he went on taking long sniffs again, and said,—

"Fee, faw, fum,
I smell the blood of an Englishman;
Let him be alive, or let him be dead,
I'll grind his bones to make my bread!"

And with that he took his great knife in his hand, and went smelling about the room, till he came to the place where Hop and his brothers were hiding. The noise the Giant made woke them all up, and he cried out in a voice like the roaring of a bull,—

"Come out there!" The poor frightened boys crept out and stood trembling before him; when he saw that they were all come out from their hiding-place, he sat down upon the box, and looking round to his wife, he roared out, "So, this is the way you deceive me! If you were not so old and tough, I would eat you up for my dinner to-morrow!" Upon which she burst into a loud laugh.

"Deceive you, indeed!" she said; "what should I deceive you for, darling? I only hid them for a bit of fun; I knew you would smell them out, and I thought it would be an agreeable surprise for you."

"Haw! haw!" laughed the Ogre; "is it so? Let us have a look at them;" and stooping down, he discovered poor little Hop for the first time. "Why, what have we here?" he exclaimed, as he lifted him up between his great finger and thumb. "Well, this is a delicate morsel!" and he was going to pop him into his ugly mouth, that looked like a great coal-tub; but although poor Hop was dreadfully frightened, he did not lose his senses, but cried out aloud to the Giant-Ogre for mercy, and to spare him; and the brothers, seeing their dear little Hop in such danger, all went down on their knees and cried out to the Ogre to spare their little brother.

*After escaping from the Ogre, and stealing his Seven-League Boots (which enable him to cover great distances with a single step), Hop and his brothers return home, present the boots to the King, and, of course, live happily ever after.*

# *Fairy Tales from All Nations*

*By Anthony Reubens Montalba*
*Illustrations by Richard Doyle*

*As this story from Upper Lusatia (a part of Germany) makes plain, hospitality to a stranger can have unexpected results.*

## THE LITTLE MAN IN GRAY

MINER, a blacksmith, and a nun were traveling together through the wide world. One day they were bewildered in a dark forest, and were so wearied with wandering that they thought themselves right fortunate when they saw at a distance, a building wherein they hoped to find shelter. They went up to it, and found that it was an ancient castle, which, although half in ruins, still was in condition to afford habitation for such distressed pilgrims as they. They resolved therefore to enter, and held a council how they might best establish themselves in it, and they very soon agreed that it would be best that one of them should always remain at home while the other two went out in search of provisions. They then cast lots who should first stay behind, and the lot fell on the nun.

So when the miner and the blacksmith were gone out into the forest, she prepared the food, and when noon arrived and her companions did not return, she ate her share of the provisions. As soon as she had finished her meal a little man clad in gray, came to the door, and shivering said: "Oh, I am so cold!"

Then the nun said to him: "Come to the

fire and warm thyself."

The little man did as the nun desired him, but presently after he exclaimed: "Oh, how hungry I am!"

Then the nun said to him: "There is food by the fire; eat some of it."

The little man fell upon the food, and in a very short time devoured it all. When the nun saw what he had done she was very angry, and scolded him for not having left any food for her companions. Upon this the little man flew into a great passion, seized the nun, beat her, and threw her from one wall to the other. He then quitted the castle and went his way, leaving the nun on the floor. Toward evening the two companions returned home very hungry, and when they found no food they reproached the nun bitterly, and would not believe her when she told them what had happened.

The following day the miner proposed to keep watch in the castle, and said he would take good care that no one should have to go to bed fasting. So the two others went into the forest, and the miner looked after the cooking, ate his share, and put the rest by on the oven. The little gray clad man came as before, but how terrified was the miner when he perceived that this time the little man had two heads. He shivered, as on the preceding day, saying: "Oh, how cold I am!"

Much frightened the miner pointed to the hearth. Then the little man said: "Oh, how hungry I am!"

"There is food on the oven," said the miner; "eat some."

Then the little man fell to with both his heads, and soon ate it all up, and licked the plates clean. When the miner reproached him for eating all up, he got for his pains just the same treatment as the nun. The little man beat him black and blue, and flung him against the walls till they cracked; the poor miner lost both sight and hearing, and at last the little man left him lying there, and went his way.

When the blacksmith and the nun returned hungry in the evening, and found no supper, the blacksmith fell into a great rage with the miner, and declared that when his turn should come next day to watch the castle, no one should want a supper. The next day, at meal time, the little man appeared again, but this time he had three heads. He complained of cold, and was bidden by the blacksmith to sit by the hearth. When he said he was hungry, the blacksmith gave him a portion of the food, the little man dispatched that, and looked greedily round with his six eyes, asking for more food, and when the blacksmith hesitated to give it to him, he tried to treat him as he had done the nun and the miner; the blacksmith, however, was no coward, and seizing a great smith's hammer, he rushed on the little man, and struck off two of his heads, so that he made off as fast as

he could with his remaining head. But the blacksmith chased him through the forest along many a pathway, till at last he suddenly disappeared through an iron door. The blacksmith was thus obliged to give up the pursuit, but promised himself not to rest until, with the aid of his two companions, he should have brought the matter to a satisfactory conclusion.

Meantime the nun and the miner had returned home. The smith set their supper before them as he had undertaken to do, and then related his adventure, showing them the two heads he had cut off, with their staring glazed eyes. They then all three resolved to free themselves altogether, if possible, from the little gray man, and the very next day they set to work. They searched a long time before they could find the iron door through which he had disappeared the preceding day, and great toil did it cost them before they were able to break it open. They then found themselves in a great vaulted chamber wherein sat a beautiful maiden at a table, working. She started up, and threw herself at their feet, thanking them as her deliverers, and told them that she was the daughter of a king, and had been confined there by a powerful sorcerer. Yesterday afternoon she had suddenly felt that the spell was loosened, and from that moment she had hourly expected her freedom, but that besides herself there was the daughter of another king confined in the same place. They then went in search of the other king's daughter, and set her at liberty also. She thanked them joyfully, in like manner, and said that she also had felt since yesterday afternoon that the spell was unbound. The two royal maidens now informed their liberators that in concealed caves of the castle great treasures were hoarded, which were guarded by a terrible dog. They went in search of them and at length came upon the dog, whom the blacksmith slew with his hammer, although he endeavored to defend himself.

The treasure consisted of whole tons of gold and silver, and a handsome young man sat beside them, as if to guard them. He came to meet them, and thanked them for setting him free. He was the son of a king, but had been transformed by a sorcerer into the three-headed little man and banished to that castle. By the loss of two of his heads the spell was taken off the two royal maidens, and when the blacksmith slew the terrible dog he himself was delivered from it. For that service the whole of the treasure should be theirs.

The treasure was then divided, and it was a long time before they could complete the distribution. The two princesses, however, out of gratitude to their deliverers, married the miner and the blacksmith, and the handsome prince married the nun; and so they passed the rest of their lives in peace and joy.

# *Laboulaye's Fairy Book*

*By Edouard Laboulaye*
*Illustrations by Yan Dargent*

*This story from central Europe tells about a bagpiper who played for the Devil. It inspired a famous opera.*

## SSWANDA, THE PIPER: A BOHEMIAN TALE

Sswanda, the Piper, was a jolly companion. Like every true musician, he was born with an unquenchable thirst; besides, he was madly fond of play, and would have risked his soul at strajak, the favorite game at cards in Bohemia. When he had earned a little money, he would throw aside his pipes, and drink and play with the first comer till he returned to his home as light in pocket as when he had left it. But he was always so merry, witty, and good-natured that not a drinker ever left the table while the piper was there, and his name still lives in Bohemia as the prince of good fellows.

One day there was a festival at Mokran, and no merrymaking was ever complete without the piper. Sswanda, after blowing his pipe till midnight and earning twenty zwanzigers, determined to amuse himself on his own account. Neither prayers nor promises could persuade him to go on with his music; he was determined to drink his fill and to shuffle the cards at his ease; but, for the first time in his life, he found no one to play with him.

Sswanda was not the man to quit the inn so long as he had a kreutzer in his pocket, and on that day he had many of them. By dint of talking, laughing, and drinking, he took one of those fixed ideas which are not uncommon

among those who look too often in the bottom of their glass, and determined to play at any price; but all his neighbors refused his challenge. Furious at finding no partner, he rose with an unsteady step, paid for what he had drunk, and left the inn. "I will go to Drazic," said he; "the schoolmaster and the bailiff there are honest people who are not afraid of play, and I shall find partners. Hurrah!"

The night was clear, and the moon shone like a fish's eye. On reaching a cross-road, Sswanda raised his eyes by chance, and stopped mute and motionless. A flock of ravens were croaking over his head, and in front of him rose four posts, standing like pillars, and connected at the top by cross-beams, from each of which swung a half-devoured corpse. It was a robbers' gallows, a spectacle by no means amusing to a less stoical spirit than that of Sswanda.

He had not recovered from the first shudder when suddenly there appeared before him a man dressed in black, with pale and hollow cheeks, and eyes that glittered like carbuncles.

"Where are you going so late, friend Piper?" asked he, in a soft voice.

"To Drazic, Mr. Black Coat," answered the intrepid Sswanda.

"Would you like to earn something by your music?"

"I am tired of blowing," returned Sswanda. "I have some silver in my pocket, and wish to amuse myself."

"Who talks to you of silver? It is with gold that we pay."

Saying this, the stranger flashed before his eyes a handful of shining ducats. The piper was the son of a thrifty mother; he knew not how to resist such an invitation, and followed the black man and his gold.

How the time passed he never could remember. It is true that his head was a little heavy. The only thing that he recollected was that the black man warned him to accept whatever was offered him, whether gold or wine, but never to return thanks except by saying "Good luck, brother!"

Without knowing how he had entered, he found himself in a dark room where three men, dressed in black like his guide, were playing at strajak by no other light than their glittering eyes. On the table were piles of gold, and a jug from which each one drank in his turn.

"Brothers," said the black man, "I bring you friend Sswanda, whom you have long known by reputation. I thought to please you on this feast-day by giving you a little music."

"A good idea!" said one of the players. Then, taking the jug, he handed it to Sswanda, saying, "Here, Piper, drink and play."

Sswanda had some scruples; but, after all, it is impossible to have charcoal without putting your fingers into the ashes. The wine, though rather warm, was not bad. He replaced the jug on the table, and raising his hat, said, "Good luck, brother!" as he had been advised.

He began to play, and never had his music produced such an effect. Each note made the players leap for joy. Their eyes shot forth flames; they moved about uneasily in their chairs; they staked the ducats by handfuls; they shouted and burst into loud fits of laughter without stirring a muscle of their pallid faces. The jug passed from hand to hand, always full, though replenished by no one.

As soon as Sswanda finished an air, they handed him the jug, from which he never failed to drink deeply, and threw handfuls of gold into his hat. "Good luck, brother!" he repeated, astounded at his fortune—"good luck!"

The feast lasted a long time. At last, the piper having struck up a polka, the black men, in a transport of mirth, quitted the table, and danced and waltzed with an ardor and frenzy which ill accorded with their icy faces. One of the dancers gathered up all the gold that was heaped on the table, and, pouring it into Sswanda's hat, "Here," said he, "take this for the pleasure that you have given us."

"God bless you, my good lords!" said the dazzled piper. Scarcely had he spoken when men, room, and cards vanished.

In the morning a peasant on his way to the fields heard the sound of a pipe as he approached the cross-road. "It is Sswanda," said he. But where was the piper? Seated on a corner of the gallows, he was blowing with all his might, while the corpses of the robbers danced in the wind to his music.

"Halloo, comrade!" cried the peasant, "how long have you been playing the cuckoo up there?"

Sswanda started, dropped his pipe, opened his eyes, and glided, bewildered, down the gallows. His first thought, however, was for his ducats. He rummaged his pockets, and turned his hat inside out, but all in vain; there was not even a kreutzer!

"My friend," said the peasant, making the sign of the cross, "God has punished you by giving you the devil for a partner; you love cards too well."

"You are right," said Sswanda, trembling; "I will never touch them again in my life."

He kept his word; and, to thank Heaven for having preserved him from such peril, he took the fatal pipe to which the devil had danced, and suspended it as a votive offering in the church of Strakonic, his birth-place, where it may be seen to this day. The pipe of Strakonic has become a proverb, and it is said that its sound is heard every year at the day and hour when Sswanda played for Satan and his friends.

# *Irish Fairy Tales*

*By James Stephens*
*Illustrations by Arthur Rackham*

*Two Irish heroes, Fionn, the soldier-poet, and his friend Conán, have been bewitched by the Faery king Conaran while out hunting. Here we see what happens when they and their brave band meet the king's daughters.*

## THE ENCHANTED CAVE OF CESH CORRAN

By his arts Conaran changed the sight of Fionn's eyes, and he did the same for Conán.

In a few minutes Fionn stood up from his place on the mound. Everything was about him as before, and he did not know that he had gone into Faery. He walked for a minute up and down the hillock. Then, as by chance, he stepped down the sloping end of the mound and stood with his mouth open, staring. He cried out:

"Come down here, Conán, my darling."

Conán stepped down to him.

"Am I dreaming," Fionn demanded, and he stretched out his finger before him.

"If you are dreaming," said Conán, "I'm dreaming too. They weren't here a minute ago," he stammered.

Fionn looked up at the sky and found that it was still there. He stared to one side and saw the trees of Kyle Conor waving in the distance. He bent his ear to the wind and heard the shouting of hunters, the yapping of dogs, and the clear whistles, which told how the hunt was going.

"Well!" said Fionn to himself.

"By my hand!" quoth Conán to his own soul.

And the two men stared into the hillside as though what they were looking at was too wonderful to be looked away from.

"Who are they?" said Fionn.

"What are they?" Conán gasped.

And they stared again.

For there was a great hole like a doorway in the side of the mound, and in that doorway the daughters of Conaran sat spinning. They had three crooked sticks of holly set up before the cave, and they were reeling yarn off these. But it was enchantment they were weaving.

"One could not call them handsome," said Conán.

"One could," Fionn replied, "but it would not be true."

"I cannot see them properly," Fionn complained. "They are hiding behind the holly."

"I would be contented if I could not see them at all," his companion grumbled.

"I want to make sure that it is whiskers they are wearing."

"Let them wear whiskers or not wear them," Conán counselled. "But let us have nothing to do with them."

"One must not be frightened of anything," Fionn stated.

"I am not frightened," Conán explained. "I only want to keep my good opinion of women, and if the three yonder are women, then I feel sure I shall begin to dislike females from this minute out."

"Come on, my love," said Fionn, "for I must find out if these whiskers are true."

He strode resolutely into the cave. He pushed the branches of holly aside and marched up to Conaran's daughters, with Conán behind him.

The instant they passed the holly a strange weakness came over the heroes. Their fists seemed to grow heavy as lead, and went dingle-dangle at the ends of their arms; their legs became as light as straws and began to bend in and out; their necks became too delicate to hold anything up, so that their heads wibbled and wobbled from side to side.

"What's wrong at all?" said Conán, as he stumbled to the ground.

"Everything is," Fionn replied, and he tumbled beside him.

The three sisters then tied the heroes with every kind of loop and twist and knot that could be thought of.

"Those are the whiskers!" said Fionn.

"Alas!" said Conán. "What a place you must hunt whiskers in!" he mumbled savagely. "Who wants whiskers?" he groaned.

But Fionn was thinking of other things.

"If there was any way of warning the Fianna not to come here," Fionn murmured.

"There is no way, my darling," said Caevóg, and she smiled a smile that would have killed Fionn, only that he shut his eyes in time.

After a moment he murmured again:

"Conán, my dear love, give the warning whistle so that the Fianna will keep out of this place."

A little whoof, like the sound that would be made by a baby and it asleep, came from Conán.

"Fionn," said he, "there isn't a whistle in me. We are done for," said he.

"You are done for, indeed," said Cuillen, and she smiled a hairy and twisty and fangy smile that almost finished Conán.

By that time some of the Fianna had returned to the mound to see why Bran and Sceólan were barking so outrageously. They saw the cave and went into it, but no sooner had they passed the holly branches than their strength went from them, and they were seized and bound by the vicious hags. Little by little all the members of the Fianna returned to the hill, and each of them was drawn into the cave, and each was bound by the sisters.

Oisín and Oscar and mac Lugac came, with the nobles of clann-Baiscne, and with those of clann-Corcoran and clann-Smól; they all came, and they were all bound.

It was a wonderful sight and a great deed this binding of the Fianna, and the three sisters laughed with a joy that was terrible to hear and was almost death to see. As the men were captured they were carried by the hags into dark mysterious holes and black perplexing labyrinths.

"Here is another one," cried Caevóg as she bundled a trussed champion along.

"This one is fat," said Cuillen, and she rolled a bulky Fenian along like a wheel.

"Here," said Iaran, "is a love of a man. One could eat this kind of man," she murmured, and she licked a lip that had whiskers growing inside as well as out.

And the corded champion whimpered in her arms, for he did not know but eating might indeed be his fate, and he would have preferred to be coffined anywhere in the world rather than to be coffined inside of that face.

The story ends with the rescue of the heroes and their men just as the hags were preparing to slay them. The brave Fianna live to fight (and die) another day.

# *Juvenile Calendar and Zodiac of Flowers*

*By Mrs. T. K. Hervey*
*Illustrations by Richard Doyle*

*Each month has its special flowers, birds, and insects, all of them subjects of the king and queen of the Fairies.*

*"Where Oxlips and the nodding Violet grow,*
*There sleeps Titania sometime of the night."*

# MARCH

| FLOWERS | BIRDS | INSECTS |
|---|---|---|
| White Violet | Sky-lark | Black Ant |
| Purple Violet | Blackbird | Stag Beetle |
| Daffodil | Thrush | March Moth |
| Arum, or Lords and Ladies | Linnet | Twenty-two-spotted Lady-bird |
| Pilewort | Greenfinch | Humming Bird |
| Iris | Ring-dove | Water Flea |

The Fairies had a queen, whose name was Titania. Oberon, their king, loved her very dearly.

Now, it happened that one day, very early in the breezy month of March, Oberon was called away from her side,—where he ever loved best to be,—in order to instruct some of his subjects in the duties they were expected to fulfill during the coming season.

To the fairy Bell-rocker, one of the most active of his retainers, Oberon gave the task of opening and shutting the jaws of the flower Snap-dragon, for the purpose of catching and making prisoner the little black Pismire, which had annoyed his Majesty greatly all the last summer by settling upon and tickling his lips,—and so causing him to rub off the sweet kisses that Titania bestowed on him.

He next charged the fairy Float-away not to forget to ride, for one whole minute each day, upon the horns of the Stag-beetle,—as a punishment to that insect for having goaded him under the left ribs, and so caused him suddenly to laugh just at the precise moment when his beloved Titania began to weep over the loss of some of the clearest notes of her voice, which the Sky-lark had borne away, and was trilling far off, up above the cloud-fleece.

The office which he gave to the fairy Bough-swinger was that of transforming a few of the "lords and ladies" of his court, who had occasionally defied his kingly authority, into flowers, which were, by his command, from that time forth to be called "Arums."

Having now dispatched so many of his suite upon these various errands, he turned to his favourite Puck, or Robin Goodfellow; and, as he knew that little fairy (though he loved mischief sometimes) to be happiest when employed in kind offices, Oberon instructed him to go and help the Gossamer-spider to spread out his filmy net upon the grass, for the purpose of catching the brightest drops of the morning dew. These were to be strung on the thread of the silk-worm, as a present to Titania:—for, of all the ornaments under the sun, Titania best liked the pearly dew-beads for a necklace.

# AESOP'S FABLES

*We don't really know who Aesop was, or even if he ever existed, though some think that the fables might have been told by a Greek slave who lived about 600* B.C. *What we do know is that these brief tales have been enjoyed by children and adults in many lands since ancient times. I have chosen a few of them, illustrated by different artists over the past five hundred years, to show the many ways Aesop's fables have been retold and illustrated.*

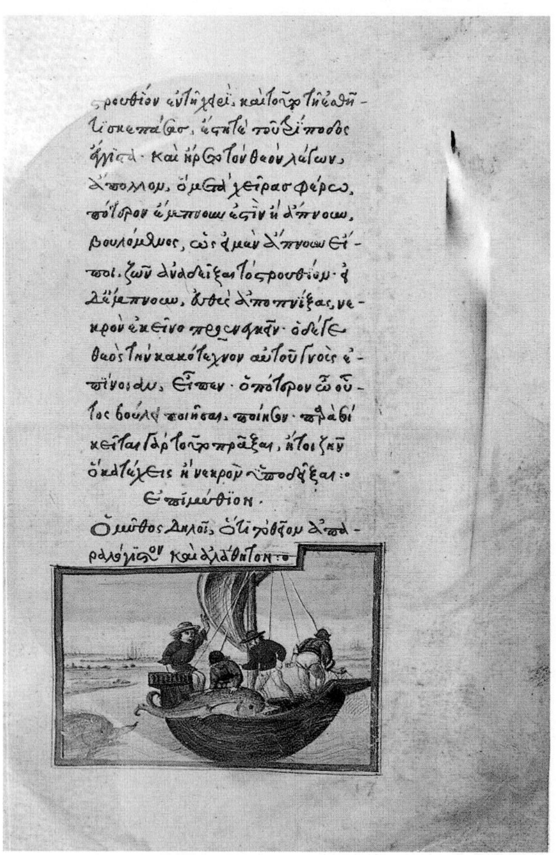

## THE FISHERMEN AND THE TUNA

A boat load of fishermen had been out all day without a catch. They decided that it was no use to continue on, and began to sail home. At that moment a huge tuna fish, panicking as he tried to escape from some fishy foe, jumped right into their boat. So they killed him, took him back to port, and sold him.

*MORAL: Good luck often brings what hard work fails to achieve.*

# *Aesop in the Fifteenth Century*

*The two fables illustrated here were written in Greek around 1490 in an illuminated manuscript from Italy, now in the Spencer Collection of the New York Public Library.*

## THE THIEVES AND THE ROOSTER

Some robbers broke into a house, and the only thing they could find to steal was a rooster. They carried him off, and as they were about to kill and eat him, he cried out and begged them to spare his life. He was quite useful to men, he claimed, since he woke people up for work. The thieves responded that this was an excellent reason for them to slaughter him, since, in waking people up, he could keep them from being robbed.

*MORAL: "One man's Mede is another man's Persian."*

# *Aesop in the Seventeenth Century*

*The fables in this version were printed in London in 1666 in three languages—English, French, and Latin—and illustrated by Francis Barlow.*

## THE EAGLE AND THE FOX

The Eagle and the Fox became friendly, so friendly, in fact, that they decided to build their houses near to one another. This, they thought, would allow them to meet and talk more often and would make their friendship firmer. So the Eagle built her nest on a tall tree beneath which the Fox built her den and put her kits into it. One day, while the Fox was out looking for food for her family, the Eagle, who also needed food, flew down to the den and stole the kits. She fed them to her children.

When the Fox came home and discovered the cruel loss of her children, she was very angry. But she knew that she wasn't able to take revenge on the Eagle, who could easily fly away from any attack. Instead, she cursed the Eagle, wishing the worst for her and her family, with all the rage of a friend betrayed.

A few days later, there was a burnt offering to the gods in a nearby field. Some people had sacrificed a rabbit, and they went away and left it on the fire. The Eagle flew over the site of the sacrifice and scooped up the rabbit. She didn't realize that she was also picking up some twigs that were still burning. She brought the cooked rabbit back to her nest, where a fire started in the dry twigs that her home was made of. Her children, not being able to fly as yet, jumped from the fiery nest to the ground, where the Fox instantly ate them up, while their mother watched in horror.

*MORAL: Those who have false friends should be careful where they build their houses.*

# *Aesop in the Nineteenth Century*
# *Aesop's Fables*

*By the Reverend Thomas James, M.A.*
*Illustrations by John Tenniel*

*The artist who illustrated this fable is best known for his drawings in the original* Alice's Adventures in Wonderland.

## THE WOLF AND THE CRANE

A Wolf had got a bone stuck in his throat, and in the greatest agony ran up and down, beseeching every animal he met to relieve him: at the same time hinting at a very handsome reward to the successful operator. A Crane, moved by his entreaties and promises, ventured her long neck down the Wolf's throat, and drew out the bone. She then modestly asked for the promised reward. To which, the Wolf, grinning and showing his teeth, replied with seeming indignation, "Ungrateful creature! to ask for any other reward than that you have put your head into a Wolf's jaws, and brought it safe out again!"

*MORAL: Those who are charitable only in the hope of a return, must not be surprised if, in their dealings with evil men, they meet with more jeers than thanks.*

# *Aesop in the Twentieth Century*
# *The Fables of Aesop, According to Sir Roger L'Estrange*

*Illustrations by Alexander Calder*

*Although the language of this fable is seventeenth-century English, the illustration by a famous twentieth-century artist and sculptor is purely of our time.*

## THE KITE, HAWK, AND PIGEONS

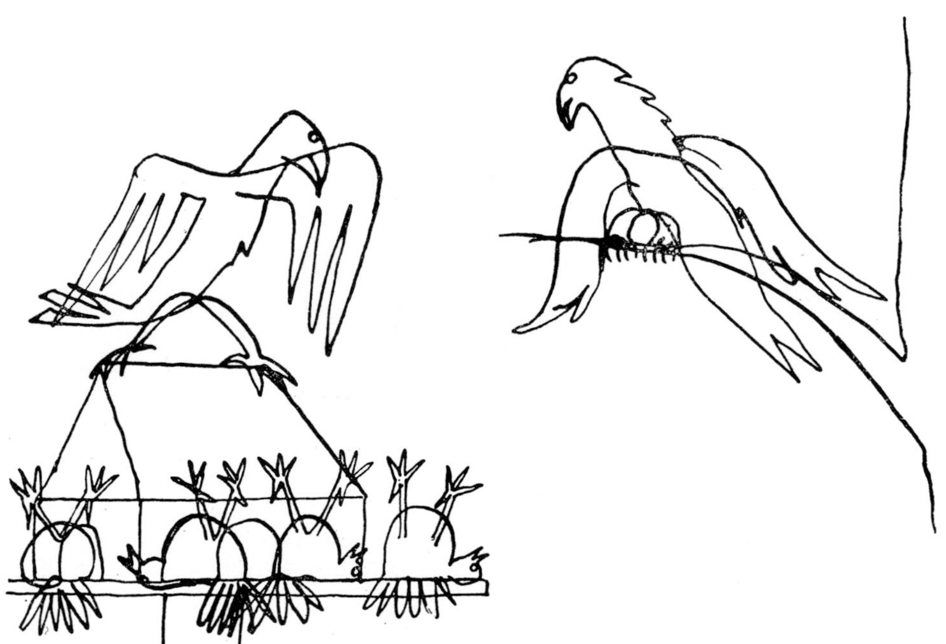

The pigeons finding themselves persecuted by the kite, made choice of the hawk for their guardian. The hawk sets up for their protector; but under countenance of that authority, makes more havock in the dove-house in two days than the kite could have done in twice as many months.

*MORAL: 'Tis a dangerous thing for people to call in a powerful and an ambitious man for their protector; and upon the clamour of here and there a private person, to hazard the whole community.*

# *Stories by Leo Tolstoy*

*Best known for his long novels, among them* War and Peace, *Tolstoy also wrote these brief animal stories very much in the style of Aesop.*

## THE WOLF AND THE DOG

A lean and hungry wolf was walking past a village and met a fat dog. The wolf asked the dog: "Tell me, dog, where do you get your food?"

"People give it to me," the dog answered.

"That means you work hard for these people," said the wolf.

"No, we dogs don't work hard. All we do is guard the yard at night," the dog said.

"And for doing only this service they feed you so well?" wondered the wolf. "I would accept this kind of job at once. It is hard for us wolves to find food."

"Well, go ahead," said the dog. "My master will feed you then as well as he feeds me."

The wolf was glad and went with the dog to work for people. As the dog was entering his yard, the wolf noticed that some of the fur on his neck had been rubbed away.

"How did this happen to you, dog?" he said.

"Oh, it just happened," answered the dog.

"What do you mean 'it just happened'?" asked the wolf.

"It just happened . . . from the chain. They chain me during the day and the chain rubs away the fur on my neck."

"Well," said the wolf, "if that is so, then good-bye, dog. I will not live with people. I would rather be hungry, but free."

## THE CZAR AND THE FALCON

A czar once went hunting. He let loose from his arm his favorite falcon to have him catch a hare.

The falcon caught the hare. The czar took it from him and then began to look for water to quench his thirst. He found water coming, drop by drop, from a weeping rock. He took a cup and placed it under the rock. When the cup was full, the czar raised it to his mouth and was about to drink from it when the falcon became agitated, flapped his wings against the czar's hand causing all the water to spill from the cup. Again the czar placed the cup under the rock. He waited a long time for it to fill up. And when he raised it to his mouth, the falcon once more spilled the water.

When the czar filled the cup for the third time and raised it to his mouth, the falcon spilled the water for the third time. The czar grew very angry. With all his strength he dashed the falcon against a stone and killed him. At that moment the czar's servants rode up to him. One of them climbed up the hill to the spring that fed the weeping rock and where there was more water, so that a cup could be filled more quickly. But the servant came back with the empty cup and said: "You must not drink this water; there is a serpent in the spring. It poured its poison into the water. It was lucky that the falcon spilled the water. If you had drunk it, you would have died."

The czar then said: "Badly have I repaid the falcon. He saved my life and I killed him."

# THE LION AND THE PUPPY

Some wild beasts were on view in a London zoo. As payment for seeing them either money was accepted or dogs and cats which were used to feed the animals.

A man wanted to see the beasts. He picked up a puppy in the street and brought it to the zoo. They let him in, took the puppy from him, and threw it into the lion's cage for him to eat.

The little dog drew in its tail and pushed himself against the corner of the cage. The lion approached it and smelled it.

The puppy turned on its back, raised its little paws, and began to wave its little tail.

The lion touched it lightly and turned it over.

The puppy jumped up and stood before the lion on its hind legs.

The lion kept looking at the little dog but did not harm it.

When the keeper threw some meat to the lion, he tore off a piece and left it for the puppy.

In the evening, when the lion lay down to sleep, the puppy lay down against his side and put its head on the lion's paw.

From that day on the little dog lived in the cage with the lion.

The lion never hurt it, but slept near it, and at times played with it.

One day a gentleman came to the zoo, noticed the little dog and claimed that it was his. He asked the keeper to give it to him. The keeper wanted to do it, but as soon as they began to call to the puppy, the lion bristled and roared.

The lion and the little dog continued to live together in the same cage for a whole year. At the end of the year the little dog got sick and died. The lion stopped eating, kept smelling the puppy and touching it gently with his paw.

When the lion understood that the puppy was dead, he suddenly jumped up, bristled, began to whip his sides with his tail, threw himself at the bars of the cage, and tore at them.

For a whole day he rushed about the cage and roared. Then he lay down near the dead little dog, embraced it with his paws, and remained there for the next five days.

On the sixth day the lion died.

# *Ivanhoe*

*By Sir Walter Scott*
*Illustrations by Frank E. Schoonover*

*This account of a jousting tournament, in which Ivanhoe is the mysterious champion, shows us what a popular sport was like in the Middle Ages.*

As far as could be judged of a man sheathed in armour, the new adventurer did not greatly exceed middle size, and seemed to be rather slender than strongly made. His suit of armour was formed of steel, richly inlaid with gold, and the device on his shield was a young oak-tree pulled up by the roots, with the Spanish word *Desdichado*, signifying Disinherited. He was mounted on a gallant black horse, and as he passed through the lists he gracefully saluted the Prince and the ladies by lowering his lance. The dexterity with which he managed his steed, and something of youthful grace which he displayed in his manner, won him the favour of the multitude, which some of the lower classes expressed by calling out. "Touch Ralph de Vipont's shield—touch the Hospitaller's shield; he has the least sure seat, he is your cheapest bargain."

The champion, moving inward amid these well-meant hints, ascended the platform by the sloping alley which led to it from the lists, and, to the astonishment of all present, riding straight up to the central pavilion, struck with the sharp end of his spear the shield of Brian de Bois-Guilbert until it rung again. All stood astonished at his presumption, but none more than the redoubted Knight whom he had thus defied to mortal combat, and who, little expecting so rude a challenge, was standing carelessly at the door of the pavilion.

"Have you confessed yourself, brother," said the Templar, "and have you heard mass this morning, that you peril your life so frankly?"

"I am fitter to meet death than thou art," answered the Disinherited Knight; for by this name the stranger had recorded himself in the books of the tourney.

"Then take your place in the lists," said Bois-Guilbert, "and look your last upon the sun; for this night thou shalt sleep in paradise."

"Gramercy for thy courtesy," replied the Disinherited Knight, "and to requite it, I advise thee to take a fresh horse and a new lance, for by my honour you will need both."

Having expressed himself thus confidently, he reined his horse backward down the slope which he had ascended, and compelled him in the same manner to move backward through the lists, till he reached the northern extremity, where he remained stationary, in expectation of his antagonist. This feat of horsemanship again attracted the applause of the multitude.

However incensed at his adversary for the precautions which he recommended, Brian de Bois-Guilbert did not neglect his advice; for his honour was too nearly concerned, to permit his neglecting any means which might ensure victory over his presumptuous opponent. He changed his horse for a proved and fresh one of great strength and spirit. He chose a new and a tough spear, lest the wood of the former might have been strained in the previous encounters he had sustained. Lastly, he laid aside his shield, which had received some little damage, and received another from his squires. His first had only borne the general device of his rider, representing two knights upon one horse, an emblem expressive of the original humility and poverty of the Templars, qualities which they had since exchanged for the arrogance and wealth that finally occasioned their suppression. Bois-Guilbert's new shield bore a raven in full flight, holding in its claws a skull, and bearing the motto, *Gare le Corbeau.*

When the two champions stood opposed to each other at the two extremities of the lists, the public expectation was strained to the highest pitch. Few augured the possibility that the encounter could terminate well for the Disinherited Knight, yet his courage and gallantry secured the general good wishes of the spectators.

The trumpets had no sooner given the signal, than the champions vanished from their posts with the speed of lightning, and closed in the centre of the lists with the shock of a thunderbolt. The lances burst into shivers up to the very grasp, and it seemed at the moment that both knights had fallen, for the shock had made each horse recoil backwards upon its haunches. The address of the riders recovered their steeds by use of the bridle and spur; and having glared on each other for an instant with eyes which seemed to flash fire through the bars of their visors, each made a demi-volte, and, retiring to the extremity of the lists, received a fresh lance from the attendants.

A loud shout from the spectators, waving of scarfs and handkerchiefs, and general acclamations, attested the interest taken by the spectators in this encounter; the most equal, as well as the best performed, which had graced the day. But no sooner had the knights resumed their station, than the clamour of applause was hushed into a silence, so deep and so dead, that it seemed the multitude were afraid even to breathe.

A few minutes' pause having been allowed, that the combatants and their horses might recover breath, Prince John with his truncheon signed to the trumpets to sound the onset. The champions a second time sprung from their stations, and closed in the center of the lists, with the same speed, the same dexterity, the same violence, but not the same equal fortune as before.

In this second encounter, the Templar aimed at the center of his antagonist's shield, and struck it so fair and forcibly, that his spear went to shivers, and the Disinherited Knight reeled in his saddle. On the other hand, that champion had, in the beginning of his career, directed the point of his lance towards Bois-

Guilbert's shield, but, changing his aim almost in the moment of the encounter, he addressed it to the helmet, a mark more difficult to hit, but which if attained, rendered the shock more irresistible. Fair and true he hit the Norman on the visor, where his lance's point kept hold of the bars. Yet, even at this disadvantage, the Templar sustained his high reputation, and had not the girths of his saddle burst, he might not have been unhorsed. As it chanced, however, saddle, horse, and man, rolled on the ground under a cloud of dust.

To extricate himself from the stirrups and fallen steed, was to the Templar scarce the work of a moment; and, stung with madness, both at his disgrace and at the acclamations with which it was hailed by the spectators, he drew his sword and waved it in defiance of his conqueror. The Disinherited Knight sprung from his steed, and also unsheathed his sword. The marshals of the field, however, spurred their horses between them, and reminded them, that the laws of the tournament did not, on the present occasion, permit this species of encounter.

"We shall meet again, I trust," said the Templar, casting a resentful glance at his antagonist; "and where there are none to separate us."

"If we do not," said the Disinherited Knight, "the fault shall not be mine. On foot or horseback, with spear, with axe, or with sword, I am alike ready to encounter thee."

More and angrier words would have been exchanged, but the marshals, crossing their lances betwixt them, compelled them to separate. The Disinherited Knight returned to his first station, and Bois-Guilbert to his tent, where he remained for the rest of the day in an agony of despair.

Without alighting from his horse, the conqueror called for a bowl of wine, and opening the beaver, or lower part of his helmet, announced that he quaffed it, "To all true English hearts, and to the confusion of foreign tyrants." He then commanded his trumpet to sound a defiance to the challengers, and desired a herald to announce to them, that he should make no election, but was willing to encounter them in the order in which they pleased to advance against him.

The gigantic Front-de-Boeuf, armed in sable armour, was the first who took the field. He bore on a white shield a black bull's head, half defaced by the numerous encounters which he had undergone, and bearing the arrogant motto, *Cave, adsum.* Over this champion the Disinherited Knight obtained a slight but decisive advantage. Both Knights broke their lances fairly, but Front-de-Boeuf, who lost a stirrup in the encounter, was adjudged to have a disadvantage.

In the stranger's third encounter with Sir Philip Malvoisin, he was equally successful; striking that baron so forcibly on the casque, that the laces of the helmet broke, and Malvoisin, only saved from falling by being unhelmeted, was declared vanquished like his companions.

In his fourth combat with De Grantmesnil, the Disinherited Knight showed as much courtesy as he had hitherto evinced courage and dexterity. De Grantmesnil's horse, which was young and violent, reared and plunged in the course of the career so as to disturb the rider's aim, and the stranger, declining to take the advantage which this accident afforded him, raised his lance, and passing his antagonist without touching him, wheeled his horse and rode back again to his own end of the lists, offering his antagonist, by a herald, the chance of a second encounter. This De Grantmesnil declined, avowing himself vanquished as much by the courtesy as by the address of his opponent.

Ralph de Vipont summed up the list of the stranger's triumphs, being hurled to the ground with such force, that the blood gushed from his nose and his mouth, and he was borne senseless from the lists.

The acclamations of thousands applauded the unanimous award of the Prince and marshals, announcing that day's honours to the Disinherited Knight.

# *The Selfish Giant*

*By Oscar Wilde*
*Illustrations by Everett Shinn*

*Giants and little children don't always get along, but in this story the giant has a change of heart.*

Every afternoon, as they were coming from school, the children used to go and play in the Giant's garden.

It was a large lovely garden, with soft green grass. Here and there over the grass stood beautiful flowers like stars, and there were twelve peach-trees that in the spring-time broke out into delicate blossoms of pink and pearl, and in the autumn bore rich fruit. The birds sat on the trees and sang so sweetly that the children used to stop their games in order to listen to them. "How happy we are here!" they cried to each other.

One day the Giant came back. He had been to visit his friend the Cornish ogre, and had stayed with him for seven years. After the seven years were over he had said all that he had to say, for his conversation was limited, and he determined to return to his own castle. When he arrived he saw the children playing in his garden.

"What are you doing there?" he cried in a very gruff voice, and the children ran away.

"My own garden is my own garden," said the Giant; "anyone can understand that, and I will allow nobody to play in it but myself." So he built a high wall around it, and put up a notice-board.

TRESPASSERS
WILL BE
PROSECUTED

He was a very selfish Giant.

The poor children had now nowhere to play. They tried to play on the road, but the road was very dusty and full of hard stones, and they did not like it. They used to wander round the high wall when their lessons were over, and talk about the beautiful garden inside. "How happy we were there," they said to each other.

Then the Spring came, and all over the country there were little blossoms and little birds. Only in the garden of the Selfish Giant it was still winter. The birds did not care to sing in it as there were no children, and the trees forgot to blossom. Once a beautiful flower put its head out from the grass, but when it saw the notice-board it was so sorry for the children that it slipped back into the ground again, and went off to sleep. The only people who were pleased were the Snow and the Frost. "Spring has forgotten this garden," they cried, "so we will live here all the year round." The Snow covered up the grass with her great white cloak, and the Frost painted all the trees silver. Then they invited the North Wind to stay with them, and he came. He was wrapped in furs, and he roared all day about the garden, and blew the chimney-pots down. "This is a delightful spot," he said, "we must ask the Hail on a visit." So the Hail came. Every day for three hours he rattled on the roof of the castle till he broke most of the slates, and then he ran round and round the garden as fast as he could go. He was dressed in grey, and his breath was like ice.

"I cannot understand why the Spring is so late in coming," said the Selfish Giant, as he sat at the window and looked out at his cold white garden; "I hope there will be a change in the weather."

But the Spring never came, nor the Summer. The Autumn gave golden fruit to every garden, but to the Giant's garden she gave none. "He is too selfish," she said. So it was always Winter there, and the North Wind, and the Hail, and the Frost, and the Snow danced about through the trees.

One morning the Giant was lying awake in bed when he heard some lovely music. It sounded so sweet to his ears that he thought it must be the King's musicians passing by. It was really only a little linnet singing outside his window, but it was so long since he had heard a bird sing in his garden that it seemed to him to be the most beautiful music in the world. Then the Hail stopped dancing over his head, and the North Wind ceased roaring, and a delicious perfume came to him through the open casement. "I believe the Spring has come at last," said the Giant; and he jumped out of bed and looked out.

What did he see?

He saw a most wonderful sight. Through a little hole in the wall the children had crept in, and they were sitting in the branches of the trees. In every tree that he could see there was a little child. And the trees were so glad to have the children back again that they had covered themselves with blossoms, and were waving their arms gently above the children's heads. The birds were flying about and twittering with delight, and the flowers were looking up through the green grass and laughing. It was a lovely scene, only in one corner it was still winter. It was the farthest corner of the garden, and in it was standing a little boy. He was so small that he could not reach up to the branches of the tree, and he was wandering all round it, crying bitterly. The poor tree was still quite covered with frost and snow, and the North Wind was blowing and roaring above it. "Climb up! little boy," said the Tree, and it bent its branches down as low as it could; but the boy was too tiny.

And the Giant's heart melted as he looked out. "How selfish I have been!" he said; "now I know why the Spring would not come here. I will put that poor little boy on the top of the tree, and then I will knock down the wall, and my garden shall be the children's playground for ever and ever." He was really very sorry for what he had done.

So he crept downstairs and opened the front door quite softly, and went out into the garden. But when the children saw him they were so frightened that they all ran away, and the garden became Winter again. Only the little boy did not run, for his eyes were so full of tears that he did not see the Giant coming. And the Giant stole up behind him and took him gently in his hand, and put him up into the tree. And the tree broke at once into blossom, and the birds came and sang on it, and the little boy stretched out his two arms and flung them round the Giant's neck, and kissed him. And the other children, when they saw that the Giant was not wicked any longer, came running back, and with them came the Spring. "It is your garden now, little children," said the Giant, and he took a great axe and knocked down the wall. And when the people were going to market at twelve o'clock they found the Giant playing with the children in the most beautiful garden they had ever seen.

All day long they played, and in the evening they came to the Giant to bid him good-bye.

"But where is your little companion?" he said: "the boy I put into the tree." The Giant loved him the best because he had kissed him.

"We don't know," answered the children; "he has gone away."

"You must tell him to be sure and come here to-morrow," said the Giant. But the children said that they did not know where he lived, and had never seen him before; and the Giant felt very sad.

Every afternoon, when school was over, the children came and played with the Giant. But the little boy whom the Giant loved was never seen again. The Giant was very kind to all the children, yet he longed for his first little friend, and often spoke of him. "How I would like to see him!" he used to say.

Years went over, and the Giant grew very old and feeble. He could not play about any more, so he sat in a huge armchair, and watched the children at their games, and admired his garden. "I have many beautiful flowers," he said; "but the children are the most beautiful flowers of all."

One winter morning he looked out of his window as he was dressing. He did not hate the Winter now, for he knew that it was merely the Spring asleep, and that the flowers were resting.

Suddenly he rubbed his eyes in wonder, and looked and looked. It certainly was a marvellous sight. In the farthest corner of the garden was a tree quite covered with white blossoms. Its branches were all golden, and silver fruit hung down from them, and underneath it stood the little boy he had loved.

Downstairs ran the Giant in great joy, and out into the garden. He hastened across the grass, and came near to the child. And when he came quite close his face grew red with anger, and he said, "Who hath dared to wound thee?" For on the palms of the child's hands were the prints of two nails, and the prints of two nails were on the little feet.

"Who hath dared to wound thee?" cried the Giant; "tell me, that I may take my sword and slay him."

"Nay!" answered the child; "but these are the wounds of Love."

"Who art thou?" said the Giant, and a strange awe fell on him, and he knelt before the little child.

And the child smiled on the Giant, and said to him, "You let me play once in your garden, to-day you shall come with me to my garden, which is Paradise."

And when the children ran in that afternoon, they found the Giant lying dead under the tree, all covered with white blossoms.

# *The Merry Adventures of Robin Hood*

*Written and illustrated by Howard Pyle*

*In this segment of the tale, we see one of Robin's merry men recruit a new member for the band of outlaws in a curious fashion.*

## THE MIGHTY FIGHT BETWIXT: LITTLE JOHN AND THE COOK

"Now, by my faith," cried the Cook, as he rattled the pottle against the sideboard, "I like that same song hugely, and eke the motive of it, which lieth like a sweet kernel in a hazel-nut."

"Now thou art a man of shrewd opinions," quoth Little John, "and I love thee truly as thou wert my brother."

"And I love thee, too. But the day draweth on, and I have my cooking to do ere our master cometh home; so let us e'en go and settle this brave fight we have in hand."

"Ay, marry," quoth Little John, "and that right speedily. Never have I been more laggard in fighting than in eating and drinking. So come thou straight forth into the passage-way, where there is good room to swing a sword, and I will try to serve thee."

Then they both stepped forth into the broad passage that led to the Steward's pantry, where each man drew his sword again, and without more ado fell upon the other as though he would hew his fellow limb from limb. Then their swords clashed upon one another with great din, and sparks flew from each blow in showers. So they fought up and down the hall for an hour and more, neither striking the other a blow, though they strove their best to do so; for both were skilful at the fence; so nothing came of all their labor. Ever and anon they rested, panting; then, after getting their wind, at it they would go again more fiercely than ever. At last Little John cried aloud, "Hold, good Cook!" whereupon each rested upon his sword, panting.

"Now will I make my vow," quoth Little John, "thou art the very best swordsman that ever mine eyes beheld. Truly, I had thought to carve thee ere now."

"And I had thought to do the same by thee," quoth the Cook; "but I have missed the mark somehow."

"Now I have been thinking within myself," quoth Little John, "what we are fighting for; but albeit I do not rightly know."

"Why, no more do I," said the Cook. "I bear no love for that pursy Steward, but I thought that we had engaged to fight with one another, and that it must be done."

"Now," quoth Little John, "it doth seem to me that instead of striving to cut one another's throats, it were better for us to be boon companions. What sayst thou, jolly Cook, wilt thou go with me to Sherwood Forest and join with Robin Hood's band? Thou shalt live a merry life within the woodlands, and sevenscore good companions shalt thou have, one of whom is mine own self. Thou shalt have two suits of Lincoln green each year, and forty marks in pay."

"Now, thou art a man after mine own heart!" cried the Cook right heartily; "and, as

thou speakest of it, that is the very service for me. I will go with thee, and that right gladly. Give me thy palm, sweet fellow, and I will be thine own companion from henceforth. What may be thy name, lad?"

"Men do call me Little John, good fellow."

"How? And art thou indeed Little John, and Robin Hood's own right-hand man? Many a time and oft have I heard of thee, but never did I hope to set eyes upon thee. And thou art indeed the famous Little John!" And the Cook seemed lost in amazement, and looked upon his companion with open eyes.

"I am Little John, indeed, and I will bring to Robin Hood this day a right stout fellow to join his merry band. But ere we go, good friend, it seemeth to me to be a vast pity that, as we have had so much of the good Sheriff's food, we should not also carry off some of his silver plate to Robin Hood, as a present from his worship."

"Ay, marry is it," said the Cook. And so they began hunting about, and took as much silver as they could lay hands upon, clapping it into a bag, and when they had filled the sack they set forth to Sherwood Forest.

Plunging into the woods, they came at last to the greenwood tree, where they found Robin Hood and threescore of his merry men lying upon the fresh green grass. When Robin and his men saw who it was that came, they leaped to their feet. "Now welcome!" cried Robin Hood, "Now welcome, Little John! for long hath it been since we have heard from thee, though we all knew that thou hadst joined the Sheriff's service. And how hast thou fared all these long days?"

"Right merrily have I lived at the Lord Sheriff's," answered Little John, "and I have come straight thence. See, good master! I have brought thee his cook, and even his silver plate." Thereupon he told Robin Hood and his merry men that were there all that had befallen him since he had left them to go to the Fair at Nottingham Town. Then all shouted with laughter, except Robin Hood; but he looked grave.

"Nay, Little John," said he, "thou art a brave blade and a trusty fellow. I am glad thou hast brought thyself back to us, and with such a good companion as the Cook, whom we all welcome to Sherwood. But I like not so well that thou hast stolen the Sheriff's plate like some paltry thief. The Sheriff hath been punished by us, and hath lost three hundred pounds, even as he sought to despoil another; but he hath done nought that we should steal his household plate from him."

Though Little John was vexed with this, he strove to pass it off with a jest. "Nay, good master," quoth he, "if thou thinkest the Sheriff gave us not the plate, I will fetch him, that he may tell us with his own lips he giveth it all to us." So saying, he leaped to his feet, and was gone before Robin Hood could call him back.

Little John ran for full five miles till he came to where the Sheriff of Nottingham and a gay company were hunting near the forest. When Little John came to the Sheriff he doffed his cap and bent his knee. "God save thee, good master," quoth he.

"Why, Reynold Greenleaf!" cried the Sheriff, "whence comest thou and where hast thou been?"

"I have been in the forest," answered Little John, speaking amazedly, "and there I saw a sight such as ne'er before man's eyes beheld! Yonder I saw a young hart all in green from top to toe, and about him was a herd of threescore deer, and they, too, were all of green from head to foot. Yet I dared not shoot, good master, for fear lest they should slay me."

"Why, how now, Reynold Greenleaf," cried the Sheriff; "art thou dreaming, or art thou mad, that thou dost bring me such a tale?"

"Nay, I am not dreaming nor am I mad," said Little John; "and if thou wilt come with me, I will show thee this fair sight, for I have seen it with mine own eyes. But thou must come alone, good master, lest the others frighten them and they get away."

So the party all rode forward, and Little John led them downward into the forest.

# *A Wonder-Book for Girls and Boys*

*By Nathaniel Hawthorne*

*The author of* The House of Seven Gables *and* The Scarlet Letter *here recounts the fable of the Greek king who paid a terribly high price for his love of gold.*

## THE GOLDEN TOUCH

Once upon a time, there lived a very rich man, and a king besides, whose name was Midas; and he had a little daughter, whom nobody but myself ever heard of, and whose name I either never knew, or have entirely forgotten. So, because I love odd names for little girls, I choose to call her Marygold.

This King Midas was fonder of gold than of anything else in the world. He valued his royal crown chiefly because it was composed of that precious metal. If he loved anything better, or half so well, it was the one little maiden who played so merrily around her father's footstool. But the more Midas loved his daughter, the more did he desire and seek for wealth. He thought, foolish man! that the best thing he could possibly do for this dear child would be to bequeath her the immensest pile of yellow, glistening coin, that had ever been heaped together since the world was made. Thus, he gave all his thoughts and all his time to this one purpose.... When little Marygold ran to meet him, with a bunch of buttercups and dandelions, he used to say, "Poh, Poh, child! If these flowers were as golden as they look, they would be worth the plucking!"

And yet, in his earlier days, before he was so entirely possessed with this insane desire for riches, King Midas had shown a great taste for flowers.... But now, if he looked at them at all, it was only to calculate how much the garden would be worth, if each of the innumerable rose-petals were a thin plate of gold. And though he once was fond of music (in spite of an idle story about his ears, which were said to resemble those of an ass), the only music for poor Midas, now, was the chink of one coin against another.

At length (as people always grow more and

more foolish, unless they take care to grow wiser and wiser), Midas had got to be so exceedingly unreasonable, that he could scarcely bear to see or touch any object that was not gold. He made it his custom, therefore, to pass a large portion of every day in a dark and dreary apartment, under ground, at the basement of his palace. It was here that he kept his wealth. ... Here, after carefully locking the door, he would take a bag of gold coin, or a gold cup as big as a wash-bowl, or a heavy golden bar, or a peck-measure of gold dust, and bring them from the obscure corners of the room into the one bright and narrow sunbeam that fell from the dungeon-like window. He valued the sunbeam for no other reason but that his treasure would not shine without its help. And then would he reckon over the coins in the bag; toss up the bar, and catch it as it came down; sift the gold dust through his fingers; look at the funny image of his own face, as reflected in the burnished circumference of the cup; and whisper to himself, "O Midas, rich King Midas, what a happy man art thou!"...

Midas called himself a happy man, but felt that he was not yet quite so happy as he might be. The very tip-top of enjoyment would never be reached, unless the whole world were to become his treasure-room, and be filled with yellow metal which should be all his own.

Now, I need hardly remind such wise little people as you are, that in the old, old times, when King Midas was alive, a great many things came to pass, which we should consider wonderful if they were to happen in our own day and country. And, on the other hand, a great many things take place now-a-days, which seem not only wonderful to us, but at which the people of old times would have stared their eyes out. On the whole, I regard our own times as the strangest of the two; but, however that may be, I must go on with my story.

Midas was enjoying himself in his treasure-room, one day, as usual, when he perceived a shadow fall over the heaps of gold; and, looking suddenly up, what should he behold but the figure of a stranger, standing in the bright and narrow sunbeam! It was a young man, with a cheerful and ruddy face. Whether it was that the imagination of King Midas threw a yellow tinge over everything, or whatever the cause might be, he could not help fancying that the smile with which the stranger regarded him had a kind of golden radiance in it. Certainly, although his figure intercepted the sunshine, there was now a brighter gleam upon all the piled-up treasures than before....

As Midas knew that he had carefully turned the key in the lock, and that no mortal strength could possibly break into his treasure-room, he, of course, concluded that his visitor must be something more than mortal. It is no matter about telling you who he was. In those days, when the earth was comparatively a new affair, it was supposed to be often the resort of beings endowed with supernatural powers, and who used to interest themselves in the joys and sorrows of men, women and children, half playfully and half seriously. Midas had met such beings before now, and was not sorry to meet one of them again. The stranger's aspect, indeed, was so good-humored and kindly, if not beneficent, that it would have been unreasonable to suspect him of intending any mischief. It was far more probable that he came to do Midas a favor. And what could that favor be, unless to multiply his heaps of treasure?

The stranger gazed about the room; and when his lustrous smile had glistened upon all the golden objects that were there, he turned again to Midas.

"You are a wealthy man, friend Midas!" he observed. "I doubt whether any other four walls, on earth, contain so much gold as you have contrived to pile up in this room."

"I have done pretty well—pretty well," answered Midas, in a discontented tone. "But, after all, it is but a trifle, when you consider that it has taken me my whole life to get it together. If one could live a thousand years, he might have time to grow rich!"

"What!" exclaimed the stranger. "Then you are not satisfied?"

Midas shook his head.

"And pray what would satisfy you?" asked the stranger. "Merely for the curiosity of the thing, I should be glad to know."

Midas paused and meditated. He felt a presentiment that this stranger, with such a golden lustre in his good-humored smile, had come hither with both the power and the purpose of gratifying his utmost wishes. Now, therefore, was the fortunate moment, when he had but to speak, and obtain whatever possible, or seemingly impossible thing, it might come into his head to ask. So he thought, and thought, and thought, and heaped up one golden mountain upon another, in his imagination, without being able to imagine them big enough. At last, a bright idea occurred to King Midas. It seemed really as bright as the glistening metal which he loved so much.

Raising his head, he looked the lustrous stranger in the face.

"Well, Midas," observed his visitor, "I see that you have at length hit upon something that will satisfy you. Tell me your wish."

"It is only this," replied Midas. "I am weary of collecting my treasures with so much trouble, and beholding the heap so diminutive, after I have done my best. I wish everything that I touch to be changed to gold!"

The stranger's smile grew so very broad, that it seemed to fill the room like an outburst of the sun....

"The Golden Touch!" exclaimed he. "You certainly deserve credit, friend Midas, for striking out so brilliant a conception. But are you quite sure that this will satisfy you?"

"How could it fail?" said Midas.

"And will you never regret the possession of it?"

"What could induce me?" asked Midas. "I ask nothing else, to render me perfectly happy."

"Be it as you wish, then," replied the stranger, waving his hand in token of farewell. "To-morrow, at sunrise, you will find yourself gifted with the Golden Touch."

The figure of the stranger then became exceedingly bright, and Midas involuntarily closed his eyes. On opening them again, he beheld only one yellow sunbeam in the room, and, all around him, the glistening of the precious metal which he had spent his life in hoarding up.

Whether Midas slept as usual that night, the story does not say. Asleep or awake, however, his mind was probably in the state of a child's, to whom a beautiful new plaything has been promised in the morning. At any rate, day had hardly peeped over the hills, when Midas was broad awake, and, stretching his arms out of bed, began to touch the objects that were within reach. He was anxious to prove whether the Golden Touch had really come, according to the stranger's promise. So he laid his finger on a chair by the bedside, and on various other things, but was grievously disappointed to perceive that they remained of exactly the same substance as before. Indeed, he felt very much afraid that he had only dreamed about the lustrous stranger, or else that the latter had been making game of him. . . .

He lay in a very disconsolate mood, regretting the downfall of his hopes, and kept growing sadder and sadder, until the earliest sunbeam shone through the window, and gilded the ceiling over his head. It seemed to Midas that this bright yellow sunbeam was reflected in a rather singular way on the white covering of the bed. Looking more closely, what was his astonishment and delight, when he found that this linen fabric had been transmuted to what seemed a woven texture of the purest and brightest gold! The Golden Touch had come to him, with the first sunbeam!

Midas started up, in a kind of joyful frenzy, and ran about the room, grasping at everything that happened to be in his way. He seized one of the bedposts, and it became immediately a fluted golden pillar. He pulled aside a window-curtain, in order to admit a clear spectacle of the wonders which he was performing; and the tassel grew heavy in his hand—a mass of gold. He took up a book from the table. At his first touch, it assumed the appearance of such a splendidly-bound and gilt-edged volume as one often meets with, now-a-days; but, on running his fingers through the leaves, behold! it was a bundle of thin golden plates, in which all the wisdom of the book had grown illegible. He hurriedly put on his clothes, and was enraptured to see himself in a magnificent suit of gold cloth, which retained its flexibility and softness, although it burdened him a little with its weight. He drew out his handkerchief, which little Marygold had hemmed for him. That was likewise gold, with the dear child's neat and pretty stitches running all along the border, in gold thread!

Somehow or other, this last transformation did not quite please King Midas. He would rather that his little daughter's handiwork should have remained just the same as when she climbed his knee, and put it into his hand.

But it was not worth while to vex himself about a trifle. Midas now took his spectacles from his pocket, and put them on his nose, in order that he might see more distinctly what he was about. In those days, spectacles for common people had not been invented, but were already worn by kings; else, how could Midas have had any? To his great perplexity, however, excellent as the glasses were, he discovered that he could not possibly see through them. But this was the most natural thing in the world; for, on taking them off, the transparent crystals turned out to be plates of yellow metal, and, of course, were worthless as spectacles, though valuable as gold. It struck Midas as rather inconvenient, that, with all his wealth, he could never again be rich enough to own a pair of serviceable spectacles.

"It is no great matter, nevertheless," said he to himself, very philosophically. "We cannot expect any great good, without its being accompanied with some small inconvenience. The Golden Touch is worth the sacrifice of a pair of spectacles, at least, if not of one's very eyesight. My own eyes will serve for ordinary purposes, and little Marygold will soon be old enough to read to me."

Wise King Midas was so exalted by his good fortune, that the palace seemed not sufficiently spacious to contain him. He therefore went down stairs, and smiled, on observing that the balustrade of the staircase became a bar of burnished gold, as his hand passed over it, in his descent. He lifted the doorlatch (it was brass only a moment ago, but golden when his fingers quitted it), and emerged into the garden. Here, as it happened, he found a great number of beautiful roses in full bloom, and others in all the stages of lovely bud and blossom. Very delicious was their fragrance in the morning breeze. Their delicate blush was one of the fairest sights in the world; so gentle, so modest, and so full of sweet tranquillity, did these roses seem to be.

But Midas knew a way to make them far more precious, according to his way of thinking, than roses had ever been before. So he took great pains in going from bush to bush, and exercised his magic touch most indefatigably; until every individual flower and bud, and even the worms at the heart of some of them, were changed to gold. By the time this good work was completed, King Midas was summoned to breakfast; and, as the morning air had given him an excellent appetite, he made haste back to the palace.

What was usually a king's breakfast, in the days of Midas, I really do not know, and cannot stop now to investigate. To the best of my belief, however, on this particular morning, the breakfast consisted of hot cakes, some nice little brook-trout, roasted potatoes, fresh boiled eggs, and coffee, for King Midas himself, and a bowl of bread and milk for his daughter Marygold. At all events, this is a breakfast fit to set before a king; and, whether he had it or not, King Midas could not have had a better.

Little Marygold had not yet made her appearance. Her father ordered her to be called, and, seating himself at table, awaited the child's coming, in order to begin his own breakfast. To do Midas justice, he really loved his daughter, and, loved her so much the more this morning, on account of the good fortune which had befallen him. It was not a great while before he heard her coming along the passage-way, crying bitterly. This circumstance surprised him, because Marygold was one of the cheerfullest little people whom you would see in a summer's day, and hardly shed a thimble-full of tears in a twelve-month. When Midas heard her sobs, he determined to put little Marygold into better spirits, by an agreeable surprise; so, leaning across the table, he touched his daughter's bowl (which was a China one, with pretty figures all around it), and transmuted it to gleaming gold.

Meanwhile, Marygold slowly and disconsolately opened the door, and showed herself with her apron at her eyes, still sobbing as if her heart would break.

"How now, my little lady!" cried Midas. "Pray what is the matter with you, this bright morning?"

Marygold, without taking the apron from her eyes, held out her hand, in which was one of the roses which Midas had so recently transmuted.

"Beautiful!" exclaimed her father. "And what is there in this magnificent golden rose to make you cry?"

"Ah, dear father!" answered the child, as well as her sobs would let her; "it is not beautiful, but the ugliest flower that ever grew! As soon as I was dressed, I ran into the garden to gather some roses for you; because I know you like them, and like them the better when gathered by your little daughter. But, oh dear, dear me! What do you think has happened? Such a misfortune! All the beautiful roses, that smelled so sweetly and had so many lovely blushes, are blighted and spoilt! They are grown quite yellow, as you see this one, and have no longer any fragrance! What can have been the matter with them?"

"Poh, my dear little girl,—pray don't cry about it!" said Midas, who was ashamed to confess that he himself had wrought the change which so greatly afflicted her. "Sit down and eat your bread and milk! You will find it easy enough to exchange a golden rose like that (which will last hundreds of years), for an ordinary one, which would wither in a day.". . .

The child now sat down to table, but was so occupied with her grief for the blighted roses that she did not even notice the wonderful transmutation of her China bowl. Perhaps this was all the better; for Marygold was accustomed to take pleasure in looking at the queer figures, and strange trees and houses, that were painted on the circumference of the bowl; and these ornaments were now entirely lost in the yellow hue of the metal.

Midas, meanwhile, had poured out a cup of coffee; and, as a matter of course, the coffee-pot, whatever metal it may have been when he took it up, was gold when he set it down. He thought to himself, that it was rather an extravagant style of splendor, in a king of his simple habits, to breakfast off a service of gold, and began to be puzzled with the difficulty of keeping his treasures safe. The cupboard and the kitchen would no longer be a secure place of deposit for articles so valuable as golden bowls and coffee-pots.

Amid these thoughts, he lifted a spoonful of coffee to his lips, and, sipping it, was astonished to perceive that the instant his lips touched the liquid, it became molten gold, and, the next moment, hardened into a lump!

"Ha!" exclaimed Midas, rather aghast.

"What is the matter, father?" asked little Marygold, gazing at him, with the tears still standing in her eyes.

"Nothing, child, nothing!" said Midas. "Eat your milk, before it gets quite cold."

He took one of the nice little trouts on his plate, and, by way of experiment, touched its tail with his finger. To his horror, it was immediately transmuted from an admirably-fried brook-trout into a gold fish, though not one of those gold-fishes which people often keep in glass globes, as ornaments for the parlor. No; but it was really a metallic fish, and looked as if it had been very cunningly made by the nicest goldsmith in the world. Its little bones were now golden wires; its fins and tail were thin plates of gold; and there were the marks of the fork in it, and all the delicate, frothy appearance of a nicely fried fish, exactly imitated in metal. A very pretty piece of work, as you may suppose; only King Midas, just at that moment, would much rather have had a real trout in his dish than this elaborate and valuable imitation of one.

"I don't quite see," thought he to himself, "how I am to get any breakfast!"

He took one of the smoking hot cakes, and had scarcely broken it, when, to his cruel mortification, though, a moment before, it had been of the whitest wheat, it assumed a yellow hue of Indian meal.... Almost in despair, he helped himself to a boiled egg, which immediately underwent a change similar to those of the trout and the cake. The egg, indeed, might have been mistaken for one of those which the famous goose, in the story-book, was in the habit of laying; but King Midas was the only goose that had had anything to do with the matter.

"Well, this is a quandary!" thought he, leaning back in his chair, and looking quite enviously at little Marygold, who was now eating her bread and milk with great satisfaction. "Such a costly breakfast before me, and nothing that can be eaten!"

Hoping that, by dint of great despatch, he might avoid what he now felt to be a considerable inconvenience, King Midas next snatched a hot potato, and attempted to cram it into his mouth, and swallow it in a hurry. But the Golden Touch was too nimble for him. He found his mouth full, not of mealy potato, but of solid metal, which so burnt his tongue that he roared aloud, and, jumping up from the table, began to dance and stamp about the room, both with pain and affright.

"Father, dear father!" cried little Marygold, who was a very affectionate child, "pray what is the matter? Have you burnt your mouth?"

"Ah, dear child," groaned Midas, dolefully, "I don't know what is to become of your poor father!"

And, truly, my dear little folks, did you ever hear of such a pitiable case, in all your lives? Here was literally the richest breakfast that could be set before a king, and its very richness made it absolutely good for nothing. The poorest laborer, sitting down to his crust of bread and cup of water, was far better off than King Midas, whose delicate food was really worth its weight in gold. And what was to be done? Already, at breakfast, Midas was excessively hungry. Would he be less so by dinner time? And how ravenous would be his appetite for supper, which must undoubtedly consist of the same sort of indigestible dishes as those now before him! How many days, think you, would he survive a continuance of this rich fare?

These reflections so troubled wise King Midas, that he began to doubt whether, after all, riches are the one desirable thing in the world, or even the most desirable. But this was only a passing thought. So fascinated was Midas with the glitter of the yellow metal, that he would still have refused to give up the Golden Touch for so paltry a consideration as a breakfast. Just imagine what a price for one meal's victuals! It would have been the same as paying millions and millions of money (and as many millions more as would take forever to reckon up) for some fried trout, an egg, a potato, a hot cake, and a cup of coffee!

"It would be quite too dear," thought Midas.

Nevertheless, so great was his hunger, and the perplexity of his situation, that he again groaned aloud, and very grievously too. Our pretty Marygold could endure it no longer. She sat, a moment, gazing at her father, and trying, with all the might of her little wits, to find out what was the matter with him. Then, with a sweet and sorrowful impulse to comfort him, she started from her chair, and running to Midas, threw her arms affectionately about his knees. He bent down and kissed her. He felt that his little daughter's love was worth a thousand times more than he had gained by the Golden Touch.

"My precious, precious Marygold!" cried he.

But Marygold made no answer.

# *Adventures of Huckleberry Finn (Tom Sawyer's Comrade)*

*By Mark Twain*
*Illustrations by E. W. Kemble*

*To see a circus through Huck Finn's eyes is to enjoy Mark Twain's humor at its liveliest.*

I went to the circus, and loafed around the back side till the watchman went by, and then dived in under the tent. I had my twenty-dollar gold piece and some other money, but I reckoned I better save it, because there ain't no telling how soon you are going to need it, away from home and amongst strangers, that way. You can't be too careful. I ain't opposed to spending money on circuses, when there ain't no other way, but there ain't no use in *wasting* it on them.

It was a real bully circus. It was the splendidest sight that ever was, when they all come riding in, two and two, a gentleman and a lady, side by side, the men just in their drawers and under-shirts, and no shoes nor stirrups, and resting their hands on their thighs, easy and comfortable—there must a' been twenty of them—and every lady with a lovely complexion, and perfectly beautiful, and looking just like a gang of real sure-enough queens, and dressed in clothes that cost millions of dollars, and just littered with diamonds. It was a powerful fine sight; I never see anything so lovely. And then one by one they got up and stood, and went a-weaving around the ring so gentle

HE SHED SEVENTEEN SUITS.

and wavy and graceful, the men looking ever so tall and airy and straight, with their heads bobbing and skimming along, away up there under the tent-roof, and every lady's rose-leafy dress flapping soft and silky around her hips, and she looking like the most loveliest parasol.

And then faster and faster they went, all of them dancing, first one foot stuck out in the air and then the other, the horses leaning more and more, and the ring-master going round and round the centre-pole, cracking his whip and shouting "hi!—hi!" and the clown cracking jokes behind him; and by-and-by all hands dropped the reins, and every lady put her knuckles on her hips and every gentleman folded his arms, and then how the horses did lean over and hump themselves! And so, one after the other they all skipped off into the ring, and made the sweetest bow I ever see, and then scampered out, and everybody clapped their hands and went just about wild.

Well, all through the circus they done the most astonishing things; and all the time that clown carried on so it most killed the people. The ring-master couldn't ever say a word to him but he was back at him quick as a wink with the funniest things a body ever said; and how he ever *could* think of so many of them, and so sudden and so pat, was what I couldn't noway understand. Why, I couldn't a thought of them in a year. And by-and-by a drunk man tried to get into the ring—said he wanted to ride; said he could ride as well as anybody that ever was. They argued and tried to keep him out, but he wouldn't listen, and the whole show come to a standstill. Then the people begun to holler at him and make fun of him, and that made him mad, and he began to rip and tear; so that stirred up the people, and a lot of men begun to pile down off of the benches and swarm towards the ring, saying, "Knock him down! throw him out!" and one or two women begun to scream. So, then, the ring-master he made a little speech, and said he hoped there wouldn't be no disturbance, and if the man would promise he wouldn't make no more trouble, he would let him ride, if he thought he could stay on the horse. So everybody laughed and said all right, and the man got on. The minute he was on, the horse begun to rip and tear and jump and cavort around, with two circus men hanging onto his bridle trying to hold him, and the drunk man hanging onto his neck, and his heels flying in the air every jump, and the whole crowd of people standing up shouting and laughing till the tears rolled down. And at last, sure enough, all the circus men could do, the horse broke loose, and away he went like the very nation, round and round the ring, with that sot laying down on him and hanging to his neck, with first one leg hanging most to the ground on one side, and then t'other one on t'other side, and the people just crazy. It warn't funny to me, though; I was all of a tremble to see his danger. But pretty soon he struggled up astraddle and grabbed the bridle, a-reeling this way and that; and the next minute he sprung up, and dropped the bridle and stood! and the horse agoing like a house afire too. He just stood up there, a-sailing around as easy and comfortable as if he warn't ever drunk in his life—and then he begun to pull off his clothes and sling them. He shed them so thick they kind of clogged up the air, and altogether he shed seventeen suits. And then, there he was, slim and handsome, and dressed the gaudiest and prettiest you ever saw, and he lit into that horse with his whip and made him fairly hum—and finally skipped off, and made his bow and danced off to the dressing-room, and everybody just a-howling with pleasure and astonishment.

Then the ring-master he see how he had been fooled, and he was the sickest ring-master you ever see, I reckon. Why, it was one of his own men! He had got up that joke all out of his own head, and never let on to nobody. Well, I felt sheepish enough, to be took in so, but I wouldn't a been in that ring-master's place, not for a thousand dollars. I don't know; there may be bullier circuses than what that one was, but I never struck them yet. Anyways it was plenty good enough for *me*; and wherever I run across it, it can have all of *my* custom, every time.

# *The Twin Heroes: An African Myth*

*Adapted by Alphonso O. Stafford*
*Illustrations by Albert Alex Smith*

*This story is taken from* The Brownies' Book, *a magazine edited for black children by W. E. B. Du Bois, one of the founders of the NAACP.*

In that far-off time when the world was young, there lived in a town of a powerful king, a widow whose name was Isokah, and whose husband, a brave warrior, had fallen in battle.

She had two baby sons, called Mansur and Luembur. They were twins, with bodies round and shapely, the color of dull gold.

At their birth an old man, known for his gift of prophecy, said, "Twins are a gift of Anambia, the Great Spirit, and they have been sent to us for a special work."

Everyone in that town, knowing how true were the sayings of the old man, believed thereafter that the twin babes of Isokah would grow into manhood and become warriors of note and possibly heroes of great renown.

When they were six weeks old, their mother planted in her garden, a short distance apart, two seeds. With great care she watered the earth about and when the seeds sprouted and became tiny plants, her care for them did not cease.

As the years passed, Isokah's two sons grew tall, strong, and pleasing to the eye, like the graceful pine trees around their home. In play, in the hunt, and in deeds of daring, these two boys always took first place among their companions.

Meanwhile, the two plants grew into fine

trees with beautiful spreading foliage. When Mansur and Luembur were old enough to understand, Isokah took each of them to one of the trees, and said,

"This, my son, is your life tree. As it thrives, withers, or dies, so you will grow, be in peril, or perish."

After that day, Mansur and Luembur watched his own tree with increasing interest and felt for it a loving tenderness when resting under its spreading branches during the heat of the day, or in the cool of the evening, while listening to the strange cries in the jungle; or gazing with wonder at the clear sky with its brilliant stars, and the silver crescent changing nightly into a great golden ball.

How happy was Isokah as she watched her boys grow into early manhood, and the life trees thrive in strength and beauty with them.

During this time, Mansur had many strange dreams,—dreams of great perils in the jungle, dreams of different lands, but more often he had visions of Yuah, the daughter of Zambay, who was Old Mother Earth, the first daughter of the first father.

Yuah was said to be beautiful. Her beauty was like the dusk at twilight, when the stars begin to twinkle in the afterglow of the western sky.

One day, after Mansur had passed his twentieth year, he said to his mother, "The time has come for me to marry and I am going in search of Yuah, the daughter of Old Mother Earth."

Though her sorrow was great when she heard these words, Isokah knew that she could not always keep her sons near her. So she called upon Musimu, a wizard of strange powers, and asked him for some magic to help her son, Mansur, in his quest.

When this was given, she returned and gave it to him, saying, "My son, this is your magic. I shall guard your life tree while you are away and Luembur, your brother, will watch over me."

Mansur then put strong arms around his mother's shoulders, bowed his head upon her cheek, and gave her his farewell kiss. Then, taking from her the magic, he touched some grass he had plucked from the ground. One blade was changed into a horn, another into a knife, and still another into a spear.

Before leaving, he called Luembur, saying, "Brother, be ever near mother Isokah, and let no harm befall her."

For days and days Mansur travelled. What a picture of natural beauty met his eye everywhere! How verdant was the foliage of the trees, shrubs, and plants of the African plains and highlands; how sparkling the streams that foamed over rocky beds of granite and sandstone, how beautiful was the coloring of the flowers, how gay was the plumage of the birds, how graceful and striking in size were the animals that fled before him as he pushed his way onward to the land of Zambay, the mother of his desired Yuah. When overcome by hunger, Mansur called upon his magic for food.

At last, the far country of Zambay was reached. Whenever a stranger entered it, he was escorted at once to Zambay, the queen, the all powerful ruler of that land. The usual custom followed, when Mansur was seen striding forward with his spear in hand, horn across shoulder, and knife at side.

Standing near her mother, Yuah saw the stranger,—saw him in his strength and early manhood, so lithe in movement and so fearless in bearing. Straightway her heart warmed to him. How happy was Mansur when he beheld this dream-girl as a reality and saw in her eyes, a look of friendly interest that passed into admiration when he recited the story of his travels and the purpose of his visit.

Three days later, they were married. A fine feast was held, followed by joyous singing and a merry dance. The finest house in the town was given to the bride and groom, where for many months their happiness was complete.

One day, while idling in his new home, Mansur opened the door of a strange room which he had never noticed. In it were many mirrors, each covered so that the glass could not be seen. Calling Yuah, he asked her to remove the covers so that he might examine them. She took him to one, uncovered it, and Mansur immediately saw a perfect likeness of his native town; then to another, and he saw his mother and his brother, Luembur, sitting in peace beneath his life tree. In each mirror he saw something that carried his memory back to his past life and the country of his birth.

Coming to the last mirror, larger than the others, Mansur was filled with a strange foreboding. Yuah did not uncover it. "Why not let me look into it, Yuah?" asked Mansur.

"Because, my beloved one, in it you will see reflected the Land of Never Return—from it none returns who wanders there."

Now this remark made Mansur very curious, and he longed as never before, to see this mirror that could picture so strange a land or mysterious a scene.

"Do let me see it," urged Mansur. Yielding at last to his entreaties, Yuah uncovered the mirror, and her young husband saw reflected therein that dread land of the lower world—that unsought place of cruel King Kalungo, of which all men had heard. Mansur looked in the mirror a long time, then he said,

"I must go there; I must leave you, my dear."

"Nay, you will never return; please do not go, my beloved one," pleaded Yuah.

"Have no fear," answered Mansur. "The magic of Muzimu will be my protection. Should any harm befall me, my twin brother, Luembur, will come to my rescue."

Now this made Yuah cry and she was very, very sad, but her tears did not move Mansur from his desire and his purpose.

In a few hours he had departed for the Land of Never Return.

After travelling many days, Mansur came upon a weird old woman working in the fields. In her eyes, there was mystery; in her presence, there came to him a feeling of awe. Though he knew not then, she was the never sleeping spirit that guarded the secrets of the Land of Never Return.

Approaching her, Mansur said, "My good woman, please show me the road to the land whence no man returns who wanders there."

The old woman, pausing in her work, looked at him as he stood there, so tall and straight. A smile passed over her wrinkled face as she recognized in Mansur one of the true heroes for whose coming she had waited many years.

Much to his surprise, the old woman, after a long and deep gaze, said,

"Mansur, I know you and I shall direct your way, though the task before you is one of peril. Go down that hill to your right, take the narrow path, and avoid the wide one. After an hour's travel, you will come to the dread home of Kalungo, the Land of Never Return. Before reaching his abode, you must pass a fierce dog that guards his gate, fight the great serpent of seven heads within the courtyard, and destroy the mighty crocodile that sleeps in the pool."

These impending dangers did not frighten Mansur. Following the narrow path, he came within a short time to a deep ravine. Through this he walked, head erect, eyes alert, and spear uplifted. Suddenly he observed the outer gate of the Land of Never Return.

By means of his magic, he passed the fierce dog, and after a severe battle he succeeded in destroying the serpent, that seven-headed monster. Near the pool, he saw the mighty crocodile resting on its bank, and rushed forward to strike him. Then, by accident, Mansur's magic fell upon the ground, and immediately he was seized by the crocodile and disappeared within his terrible mouth.

At home, his mother, Isokah, and brother Luembur, noticed with fear that the life tree of Mansur had suddenly withered.

"Mother, my brother is in danger. I must go at once in search of him," cried Luembur.

Rushing to Muzimu, the wizard, Isokah procured some more magic, returned home and gave it to Luembur and besought him to go immediately in search of his twin brother.

As he departed, a great weakness seized her, and supporting herself for awhile against

the trunk of Luembur's life tree, she slowly sank to the ground, with a foreboding that she would never again see her sons.

When Luembur reached the town of Zambay, she was much struck with the resemblance he bore to his brother, and Yuah was overjoyed that he had come to go in search of Mansur. She noticed with pleasure that Luembur also carried the same kind of spear, horn, and knife that Mansur had.

Yuah showed him the magic mirrors, reserving for the last the fateful one that had caused Mansur to depart for the Land of Never Return.

After resting awhile, Luembur continued his journey and, as in the case of his brother, came after many days to the weird old woman working in the fields.

The story of his quest was soon told. After it was finished, she said, "I know you, also, Luembur." She then gave him the same directions.

When he reached the gates of the land of Kalungo, the fierce dog fell before the magic spear of Luembur. Then rushing to the bank of the pool where the mighty crocodile was dozing in the sun, Luembur with one great blow of his spear slew him. Then taking his knife he cut along the under side of the dead crocodile and, strange to state, Mansur jumped out, well and happy.

Swift as the wind, the twin brothers left the gates of the dread Land of Never Return and travelled upward to the place where the weird old woman worked in the field, under the rays of the glinting sun.

When she beheld them, she stood erect, a deeper mystery flashed into her age-old eyes, and in their presence, there returned to the brothers, that same feeling of awe, but now more intense.

Finally she spoke, "Brothers, by slaying the fierce dog, the terrible serpent, and the mighty crocodile, you have released the spirits of the brave, the wise, and the good, who were prisoners in the realm of cruel Kalungo. They may now return to Mother Earth when they desire, and visit the abode of their mortal existence. Your task here below is now finished.

"You, Mansur, shall be Lightning, that mortals may ever see your swift spear as it darts through the clouds; and you, Luembur, shall be Thunder, that mortals may ever hear and know the power of that flashing spear."

With these words, the sleepless spirit of the Land of Never Return touched each of the brothers, and Mansur went to the East and became the swift, darting lightning; and Luembur went to the West and became the loud, pealing thunder.

In the land of Zambay, when Yuah, through her magic mirrors, saw what had happened to the brothers, she cried with much grief. Neither by day nor by night would she be comforted.

At last her mother, Zambay, said in a gentle and sad voice, "My daughter, when your husband, Mansur, and his brother, Luembur, are angry in their home, amid the clouds, and have frightened men and beasts, here in my land, your beauty and your smile will bring them joy. At such times, your body clothed with many colors, will bend and touch me, your Mother Earth. Go hence, and live with them.

With these words, Yuah went away from the home of her mother, and we see her now as the beautiful Rainbow, after the storm clouds of Mansur and Luembur have passed on their way to the home of The All Father, the Great Sky-Spirit, Anambia.

# *The Prince and the Pauper*

*By Mark Twain*
*Illustrations by Harley and F. T. Merrill*

*In this episode the ragged pauper, Tom Canty, a poor boy who has secretly exchanged places with the prince, experiences for the first time the full sense of how it feels to be a royal person.*

## THE RIVER PAGEANT

At nine in the evening the whole vast river-front of the palace was blazing with light. The river itself, as far as the eye could reach citywards, was so thickly covered with watermen's boats and with pleasure-barges, all fringed with colored lanterns, and gently agitated by the waves, that it resembled a glowing and limitless garden of flowers stirred to soft motion by summer winds. The grand terrace of stone steps leading down to the water, spacious enough to mass the army of a German principality upon, was a picture to see, with its ranks of royal halberdiers in polished armor, and its troops of brilliantly costumed servitors flitting up and down, and to and fro, in the hurry of preparation.

Presently a command was given, and immediately all living creatures vanished from the steps. Now the air was heavy with the hush of suspense and expectancy. As far as one's vision could carry, he might see the myriads of people in the boats rise up, and shade their eyes from the glare of lanterns and torches, and gaze toward the palace. A file of forty or fifty state barges drew up to the steps. They were richly gilt, and their lofty prows and sterns were elaborately carved. . . .

The advance-guard of the expected procession now appeared in the great gateway, a troop of halberdiers. They were dressed in striped hose of black and tawny, velvet caps graced at the sides with silver roses, and doublets of murrey and blue cloth. . . . Filing off on the right and left, they formed two long lines, extending from the gateway of the palace to the water's edge. A thick, rayed cloth or carpet was then unfolded, and laid down between them by attendants in the gold-and-crimson liveries of the prince. This done, a flourish of trumpets resounded from within. A lively prelude arose from the musicians on the water; and two ushers with white wands marched with a slow and stately pace from the portal. They were followed by an officer bearing the civic mace, after whom came another carrying the city's sword; then several sergeants of the city guard, in their full accoutrements, and with badges on their sleeves; then the Garter king-at-arms, in his tabard; then several knights of the bath, each with a white lace on his sleeve; then their esquires; then the judges, in their robes of scarlet and coifs; then the lord high chancellor of Eng-

land, in a robe of scarlet, open before, and purfled with minever; then a deputation of aldermen, in their scarlet cloaks; and then the heads of the different civic companies, in their robes of state. Now came twelve French gentlemen, in splendid habiliments, consisting of pourpoints of white damask barred with gold, short mantles of crimson velvet lined with violet taffeta, and carnation-colored *hauts-de-chausses,* and took their way down the steps. They were of the suite of the French ambassador, and were followed by twelve cavaliers of the suite of the Spanish ambassador, clothed in black velvet, unrelieved by any ornament. Following these came several great English nobles with their attendants.

"TOM CANTY STEPPED INTO VIEW."

There was a flourish of trumpets within; and the prince's uncle, the future great Duke of Somerset, emerged from the gateway, arrayed in a "doublet of black cloth-of-gold, and a cloak of crimson satin flowered with gold, and ribanded with nets of silver." He turned, doffed his plumed cap, bent his body in a low reverence, and began to step backward, bowing at each step. A prolonged trumpet-blast followed, and a proclamation, "Way for the high and mighty, the Lord Edward, Prince of Wales!" High aloft on the palace walls a long line of red tongues of flame leaped forth with a thunder-crash; the massed world on the river burst into a mighty roar of welcome; and Tom Canty, the cause and hero of it all, stepped into view, and slightly bowed his princely head.

He was "magnificently habited in a doublet of white satin, with a front-piece of purple cloth-of-tissue, powdered with diamonds, and edged with ermine. Over this he wore a mantle of white cloth-of-gold, pounced with the triple-feather crest, lined with blue satin, set with pearls and precious stones, and fastened with a clasp of brilliants. About his neck hung the order of the Garter, and several princely foreign orders;" and wherever light fell upon him jewels responded with a blinding flash. O Tom Canty, born in a hovel, bred in the gutters of London, familiar with rags and dirt and misery, what a spectacle is this!

# *The King of the Golden River*

*By John Ruskin*
*Illustrations by Richard Doyle*

*In this legend from Styria, in the Austrian Alps, a dwarf king rewards a kind and generous man, having turned his two selfish brothers into black stones.*

When Gluck found that Schwartz did not come back, he was very sorry, and did not know what to do. He had no money, and was obliged to go and hire himself to a goldsmith, who worked him very hard, and gave him very little money. So, after a month, or two, Gluck grew tired, and made up his mind to go and try his fortune with the Golden River. "The little king looked very kind," thought he. "I don't think he will turn me into a black stone." So he went to the priest, and the priest gave him some holy water as soon as he asked for it. Then Gluck took some bread in his basket, and the bottle of water, and set off very early for the mountains.

If the glacier had occasioned a great deal of fatigue to his brothers, it was twenty times worse for him, who was neither so strong nor so practised on the mountains. He had several very bad falls, lost his basket and bread, and was very much frightened at the strange noises under the ice. He lay a long time to rest on the grass, after he had got over, and began to climb the hill just in the hottest part of the day. When he had climbed for an hour, he got dreadfully thirsty, and was going to drink like his brothers, when he saw an old man coming down the path above him, looking very feeble, and leaning on a staff. "My son," said the old man, "I am faint with thirst, give me some of that water." Then Gluck looked at him, and when he saw that he was pale and weary, he gave him the water; "Only pray don't drink it all," said Gluck. But the old man drank a great deal, and gave him back his bottle two-thirds empty. Then he bade him good speed, and Gluck went on again merrily. And the path became easier to his feet, and two or three blades of grass appeared upon it, and some grasshoppers began singing on the bank beside it; and Gluck thought he had never heard such merry singing.

Then he went on for another hour, and the thirst increased on him so that he thought he should be forced to drink. But, as he raised the flask, he saw a little child lying panting by the road-side, and it cried out piteously for water. Then Gluck struggled with himself, and determined to bear the thirst a little longer; and he put the bottle to the child's lips, and it drank it all but a few drops. Then it smiled on him, and got up, and ran down the hill; and Gluck looked after it, till it became as small as a little star, and then turned and began climbing again. And then there were all kinds of sweet flowers growing on the rocks, bright green moss, with pale pink starry flowers, and soft belled gentians, more blue than the sky at its deepest, and pure white transparent lilies. And crimson and purple butterflies darted hither and thither, and the sky sent down such pure light, that Gluck had never felt so happy in his life.

Yet, when he had climbed for another hour, his thirst became intolerable again; and, when he looked at his bottle, he saw that there were only five or six drops left in it, and he could not venture to drink. And, as he was hanging the flask to his belt again, he saw a little dog lying on the rocks, gasping for breath . . . . And Gluck stopped and looked at it, and then at the Golden River, not five hundred yards above him; and he thought of the dwarf's words, "that no one could succeed, except in his first attempt"; and he tried to pass the dog, but it whined so piteously, and Gluck stopped again. "Poor beastie," said Gluck, "it'll be dead when I come down again, if I don't help it." Then he looked closer and closer at it, and its eye turned on him so mournfully, that he could not stand it. "Confound the King and his gold too," said Gluck; and he opened the flask, and poured all the water into the dog's mouth.

The dog sprang up and stood on its hind legs. Its tail disappeared, its ears became long, longer, silky, golden; its nose became very red, its eyes became very twinkling; in three seconds the dog was gone, and before Gluck stood his old acquaintance, the King of the Golden River.

"Thank you," said the monarch; "but don't be frightened, it's all right"; for Gluck showed manifest symptoms of consternation at this unlooked-for reply to his last observation. "Why didn't you come before," continued the dwarf, "instead of sending me those rascally brothers of yours, for me to have the trouble of turning into stones? Very hard stones they make too."

"Oh dear me!" said Gluck, "have you really been so cruel?"

"Cruel!" said the dwarf, "they poured unholy water into my stream: do you suppose I'm going to allow that?"

"Why," said Gluck, "I am sure, sir—your majesty, I mean—they got the water out of the church font."

"Very probably," replied the dwarf; "but," and his countenance grew stern as he spoke, "the water which has been refused to the cry of the weary and dying, is unholy, though it had been blessed by every saint in heaven; and the water which is found in the vessel of mercy is holy, though it had been defiled with corpses."

So saying, the dwarf stooped and plucked a lily that grew at his feet. On its white leaves there hung three drops of clear dew. And the dwarf shook them into the flask which Gluck held in his hand. "Cast these into the river," he said, "and descend on the other side of the mountains into the Treasure Valley. And so good speed."

As he spoke, the figure of the dwarf became indistinct. The playing colours of his robe formed themselves into a prismatic mist of dewy light: he stood for an instant veiled with them as with the belt of a broad rainbow. The colours grew faint, the mist rose into the air; the monarch had evaporated.

And Gluck climbed to the brink of the Golden River, and its waves were as clear as crystal, and as brilliant as the sun. And, when he cast the three drops of dew into the stream, there opened where they fell, a small circular whirlpool, into which the waters descended with a musical noise.

Gluck stood watching it for some time, very much disappointed, because not only the river was not turned into gold, but its waters seemed much diminished in quantity. Yet he obeyed his friend the dwarf, and descended the other side of the mountains, towards the Treasure Valley; and, as he went, he thought he heard the noise of water working its way under the ground. And, when he came in sight of the Treasure Valley, behold, a river, like the Golden River, was springing from a new cleft of the rocks above it, and was flowing in innumerable streams among the dry heaps of red sand.

And as Gluck gazed, fresh grass sprang beside the new streams, and creeping plants grew, and climbed among the moistening soil. Young flowers opened suddenly along the river sides, as stars leap out when twilight is deepening, and thickets of myrtle, and tendrils of vine, cast lengthening shadows over the valley as they grew. And thus the Treasure Valley became a garden again, and the inheritance, which had been lost by cruelty, was regained by love.

And Gluck went, and dwelt in the valley, and the poor were never driven from his door: so that his barns became full of corn, and his house of treasure. And, for him, the river had, according to the dwarf's promise, become a River of Gold.

And, to this day, the inhabitants of the valley point out the place where the three drops of holy dew were cast into the stream, and trace the course of the Golden River under the ground, until it emerges in the Treasure Valley. And at the top of the cataract of the Golden River, are still to be seen two Black Stones, round which the waters howl mournfully every day at sunset; and these stones are still called by the people of the valley, The Black Brothers.

# *The Heroes; or, Greek Fairy Tales for My Children*

---

*By Charles Kingsley*
*Illustrations by W. Russell Flint*

*In this retelling of the story of Jason, we learn what made him set out in quest of the Golden Fleece. Cheiron, the wise centaur, raised him since his father was driven from the throne of Iolcos, and now Jason is ready to return to his homeland and reclaim it.*

## HOW JASON LOST HIS SANDAL IN ANAUROS

And ten years came and went, and Jason was grown to be a mighty man. Some of his fellows were gone, and some were growing up by his side. Asklepios was gone into Peloponnese to work his wondrous cures on men; and some say he used to raise the dead to life. And Heracles was gone to Thebes to fulfil those famous labours which have become a proverb among men. And Peleus had married a sea-nymph, and his wedding is famous to this day. And Æneas was gone home to Troy, and many a noble tale you will read of him, and of all the other gallant heroes, the scholars of Cheiron the just. And it happened on a day that Jason stood on the mountain, and looked north and south and east and west; and Cheiron [the centaur] stood by him and watched him, for he knew that the time was come.

And Jason looked and saw the plains of Thessaly, where the Lapithai breed their horses; and the lake of Boibe, and the stream which runs northward to Peneus and Tempe; and he looked north, and saw the mountain wall which guards the Magnesian shore; Olympus, the seat of the Immortals, and Ossa, and Pelion, where he stood. Then he looked east and saw the bright blue sea, which stretched away for ever toward the dawn. Then he looked south, and saw a pleasant land, with white-walled towns and farms, nestling along the shore of a land-locked bay, while the smoke rose blue among the trees; and he knew it for the bay of Pagasai, and the rich lowlands of Haemonia, and Iolcos by the sea.

Then he sighed, and asked, "Is it true what the heroes tell me—that I am heir of that fair land?"

"And what good would it be to you, Jason, if you were heir of that fair land?"

"I would take it and keep it."

"A strong man has taken it and kept it long. Are you stronger than Pelias the terrible?"

"I can try my strength with his," said Jason; but Cheiron sighed, and said:

"You have many a danger to go through before you rule in Iolcos by the sea: many a danger and many a woe; and strange troubles in strange lands, such as man never saw before."

"The happier I," said Jason, "to see what man never saw before."

And Cheiron sighed again, and said, "The eaglet must leave the nest when it is fledged. Will you go to Iolcos by the sea? Then promise me two things before you go."

Jason promised, and Cheiron answered, "Speak harshly to no soul whom you may meet, and stand by the word which you shall speak."

Jason wondered why Cheiron asked this of him; but he knew that the centaur was a prophet, and saw things long before they came. So he promised, and leapt down the mountain, to take his fortune like a man.

He went down through the arbutus thickets, and across the downs of thyme, till he came to the vineyard walls, and the pomegranates and the olives in the glen; and among the olives roared Anauros, all foaming with a summer flood.

And on the bank of Anauros sat a woman, all wrinkled, grey, and old; her head shook palsied on her breast, and her hands shook palsied on her knees; and when she saw Jason, she spoke whining, "Who will carry me across the flood?"

Jason was bold and hasty, and was just going to leap into the flood: and yet he thought twice before he leapt, so loud roared the torrent down, all brown from the mountain rains, and silver-veined with melting snow; while underneath he could hear the boulders rumbling like the tramp of horsemen or the roll of wheels, as they ground along the narrow channel, and shook the rocks on which he stood.

But the old woman whined all the more, "I am weak and old, fair youth. For Hera's sake, carry me over the torrent."

And Jason was going to answer her scornfully, when Cheiron's words came to his mind.

So he said, "For Hera's sake, the Queen of the Immortals on Olympus, I will carry you over the torrent, unless we both are drowned midway."

Then the old dame leapt upon his back, as nimbly as a goat; and Jason staggered in, wondering; and the first step was up to his knees.

The first step was up to his knees, and the second step was up to his waist; and the stones rolled about his feet, and his feet slipped about the stones; so he went on staggering and panting, while the old woman cried from off his back: "Fool, you have wet my mantle! Do you make game of poor old souls like me?"

Jason had half a mind to drop her, and let her get through the torrent by herself; but Cheiron's words were in his mind, and he said only, "Patience, mother; the best horse may stumble some day."

At last he staggered to the shore, and set her down upon the bank; and a strong man he needed to have been, or that wild water he never would have crossed.

He lay panting awhile upon the bank, and then leapt up to go upon his journey; but he

cast one look at the old woman, for he thought, "She should thank me once at least."

And as he looked, she grew fairer than all women, and taller than all men on earth; and her garments shone like the summer sea, and her jewels like the stars of heaven; and over her forehead was a veil, woven of the golden clouds of sunset; and through the veil she looked down on him, with great soft heifer's eyes; with great eyes, mild and awful, which filled all the glen with light.

And Jason fell upon his knees, and hid his face between his hands.

And she spoke, "I am the Queen of Olympus, Hera the wife of Zeus. As thou hast done to me, so will I do to thee. Call on me in the hour of need, and try if the Immortals can forget."

And when Jason looked up, she rose from off the earth, like a pillar of tall white cloud, and floated away across the mountain peaks, toward Olympus the holy hill.

Then a great fear fell on Jason: but after a while he grew light of heart; and he blessed old Cheiron, and said, "Surely the centaur is a prophet, and guessed what would come to pass, when he bade me speak harshly to no soul whom I might meet."

Then he went down toward Iolcos; and as he walked he found that he had lost one of his sandals in the flood.

And as he went through the streets, the people came out to look at him, so tall and fair was he; but some of the elders whispered together; and at last one of them stopped Jason, and called to him, "Fair lad, who are you, and whence come you; and what is your errand in the town?"

"My name, good father, is Jason, and I come from Pelion up above; and my errand is to Pelias your king; tell me then where his palace is."

But the old man started, and grew pale, and said, "Do you not know the oracle, my son, that you go so boldly through the town with but one sandal on?"

"I am a stranger here, and know of no oracle; but what of my one sandal? I lost the other in Anauros, while I was struggling with the flood."

Then the old man looked back to his companions; and one sighed, and another smiled; at last he said, "I will tell you, lest you rush upon your ruin unawares. The oracle in Delphi has said that a man wearing one sandal should take the kingdom from Pelias, and keep it for himself. Therefore beware how you go up to his palace, for he is the fiercest and most cunning of all kings."

Then Jason laughed a great laugh, like a war-horse in his pride. "Good news, good father, both for you and me. For that very end I came into the town."

Then he strode on toward the palace of Pelias, while all the people wondered at his bearing.

And he stood in the doorway and cried, "Come out, come out, Pelias the valiant, and fight for your kingdom like a man."

Pelias came out wondering, and "Who are you, bold youth?" he cried.

"I am Jason, the son of Æson, the heir of all this land."

Then Pelias lifted up his hands and eyes, and wept, or seemed to weep; and blessed the heavens which had brought his nephew to him, never to leave him more. "For," said he, "I have but three daughters, and no son to be my heir. You shall be my heir then, and rule the kingdom after me, and marry whichsoever of my daughters you shall choose; though a sad kingdom you will find it, and whosoever rules it a miserable man. But come in, come in, and feast."

So he drew Jason in, whether he would or not, and spoke to him so lovingly and feasted him so well, that Jason's anger passed; and after supper his three cousins came into the hall, and Jason thought that he should like well enough to have one of them for his wife.

But at last he said to Pelias, "Why do you look so sad, my uncle? And what did you mean just now when you said that this was a doleful kingdom, and its ruler a miserable man?"

Then Pelias sighed heavily again and again and again, like a man who had to tell some dreadful story, and was afraid to begin; but at last: "For seven long years and more have I never known a quiet night; and no more will he who comes after me, till the Golden Fleece be brought home."

Then he told Jason the story of Phrixus, and of the Golden Fleece; and told him, too, which was a lie, that Phrixus' spirit tormented him, calling to him day and night. And his daughters came, and told the same tale—for their father had taught them their parts—and wept, and said, "Oh who will bring home the Golden Fleece, that our uncle's spirit may rest; and that we may have rest also, whom he never lets sleep in peace?"

Jason sat awhile, sad and silent; for he had often heard of that Golden Fleece; but he looked on it as a thing hopeless and impossible for any mortal man to win it.

But when Pelias saw him silent, he began to talk of other things, and courted Jason more and more, speaking to him as if he was certain to be his heir, and asking his advice about the kingdom; till Jason, who was young and simple, could not help saying to himself, "Surely he is not the dark man whom people call him. Yet why did he drive my father out?" And he asked Pelias boldly, "Men say that you are terrible, and a man of blood; but I find you a kind and hospitable man; and as you are to me, so will I be to you. Yet why did you drive my father out?"

Pelias smiled, and sighed. "Men have slandered me in that, as in all things. Your father was growing old and weary, and he gave the kingdom up to me of his own will. You shall see him to-morrow, and ask him; and he will tell you the same."

Jason's heart leapt in him when he heard that he was to see his father; and he believed all that Pelias said, forgetting that his father might not dare to tell the truth.

"One thing more there is," said Pelias, "on which I need your advice; for, though you are young, I see in you a wisdom beyond your years. There is one neighbour of mine, whom I dread more than all men on earth. I am stronger than he now, and can command him; but I know that if he stay among us, he will work my ruin in the end. Can you give me a plan, Jason, by which I can rid myself of that man?"

After awhile Jason answered, half laughing, "Were I you, I would send him to fetch the same Golden Fleece; for if he once set forth after it you would never be troubled with him more."

And at that a bitter smile came across Pelias' lips, and a flash of wicked joy into his eyes; and Jason saw it, and started; and over his mind came the warning of the old man, and his own one sandal, and the oracle, and he saw that he was taken in a trap.

But Pelias only answered gently, "My son, he shall be sent forthwith."

"You mean me?" cried Jason, starting up, "because I came here with one sandal?" And he lifted his fist angrily, while Pelias stood up to him like a wolf at bay; and whether of the two was the stronger and the fiercer it would be hard to tell.

But after a moment Pelias spoke gently, "Why then so rash, my son? You, and not I, have said what is said; why blame me for what I have not done? Had you bid me love the man of whom I spoke, and make him my son-in-law and heir, I would have obeyed you; and what if I obey you now, and send the man to win himself immortal fame? I have not harmed you, or him. One thing at least I know, that he will go, and that gladly; for he has a hero's heart within him, loving glory, and scorning to break the word which he has given."

Jason saw that he was entrapped; but his second promise to Cheiron came into his mind, and he thought, "What if the centaur were a prophet in that also, and meant that I should win the fleece!" Then he cried aloud: "You have well spoken, cunning uncle of mine! I love glory, and I dare to keep my word. I will go and fetch this Golden Fleece. Promise me but this in return, and keep your word as I keep mine. Treat my father lovingly while I am gone, for the sake of the all-seeing Zeus; and give me up the kingdom for my own on the day that I bring back the Golden Fleece."

Then Pelias looked at him and almost loved him, in the midst of all his hate; and said, "I promise, and I will perform. It will be no shame to give up my kingdom to the man who wins that fleece."

Then they swore a great oath between them; and afterwards both went in, and lay down to sleep.

But Jason could not sleep for thinking of his mighty oath, and how he was to fulfil it, all alone, and without wealth or friends. So he tossed a long time upon his bed, and thought of this plan and of that; and sometimes Phrixus seemed to call him, in a thin voice, faint and low, as if it came from far across the sea, "Let me come home to my fathers and have rest." And sometimes he seemed to see the eyes of Hera, and to hear her words again: "Call on me in the hour of need, and see if the Immortals can forget."

# *Treasure Island*

*By Robert Louis Stevenson*
*Illustrations by N. C. Wyeth*

*In this scene from the novel, young Jim Hawkins and the old pirate Long John Silver enter the cave that holds the treasure they have pursued over the years in the ship* Hispaniola.

A gentle slope ran up from the beach to the entrance of the cave. At the top, the squire met us. To me he was cordial and kind, saying nothing of my escapade, either in the way of blame or praise. At Silver's polite salute he somewhat flushed.

"John Silver," he said, "you're a prodigious villain and impostor—a monstrous impostor, sir. I am told I am not to prosecute you. Well, then, I will not. But the dead men, sir, hang about your neck like mill-stones."

"Thank you kindly, sir," replied Long John, again saluting.

"I dare you to thank me!" cried the squire. "It is a gross dereliction of my duty. Stand back."

And thereupon we all entered the cave. It was a large, airy place, with a little spring and a pool of clear water, overhung with ferns. The floor was sand. Before a big fire lay Captain Smollett; and in a far corner, only duskily flickered over by the blaze, I beheld great heaps of coin and quadrilaterals built of bars of gold. That was Flint's treasure that we had come so far to seek, and that had cost already the lives of seventeen men from the *Hispaniola*. How many it had cost in the amassing, what blood and sorrow, what good ships scuttled on the deep, what brave men walking the plank blindfold, what shot of cannon, what shame and lies and cruelty, perhaps no man alive could tell. Yet there were still three upon that island—Silver, and old Morgan, and Ben Gunn—who had each taken his share in these crimes, as each had hoped in vain to share in the reward.

"Come in, Jim," said the captain. "You're a good boy in your line, Jim; but I don't think you and me'll go to sea again. You're too much of the born favourite for me. Is that you, John Silver? What brings you here, man?"

"Come back to my dooty, sir," returned Silver.

"Ah!" said the captain; and that was all he said.

What a supper I had of it that night, with all my friends around me; and what a meal it was, with Ben Gunn's salted goat, and some delicacies and a bottle of old wine from the *Hispaniola*. Never, I am sure, were people gayer or happier. And there was Silver, sitting back almost out of the firelight, but eating heartily, prompt to spring forward when anything was wanted, even joining quietly in our laughter—the same bland, polite, obsequious seaman of the voyage out.

# *Songs of Innocence*

*By William Blake*
*Illustrations by Geraldine Morris*

*Written by an adult, these poems convey the image of the world in a childlike way.*

Piping down the valleys wild,
   Piping songs of pleasant glee,
On a cloud I saw a child,
   And he laughing said to me:

"Pipe a song about a lamb!"
   So I piped with merry cheer.
"Piper, pipe that song again;"
   So I piped: he wept to hear.

"Drop thy pipe, thy happy pipe;
   Sing thy songs of happy cheer!"
So I sang the same again,
   While he wept with joy to hear.

"Piper, sit thee down and write
   In a book that all may read;"
So he vanished from my sight;
   And I plucked a hollow reed,

And I made a rural pen,
   And I stained the water clear,
And I wrote my happy songs
   Every child may joy to hear.

When the voices of children are heard on the hill.

# *Tom Brown at Oxford*

*By Thomas Hughes*

*A sequel to* Tom Brown's School Days, *Hughes's classic story of Victorian school life, this book rounds out the eyewitness account of the education of a young English gentleman in the middle of the last century. Here is Tom's first letter from college, an enthusiastic description of life at Oxford—with perhaps a tiny hint of homesickness at the end.*

"My dear Geordie,

"According to promise, I write to tell you how I get on up here, and what sort of a place Oxford is. Of course, I don't know much about it yet, having been only up some two weeks; but you shall have my first impressions.

"Well, first and foremost, it's an awfully idle place; at any rate, for us freshmen. Fancy now. I am in twelve lectures a week of an hour each—Greek testament, first book of Herodotus, second Æneid, and first book of Euclid! There's a treat! Two hours a day; all over by twelve, or one at the latest; and no extra work at all, in the shape of copies of verses, themes, or other exercises.

"I think sometimes I'm back in the lower fifth; for we don't get through more than we used to do there; and if you were to hear the men construe, it would make your hair stand on end. Where on earth can they have come from? unless they blunder on purpose, as I often think. Of course, I never look at a lecture before I go in, I know it all nearly by heart, so it would be a sheer waste of time. I hope I shall take to reading something or other by myself; but you know I never was much of a hand at sapping, and, for the present, the light work suits me well enough, for there's plenty to see and learn about in this place.

"We keep very gentlemanly hours. Chapel every morning at eight, and evening at seven. You must attend once a day, and twice on Sundays—at least, that's the rule of our college—and be in gates by twelve o'clock at night. Besides which, if you're a decently steady fellow, you ought to dine in hall perhaps four days a week. Hall is at five o'clock. And now you have the sum total. All the rest of your time you may just do what you like with.

"So much for our work and hours. Now for the place. Well, it's a grand old place, certainly; and I dare say, if a fellow goes straight in it, and gets creditably through his three years, he may end by loving it as much as we do the old school-house and quadrangle at Rugby. Our college is a fair specimen: a venerable old front of crumbling stone fronting the street, into which two or three other colleges look also. Over the gateway is a large room, where the college examinations go on, when there are any; and, as you enter, you pass the porter's lodge, where resides our janitor, a bustling little man, with a pot belly, whose business it is to put down the time at which the men come in at night, and to keep all discommonsed tradesmen, stray dogs, and bad characters generally, out of the college.

"The large quadrangle into which you come first, is bigger than ours at Rugby, and a much more solemn and sleepy sort of a place, with its little gables and old mullioned windows. One side is occupied by the hall and chapel; the principal's house takes up half another side; and the rest is divided into staircases, on each of which are six or eight sets of rooms, inhabited by us undergraduates, with here and there a tutor or fellow dropped down amongst us (in the first-floor rooms, of course), not exactly to keep order, but to act as a sort of ballast. This quadrangle is the show part of the college, and is generally respectable and quiet, which is a good deal more than can be said for the inner quadrangle, which you get at through a passage leading out of the other. The rooms ain't half so large or good in the inner quad; and here's where all we freshmen live, besides a lot of the older undergraduates who don't care to change their rooms. Only one tutor has rooms here; and I should think, if he's a reading man, it won't be long before he clears out; for all sorts of high jinks go on on the grass plot, and the row on the staircases is often as bad, and not half so respectable, as it used to be in the middle passage in the last week of the half year.

"My rooms are what they call garrets, right up in the roof, with a commanding view of college tiles and chimney pots, and of houses at the back. No end of cats, both college Toms and strangers haunt the neighbourhood, and I am rapidly learning cat-talk from them; but I'm not going to stand it,—I don't want to know cat-talk. The college Toms are protected by the statutes, I believe; but I'm going to buy an air-gun for the benefit of the strangers. My rooms are pleasant enough, at the top of the kitchen staircase, and separated from all mankind by a great, iron-clamped, outer door, my oak, which I sport when I go out or want to be quiet; sitting-room eighteen by twelve, bed-room twelve by eight, and a little cupboard for the scout.

"Ah, Geordie, the scout is an institution! Fancy me waited upon and valeted by a stout party in black, of quiet, gentlemanly manners, like the benevolent father in a comedy. He takes the deepest interest in all my possessions and proceedings, and is evidently used to good society, to judge by the amount of crockery and glass, wines, liquors, and grocery, which he thinks indispensable for my due establishment. He has also been good enough to recommend to me many tradesmen who are ready to supply these articles in any quantities; each of whom has been here already a dozen times, cap in hand, and vowing that it is quite immaterial when I pay,—which is very kind of them; but, with the highest respect for friend Perkins (my scout) and his obliging friends, I shall make some inquiries before "letting in" with any of them. He waits on me in hall, where we go in full fig of cap and gown at five, and get very good dinners, and cheap enough. It is rather a fine old room, with a good, arched, black oak ceiling and high paneling, hung round with pictures of old swells, bishops and lords chiefly, who have endowed the college in some way, or at least have fed here in times gone by, and for whom, "caeterisque benefactoribus nostris," we daily give thanks in a long Latin grace, which one of the undergraduates (I think it must be) goes and rattles out at the end of the high table, and then comes down again from the dais to his own place. No one feeds at the high table except the dons and the gentlemen-commoners, who are undergraduates in velvet caps and silk gowns. Why they wear these instead of cloth and serge I haven't yet made out,—I believe it is because they pay double fees; but they seem uncommonly wretched up at the high table, and I should think would sooner pay double to come to the other end of the hall.

"The chapel is a quaint little place, about the size of the chancel of Lutterworth Church. It just holds us all comfortably. The attendance is regular enough, but I don't think the men care about it a bit in general. Several I can see bring in Euclids, and other lecture books, and the service is gone through at a great pace. I couldn't think at first why some of the men seemed so uncomfortable and stiff about the legs at the morning service, but I find that they are the hunting set, and come in with pea-coats over their pinks, and trousers over their leather breeches and top-boots; which accounts for it. There are a few others who seem very devout, and bow a good deal, and turn towards the altar at different parts of the service. These are of the Oxford Highchurch school, I believe; but I shall soon find out more about them. On the whole, I feel less at home at present, I am sorry to say, in the chapel, than anywhere else.

"I was very nearly forgetting a great institution of the college, which is the buttery-hatch, just opposite the hall-door. Here abides the fat old butler (all the servants at St. Ambrose's are portly), and serves out limited bread, butter, and cheese, and unlimited beer brewed by himself, for an hour in the morning, at noon, and again at supper-time. Your scout always fetches you a pint or so on each occasion, in case you should want it, and if you don't, it falls to him; but I can't say that my fellow gets much, for I am naturally a thirsty soul, and cannot often resist the malt myself, coming up, as it does, fresh and cool, in one of the silver tankards, of which we seem to have an endless supply.

"I spent a day or two in the first week, before I got shaken down into my place here, in going round and seeing the other colleges, and finding out what great men had been at each (one got a taste for that sort of work from the Doctor, and I'd nothing else to do). Well, I never was more interested: fancy ferreting out Wycliffe, the Black Prince, our friend Sir Walter Raleigh, Pym, Hampden, Laud, Ireton, Butler, and Addison, in one afternoon. I walked about two inches taller in my trencher cap after it. Perhaps I may be going to make dear friends with some fellow who will change the history of England. Why shouldn't I? There must have been freshmen once who were chums of Wycliffe of Queen's, or Raleigh of Oriel. I mooned up and down the High-street, staring at all the young faces in caps, and wondering which of them would turn out great generals, or statesmen, or poets. Some of them will, of course, for there must be a dozen at least, I should think, in every generation of undergraduates, who will have a good deal to say to the ruling and guiding of the British nation before they die.

"But, after all, the river is the feature of Oxford, to my mind; a glorious stream, not five minutes' walk from the colleges, broad enough in most places for three boats to row abreast. I expect I shall take to boating furiously: I have been down the river three or four times already with some other freshmen, and it is glorious exercise; that I can see, though we bungle and cut crabs desperately at present.

"Here's a long yarn I'm spinning for you; and I dare say after all you'll say it tells you nothing, and you'd rather have twenty lines about the men, and what they're thinking about, and the meaning and inner life of the place, and all that. Patience, patience! I don't know anything about it myself yet, and have only had time to look at the shell, which is a very handsome and stately affair; you shall have the kernel, if I ever get at it, in due time.

"And now write me a long letter directly, and tell me about the Doctor, and who are in the Sixth, and how the house goes on, and what sort of an eleven there'll be, and what you are all doing and thinking about. Come up here and try for a scholarship; I'll take you in and show you the lions. Remember me to all old friends. —Ever yours affectionately,

T.B."

# *Bibliography*


Jacob Abbott
*Rollo Learning to Read*
Boston: Phillips, Sampson, & Co. [1855]
General Research Division

*The Adventures of Bob the Squirrel*
New York: Illman & Pilbrow [c.1830]
Rare Books and Manuscripts Division

*Aesop's Fables* [in Greek]
Illuminated manuscript, Florence, c. 1500
Spencer Collection

*Aesop's Fables* [in English, French, and Latin]
Illustrated by Francis Barlow
London: Godbid, 1666
Spencer Collection

Aesop's Fables: see also *Fables of Aesop* and The Reverend Thomas James

John Aikin
*The Farmyard Journal*
Cooperstown, N.Y.: H. & E. Phinney, 1828
Rare Books and Manuscripts Division

Louisa M. Alcott
*Lulu's Library*, 3 vols.
Boston: Roberts Bros., 1886–1901
General Research Division

*Animals in Costume*
Philadelphia: W.P. Hazard [c. 1850]
Arents Collections

Daisy Ashford
*The Young Visiters: or, Mr. Salteenas Plan* [sic]
London: Chatto & Windus [1919]
Berg Collection

*Baa Baa Black Sheep*
Illustrated by E. Caldwell
London: Marcus Ward & Co. [c.1900]
Spencer Collection

Anna Letitia Barbauld
[Mrs. Barbauld's] *Lessons for Children from Three to Four Years Old,* two parts
London: J. Johnson, 1788–91
Arents Collections

James M. Barrie
*Peter and Wendy*
Illustrated by F. D. Bedford
London: Hodder & Stoughton, 1911
Arents Collections

L. Frank Baum
*The Wonderful Wizard of Oz*
Illustrated by W. W. Denslow
Chicago and New York: G.M. Hill, 1900
Arents Collections

Charles H. Bennett
*The Stories that Little Breeches Told: and the Pictures which Charles Bennett Drew for Them*
London: Sampson Low, Son, and Co., 1863
General Research Division

Thomas Bewick
*A Cabinet of Natural History: Containing Pretty Pictures of Birds, Animals, Fishes, Reptiles, Serpents & Insects*
Illustrated by the author
Alnwick: T. Bewick, 1809
Arents Collections

William Blake
*Songs of Innocence*
Illustrated by Geraldine Morris
London and New York: John Lane, 1902
General Research Division

*The Book of Riddles*: see *Pastimes for the Parlour: The Book of Riddles*

Hablôt K. Browne
*A Pictorial Alphabet*
Manuscript, c.1860
Spencer Collection

*The Brownies' Book:* see W. E. B. Du Bois, ed.

Robert Browning
*The Pied Piper of Hamelin*
Illustrated by Arthur Rackham
London: G.G. Harrap & Co., 1934
General Research Division

Gelett Burgess
*Goop Tales*
Illustrated by the author
New York: F.A. Stokes Co. [c.1904]
General Research Division

Wilhelm Busch
*Jack Huckaback*
Illustrated by the author
New York: Stroefer and Kirchner, 1876
Central Children's Room, Donnell Library Center

R. Caldecott
*Hey Diddle Diddle and Baby Bunting*
Illustrated by the author
London: G. Routledge & Sons [c.1885]
Arents Collections

Samuel Clemens [Mark Twain]
*Adventures of Huckleberry Finn (Tom Sawyer's Comrade)*
Illustrated by E. W. Kemble
New York: C.L. Webster, 1885
Arents Collections

———.
*The Prince and the Pauper: A Tale for Young People of All Ages*
Illustrated by Harley and F.T. Merrill
London: Chatto and Windus, 1881
Rare Books and Manuscripts Division

Palmer Cox
*The Brownies: Their Book*
Illustrated by the author
New York: The Century Co. [c.1887]
Central Children's Room, Donnell Library Center

George Cruikshank
*Fairy Library*
Illustrated by the author
London: D. Bogue, 1853
Arents Collections

Countee Cullen
*The Lost Zoo: A Rhyme for the Young, But Not Too Young*
Illustrated by Charles Sebree
New York and London: Harper & Brothers [c.1940]
Schomburg Center

James Daugherty
*Andy and the Lion*
Illustrated by the author
New York: Viking, 1938
Spencer Collection

Walter de la Mare
*Peacock Pie*
Illustrated by W. Heath Robinson
London: Constable and Co. [1916]
General Research Division

Maurice Denis
*Premiers Paysages* [in French]
Illustrated by the author
Paris: H. Laurens, 1926
Spencer Collection

W. W. Denslow and Dudley A. Bragdon
*Billy Bounce*
Illustrated by W. W. Denslow
New York: G.W. Dillingham Co. [1906]
General Research Division

Catherine Ann Dorset
*The Peacock "At Home"; or, Grand Assemblage of Birds*
London: J. Harris, 1807
Rare Books and Manuscripts Division

W.E.B. Du Bois, ed.
*The Brownies' Book* [a monthly magazine for children]
New York: Du Bois and Dill, Jan. 1920 to Dec. 1921
Schomburg Center

William Pène du Bois
*Giant Otto*
Illustrated by the author
New York: Viking, 1936
Central Children's Room, Donnell Library Center

*Fables of Aesop According to Sir Roger L'Estrange*
Illustrated by Alexander Calder
Paris: Harrison, 1931
Spencer Collection

Eugene Field
*In Wink-A-Way Land*
Chicago: M.A. Donohue and Co. [1905]
General Research Division

Anatole France
*Filles et garçons: Scènes de la ville et des champs* [in French]
Illustrated by Maurice Boutet de Monvel
Paris: Hachette, 1915
Spencer Collection

Gerald Friedlander, translator and adaptor
*The Jewish Fairy Book*
Great Neck, N.Y.: Core, 1977
Jewish Division

A.B. Frost
*Stuff and Nonsense*
Illustrated by the author
New York: C. Scribner's Sons, 1884
Spencer Collection

Wanda Ga'g
*Wanda Ga'g's Story Book*
Illustrated by the author
New York: Coward–McCann, 1932
Central Children's Room, Donnell Library Center

Kenneth Grahame
*The Wind in the Willows*
Illustrated by Ernest H. Shepard
New York: C. Scribner's Sons, 1933
General Research Division

Kate Greenaway
*Mother Goose; or, The Old Nursery Rhymes*
Manuscript, c. 1880
Arents Collections

Jacob and Wilhelm Grimm
*The Fairy Tales of the Brothers Grimm*
Illustrated by Arthur Rackham
London: Macmillan, 1921
Spencer Collection

Ernest Griset
*Griset's Grotesques; or, Jokes Drawn on Wood, with Rhymes by Tom Hood*
Illustrated by the author
Boston: Roberts, 1867
General Research Division

Johnny Gruelle
*Raggedy Andy Stories*
Joliet, Ill.: The P.F. Volland Co. [c.1920]
General Research Division

Nathaniel Hawthorne
*A Wonder-Book for Girls and Boys*
Illustrated by Baker after Hammatt Billings
Boston: Ticknor, Reed, and Fields, 1852
Rare Books and Manuscripts Division

Lafcadio Hearn
*Japanese Fairy Tales*
Tokyo: Hasegawa [c. 1895]
Arents Collections

Mrs. T.K. Hervey
*Juvenile Calendar and Zodiac of Flowers*
Illustrated by Richard Doyle
London: A. Hall, Virtue and Co., 1850
General Research Division

*The History of an Apple Pie*
New York: Turner and Fisher [c.1840]
Rare Books and Manuscripts Division

Heinrich Hoffmann-Donner
*The English Struwwelpeter; or, Pretty Stories and Funny Pictures for Little Children*
Leipzig: Volckmar, 1848
Spencer Collection

Thomas Hughes
*Tom Brown at Oxford*
Cambridge and London: Macmillan & Co., 1861
Arents Collections

*Humpty Dumpty*
London: 1843
Central Children's Room, Donnell Library Center

The Reverend Thomas James
*Aesop's Fables: A New Version*
Illustrated by John Tenniel
London: J. Murray, 1848
Spencer Collection

Charles Kingsley
*The Heroes; or Greek Fairy Tales for My Children*
Illustrated by W. Russell Flint
London: P.L. Warner, 1912
Rare Books and Manuscripts Division

———.
*The Water-Babies: Fairy Tale for a Land-Baby*
Illustrated by J. Noel Paton
Boston: Burnham, 1864
General Research Division

Rudyard Kipling
*Just So Stories for Little Children*
Illustrated by the author
London: Macmillan, 1902
Berg Collection

Edouard Laboulaye
*Laboulaye's Fairy Book*
Illustrated by Yan Dargent
New York: Harper & Bros., 1866
General Research Division

Andrew Lang, ed.
*The Red Fairy Book*
Illustrated by H.J. Ford and Lancelot Speed
London: Longmans, Green, and Co., 1895
General Research Division

Edward Lear
*A Book of Nonsense*
Illustrated by the author
London: McLean, 1846
Arents Collections

El Lissitsky
[About two squares, in Russian]
Berlin: Verlag Skythen, 1922
Spencer Collection

Carlo Lorenzini [C. Collodi]
*Le Avventure di Pinocchio* [in Italian]
Florence: F. Paggi, 1883
Rare Books and Manuscripts Division

George MacDonald
*At the Back of the North Wind*
Illustrated by Jessie Willcox Smith
Philadelphia: D. McKay, 1919
General Research Division

Mark Merriwell [pseud.], ed.
*My Own Treasury: A Gift Book for Boys and Girls*
New York: Wiley and Putnam, 1847
Rare Books and Manuscripts Division

Anthony Reubens Montalba, ed.
*Fairy Tales from All Nations*
Illustrated by Richard Doyle
New York: Harper and Bros., 1850
General Research Division

Clement Clarke Moore
*A Visit from St. Nicholas*
Illustrated by Boyd
New York: Spalding and Shepard, 1849
Rare Books and Manuscripts Division

Miriam Morton, ed.
*A Harvest of Russian Children's Literature*
Berkeley and Los Angeles: University of California Press, 1967
Slavonic Division

Charles Nodier
*The Woodcutter's Dog*
Illustrated by Claud Lovat Fraser
London: D. O'Connor, 1921
Rare Books and Manuscripts Division

*Old Mother Hubbard*
New York: McLoughlin Bros. [c.1875]
Arents Collections

*Pastimes for the Parlour: The Book of Riddles, Containing Charades, Enigmas, Conundrums, Rebuses, Puzzles, Anagrams, Acting Charades, Acting Proverbs, &c.*
London: Darton and Co., 1851
General Research Division

Charles Perrault
*Contes* [in French]
Illustrated by Gustave Doré
Paris: J. Hetzel, 1869
General Research Division

*The Picture Riddler*
Boston: Munroe and Francis [c.1830]
Rare Books and Manuscripts Division

Alexander Pushkin
*The Golden Cockerel*
Illustrated by Ivan Bilibin
New York: I. Obolensky, 1962
Slavonic Division

Howard Pyle
*The Merry Adventures of Robin Hood*
Illustrated by the author
New York: C. Scribner's Sons, 1883
Central Children's Room, Donnell Library Center

William Roscoe
*The Butterfly's Ball and the Grasshopper's Feast: Said to be Written for the Use of Children*
Illustrated by William Mulready
London: J. Harris, 1807
Spencer Collection

Christina Rossetti
"An Alphabet from England" in:
*St. Nicholas* [a magazine published by C. Scribner's Sons, New York] Nov. 1875

John Ruskin
*The King of the Golden River; or the Black Brothers: A Legend of Stiria*
Illustrated by Richard Doyle
London: Smith, Elder & Co., 1856
Spencer Collection

Carl Sandburg
*Rootabaga Country*
Illustrated by Peggy Bacon
New York: Harcourt, Brace and Co. [c.1929]
General Research Division

Sir Walter Scott
*Ivanhoe*
Illustrated by Frank E. Schoonover
New York and London: Harper & Bros., 1922
General Research Division

Edward Steichen and Dr. Mary Steichen Calderone
*First and Second Picture Books*
New York: Harcourt, 1930–31
Central Children's Room, Donnell Library Center

James Stephens
*Irish Fairy Tales*
Illustrated by Arthur Rackham
London: Macmillan & Co., 1920
Spencer Collection

Robert Louis Stevenson
*Treasure Island*
Illustrated by N.C. Wyeth
New York: C. Scribner's Sons, 1905
General Research Division

*Susan and Edward; Or, A Visit to Fulton Market*
New York: Mahlon Day [1831]
Rare Books and Manuscripts Division

*Tit, Tiny and Tittens, the Three White Kittens*
London and Edinburgh: T. Nelson & Sons [c. 1860]
Central Children's Room, Donnell Library Center

Leo Tolstoy: see Miriam Morton, ed.

Mary and Newman Tremearne
*Fables and Fairy Tales for Little Folk; Or Uncle Remus in Hausaland*
Cambridge, England: W. Heffer and Sons, 1910
Schomburg Center

Pura Belpré White
*Once in Puerto Rico*
Illustrated by Christine Price
New York: F. Warne, 1973
Central Children's Room, Donnell Library Center

Oscar Wilde
*The Happy Prince, and Other Tales*
Illustrated by Everett Shinn
Philadelphia: J.C. Winston Co. [1940]
General Research Division

Jack B. Yeats
*The Bosun and the Bob-tailed Comet*
Illustrated by the author
London: E. Mathews [c. 1904]
Berg Collection

# *Acknowledgments*

The stories, poems, and illustrations herein are reproduced, with permission, from the collections of The New York Public Library, Astor, Lenox and Tilden Foundations. Grateful acknowledgment is made to the following authors, illustrators, publishers, and other copyright holders for permission to reprint copyrighted materials:

Alexander Pushkin, "The Golden Cockerel"; Elizabeth Hulick, tr.; From *The Golden Cockerel* copyright © 1962 by Ivan Obolensky, Inc.; reprinted by permission of Astor-Honor, Inc., New York, New York 10017.

Edward Steichen and Dr. Mary Steichen Calderone, *First and Second Picture Books:* Reprinted by permission of the copyright owner, Mary Steichen Calderone.

Leo Tolstoy, "The Wolf and the Dog," "The Czar and the Falcon," and "The Lion and the Puppy"; Miriam Morton, tr.; From Miriam Morton, ed. *A Harvest of Children's Literature* © 1967 by The Regents of the University of California.

Mary and Newman Tremearne, "Why Hawa Prevented the Beasts from Drinking": From *Fables and Fairy Tales for Little Folk* (Cambridge, England: W. Heffer and Sons Ltd., 1910); reprinted courtesy of F.R. Collieson, Director, W. Heffer & Sons Ltd.

Carl Sandburg, "Shush Shush, the Big Buff Banty Hen Who Laid an Egg in the Postmaster's Hat"; Peggy Bacon, illus.: From *Rootabaga Pigeons* by Carl Sandburg, copyright 1923 by Harcourt Brace Jovanovich, Inc., renewed 1951 by Carl Sandburg; reprinted by permission of the publisher.

Countee Cullen, "The Sleepamitemore": From *The Lost Zoo* by Christopher Cat and Countee Cullen, copyright 1940, copyright renewed 1968 by Ida M. Cullen; reprinted by permission of Harper & Row, Publishers, Inc.

James M. Barrie, "Wendy's Story"; F.D. Bedford, illus.: From *Peter and Wendy* by J.M. Barrie, copyright by Hodder & Stoughton 1911; reprinted by permission of the publisher.

Carlo Collodi, "Pinocchio"; Walter S. Cramp, tr.; From *Pinocchio* (New York: The Limited Editions Club, 1937); reprinted courtesy of the publisher.

Walter de la Mare, "Then", "Full Moon", and "Beasts: The Pigs and the Charcoal Burner": Reprinted by permission of the Literary Trustees of Walter de la Mare and The Society of Authors, London, as their representative.

James Stephens, "The Enchanted Cave of Cesh Corran"; Arthur Rackham, illus.: From

*Irish Fairy Tales* copyright 1920 by Macmillan Publishing Company, copyright renewed 1948 by James Stephens; reprinted by permission of Macmillan Publishing Company. For the British Commonwealth (excluding Canada): Reprinted courtesy The Society of Authors, London, on behalf of the copyright owner, Mrs. Iris Wise.

Johnny Gruelle, "The Taffy Pull": From *Raggedy Andy Stories* copyright 1920 by Macmillan, Inc., All Rights Reserved.

Wanda Ga'g, "Millions of Cats": From *Millions of Cats* and *Wanda Ga'g's Storybook* copyright 1932 by Coward-McCann, Inc., copyright renewed © 1960 by Robert Janssen; reprinted courtesy of The Putnam Publishing Group. For the British Commonwealth (excluding Canada): Reprinted by permission of Faber and Faber Ltd. from *Millions of Cats* by Wanda Ga'g.

N. C. Wyeth, illus.; Robert Louis Stevenson, *Treasure Island*: Illustration by N. C. Wyeth from *Treasure Island* copyright 1911 by Charles Scribner's Sons, copyright renewed 1939 by N. C. Wyeth; reproduced with the permission of Charles Scribner's Sons.

E. H. Shepard, illus.; Kenneth Grahame, *The Wind in the Willows*; Illustration copyright 1933 by Charles Scribner's Sons, copyright renewed © 1961 by Ernest H. Shepard; reprinted by permission of Charles Scribner's Sons. For the British Commonwealth (excluding Canada): Line illustration by E. H. Shepard copyright under the Berne Convention; reprinted by permission of the agent for the estate of E. H. Shepard, Curtis Brown Ltd.

James Daugherty, *Andy and the Lion*: Copyright 1938, copyright renewed © 1966 by James Daugherty; reprinted by permission of Viking Penguin Inc.

Pura Belpré White, "The Legend of the Royal Palm"; Christine Price, illus.: From *Once in Puerto Rico* copyright © 1973 by Pura Belpré; reprinted by permission of Viking Penguin Inc.

William Pène du Bois, *Giant Otto*: Copyright 1936 by William Pène du Bois, copyright renewed 1964 by William Pène du Bois; reprinted by permission of the Watkins, Loomis Agency, Inc.

# *Index*


Abbott, Jacob, 26
*About Two Squares* (Lissitsky), 42–44
*Adventures of Bob the Squirrel, The* 56–59
*Adventures of Huckleberry Finn* (Twain), 237–39
*Aesop's Fables*, 214–18
Alcott, Louisa May, 182–83
*Alphabet from England, An* (Rossetti), 36–39
*Andy and the Lion* (Daugherty), 157–59
*Animals in Costume*, 60–62
Ashford, Daisy, 118–21
*Askalotte* (Burgess), 75
*At the Back of the North Wind* (MacDonald), 172–74

*Baa Baa Black Sheep*, 17–19
Bacon, Peggy, 86, 87
Barbauld, Anna Letitia, 45
Barlow, Francis, 216
Barrie, James M., 100–104
Baum, L. Frank, 2, 4, 160–63
Bedford, F.D., 100, 103
Bennett, Charles, 122–23
Bewick, Thomas, 54–55
*Big Boy's Mistake, The* (France), 98–99
Bilibin, Ivan, 190, 191
*Billy Bounce* (Denslow and Bragdon), 105–8
Blake, William, 258–59
*Book of Nonsense, A* (Lear), 63–65
*Book of Riddles, The*, 117
*Bosun and the Bob-Tailed Comet, The* (Yeats), 66–71
Boutet de Monvel, Maurice, 98–99
*Boy Who Drew Cats, The* (Hearn), 175–78
Boyd, 88–90
Bragdon, Dudley A., 105–8
Browne, H.K., 31
*Brownies' Book, The* (Du Bois), 240
*Brownies on Skates, The* (Cox), 148–50
*Brownies: Their Book, The* (Cox), 148–50
Browning, Robert, 164–66
Burgess, Gelett, 75–76
Busch, Wilhelm, 142–47
*Butterfly's Ball and the Grasshopper's Feast, The* (Roscoe), 52–53

Caldecott, Randolph, 23–25
Calder, Alexander, 218
Calderone, Mary Steichen, 40–41
Caldwell, E., 17–19
*Cat's-Eyes* (Bennett), 122–23
*Cleanliness*, 60
Clemens, Samuel (Mark Twain), 237–39, 245–47
Clifford, Carrie W., 11
Collodi, Carlo, 136–39
Cox, Palmer, 148–50
*Cross Patch, lift the latch*, 22
Cruikshank, George, 199–202
Cullen, Countee, 109–10
*Czar and the Falcon, The* (Tolstoy), 219

*Daffy-down-dilly*, 20
Dargent, Yan, 206, 207
Daugherty, James, 157–59
Davison, W., 54–55
De la Mare, Walter, 167–69
Denis, Maurice, 140–41
Denslow, W.W., 105–8, 160, 161, 163
*Destroya* (Burgess), 76
*Dinkey-Bird, The* (Field), 170
*Disorder*, 61
Doré, Gustave, 184–87
Dorset, Catherine Anne, 46–47
Doyle, Richard, 203–5, 212, 248, 249
Du Bois, W.E.B., 240
du Bois, William Pène, 77–80

*Eagle and the Fox, The* (Aesop), 216
*Elephant's Child, The* (Kipling), 81–85
*Enchanted Cave of Cesh Corran, The* (Stephens), 209–11

*Fables and Fairy Tales for Little Folk; or, Uncle Remus in Hausaland* (Tremearne), 179–81
*Fables of Aesop According to Sir Roger L'Estrange, The*, 218
*Fairy Library* (Cruikshank), 199, 202
*Fairy Tales from All Nations* (Montalba), 203–5
*Fairy Tales of the Brothers Grimm* (Rackham), 195–98
*Farmyard Journal, The* 96–97
*Fatal Mistake, The* (Frost), 48–51
*Fictitious Stories* (Abbott), 26
*Fiddle-Dee-Dee* (Field), 171

*Fidelity*, 61
Field, Eugene, 170–71
*First and Second Picture Books* (Steichen and Calderone), 40–41
*First Landscapes* (Denis), 140–41
*Fisherman and the Tuna, The* (Aesop), 214
Flint, W. Russell, 251, 253
France, Anatole, 98–99
Fraser, Claud Lovat, 113–15
Friedlander, Gerald, 189
Frost, A.B., 48–51
*Full Moon* (De la Mare), 168

Ga'g, Wanda, 154–56
*Generosity*, 62
*Giant Otto* (du Bois), 77–80
*Girls and Boys: Scenes from Town and Country* (France), 98–99
*Goblick* (Burgess), 75
*Golden Cockerel, The* (Pushkin), 190–91
*Golden Touch, The* (Hawthorne), 231–36
*Goop Tales* (Burgess), 75–76
*Gossip*, 61
Grahame, Kenneth, 126–27
Greenaway, Kate, 20–22
Grimm, Jacob and Wilhelm, 195–98
Griset, Ernest, 124–25
*Griset's Grotesques* (Hood), 124–25
Gruelle, Johnny, 128–32

*Haughtiness*, 62
Hawkins, Marcellus, 11
Hawthorne, Nathaniel, 231–36
Hearn, Lafcadio, 175–78
*Heedlessness*, 62
*Heroes, The: or, Greek Fairy Tales for My Children* (Kingsley), 251–55
Hervey, T.K., 212–13
*Hey Diddle Diddle*, 23–25
*History of an Apple Pie, The*, 32–35
Hoffmann-Donner, Heinrich, 74
Hood, Tom, 124–25
*Hop-o' my-Thumb and the Seven-League Boots* (Cruikshank), 199–202
*How Jason Lost His Sandal in Anauros* (Kingsley), 251–55
Hughes, Thomas, 260–62
*Humpty Dumpty*, 27–29

*Imitation*, 61
*In Wink-A-Way Land* (Field), 170–71
*Inkfinga* (Burgess), 76
*Irish Fairy Tales* (Stephens), 209–11
*Ivanhoe* (Scott), 221–24

*Jack Huckaback* (Busch), 142–47
*Jack Sprat could eat no fat*, 20
James, Thomas, 217
*Jewish Fairy Book, The* (Friedlander), 189
*Just So Stories* (Kipling), 81–85
*Juvenile Calendar and Zodiac of Flowers* (Hervey), 212–13

Kemble, E.W., 238
*Kindergarten Song, A* (Clifford), 11
*King of the Golden River, The* (Ruskin), 248–50
Kingsley, Charles, 133–35, 251–55
Kipling, Rudyard, 81–85
*Kite, Hawk and Pigeons, The* (Aesop), 218

Laboulaye, Edouard, 206–8
*Laboulaye's Fairy Book* (Laboulaye), 206–8
Lang, Andrew, 192–94
Lear, Edward, 63–65
*Legend of the Royal Palm, The* (White), 151–53
*Lion and the Puppy, The* (Tolstoy), 220
Lissitsky, El, 42–44
*Little Man in Gray, The* (Montalba), 203–5
*Lost Zoo, The (A Rhyme for the Young but Not Too Young)* (Cullen), 109–10
*Lucy Locket, lost her pocket*, 22
*Lulu's Library* (Alcott), 182–83

MacDonald, George, 172–74
*Mary, Mary, quite contrary*, 20
Merrill, Harley and F.T., 246, 247
Merriwell, Mark, 91–95
*Merry Adventures of Robin Hood, The* (Pyle), 228–30
*Millions of Cats* (Ga'g), 154–56

Montalba, Anthony Reubens, 203–5
Moore, Clement C., 88–90
Morris, Geraldine, 258, 259
*Mother Goose and Old Nursery Rhymes* (Greenaway), 20–22
*Mrs. Barbauld's Lessons for Children from Three to Four Years Old* (Barbauld), 45
Mulready, William, 52–53
*My Own Treasury: A Gift Book for Boys and Girls* (Merriwell), 91–95

*Natural History of British Quadrupeds, A* (Davison), 54–55
Nodier, Charles, 113–15

*Old Mother Hubbard*, 12–16
*Once in Puerto Rico* (White), 151–53

Paton, J. Noel, 133, 135
*Peacock "At Home," The*, 46–47
*Peacock Pie: A Book of Rhymes* (De la Mare), 167–69
Perrault, Charles, 184–88
*Peter and Wendy* (Barrie), 100–104
*Pictorial Alphabet* (Browne), 31
*Picture Riddler*, 116
*Pied Piper of Hamelin, The* (Browning), 164–66
*Piggy Girl, The* (Alcott), 182–83
*Pigs and the Charcoal-Burner, The* (De la Mare), 169
*Pinocchio: The Adventures of a Marionette* (Collodi), 136–39
*Polly put the kettle on*, 20
Price, Christine, 151–53
*Prince and the Pauper, The* (Twain), 245–47
Pushkin, Alexander, 190–91
*Puss in Boots* (Perrault), 184–88
Pyle, Howard, 228–30

Rackham, Arthur, 164, 165, 195, 196, 209, 210
*Raggedy Andy Stories* (Gruelle), 128–32
*Rebellious Waters, The* (Friedlander), 189
*Red Fairy Book, The* (Lang), 192–94

*Ring a ring a' roses*, 22
Robinson, W. Heath, 167–69
*Rollo Books, The* (Abbott), 26
*Rootabaga Country* (Sandburg), 86–87
Roscoe, Mr., 52–53
Rossetti, Christina G., 36–39

Sandburg, Carl, 86–87
Schoonover, Frank E., 221, 223
Scott, Sir Walter, 221–24
*Self-satisfaction*, 62
*Selfish Giant, The* (Wilde), 225–27
Shepard, Ernest H., 126–27
Shinn, Everett, 225
*Shock-headed Peter* (Hoffmann-Donner), 74
*Shush Shush, the Big Buff Banty Hen Who Laid an Egg in the Postmaster's Hat* (Sandburg), 86–87
*Sleepamitemore* (Cullen), 109–10
Smith, Albert Alex, 240, 243
Smith, Jessie Willcox, 172, 173
*Songs of Innocence* (Blake), 258–59
Speed, Lancelot, 192, 194
*Sswanda, the Piper: A Bohemian Tale* (Laboulaye), 206–8
Stafford, Alphonso O., 240–44
Steichen, Edward, 40–41
Stephens, A.L., 36–39
Stephens, James, 209–11
Stevenson, Robert Louis, 256–57
*Stories That Little Breeches Told, The* (Bennett), 122–23
*Struwwelpeter* (Hoffmann-Donner), 74
*Susan and Edward; or, A Visit to Fulton Market*, 111–12

*Taffy-Pull, The* (Gruelle), 128–32
*Tales of Perrault, The* (Perrault), 184–88
Tenniel, John, 217
*Theft*, 60
*Then* (De la Mare), 167
*There was a little man*, 20
*Thieves and the Rooster, The* (Aesop), 215
*Tit, Tiny and Tittens, the Three White Kittens*, 72–73
Tolstoy, Leo, 219–20
*Tom Brown at Oxford* (Hughes), 260–62
*Tom Thumb* (Grimm), 195–98
*Treasure Island* (Stevenson), 256–57
Tremearne, Mary and Newman, 179–81
*True History of Little Golden-hood, The* (Lang), 192–94
Twain, Mark. *See* Clemens, Samuel
*Twin Heroes, The: An African Myth* (Stafford), 240–44

*Ugly Little Duck, The*, 91–95

*Visit from St. Nicholas, A* (Moore), 88–90

*Wanda Ga'g's Story Book* (Ga'g), 154–56
*Water-Babies, The: A Fairy Tale for a Land-Baby* (Kingsley), 133–35
White, Pura Belpré, 151–53
*Why Hawa Prevented the Beasts from Drinking* (Tremearne), 179–81
Wilde, Oscar, 225–27
*Wind in the Willows, The* (Grahame), 126–27
*Wolf and the Crane, The* (Aesop), 217
*Wolf and the Dog, The* (Tolstoy), 219
*Wonder-Book for Girls and Boys, A* (Hawthorne), 231–36
*Wonderful Wizard of Oz, The* (Baum), 160–63
*Woodcutter's Dog, The* (Nodier), 113–15
Wyeth, N.C., 256, 257

Yeats, Jack B., 66–71
*Young Visiters, The; or, Mr. Salteena's Plan* (Ashford), 118–21